Yours as Ever, Sam
Based on the true story of a sometime hero.

(Winner of second place in Critique Match New York's, fiction five literary competition 2022)

Mila Douglas

Copyright © Mila Douglas 2023

First published in 2023 by Bodoni Books

YOURS AS EVER, SAM is a work of historical fiction written around a true story.

The main characters are closely based on real people wherever possible. Information has been taken from family anecdotal evidence, transcribed interviews, news articles, military records and relevant accounts in books. Any resemblance between the minor characters in this book and persons living or dead is coincidental.

All rights reserved. No part of this book may be reproduced or used in any manner without written permission of the copyright owner except for the use of quotations in a book review. For more information contact miladouglas@miladouglas.com.au

Book design by Marten Norr

Interior formatting by Robert Harrison

ISBN 978-0-6457216-4-5 e-book

ISBN 978-0-6457216-5-2 paperback

www.miladouglas.com.au

To the remarkable individuals who generously shared the knowledge that brought Sam's story to life:

First and foremost, I extend my heartfelt thanks to my beloved father-in-law, James—a man larger than life, who often reminded me of the legendary character Edward Bloom in 'Big Fish.' He spun countless exaggerated and unbelievable tales. Following his passing, I embarked on a lengthy and seemingly fruitless quest to uncover his past. It wasn't until a DNA match led me to Bek Saltmarsh; who came across my plea on Ancestry.com, that the pieces began to fall into place.

Bek, with her exceptional detective skills, connected me to the truth and introduced me to two extraordinary individuals: John and Bette Solonsch. Bette and John had undertaken an impressive journey of research, diligently documenting events that included family anecdotes, encounters with commanding officers, and interviews with former POWs who had known Sam during his time in Java.

Meanwhile, Bek Saltmarsh had also gathered colourful stories from other family members, along with photographs and more.

Armed with this invaluable trove of resources, and after countless additional hours of my own investigation, I made a profound discovery. Many of my father-in-law's stories were not about himself but were tales he had been told by or about his father—the sometime hero of this novel. To these remarkable people, I extend my profound gratitude. You have become an indelible part of my extended family—a testament to the power of shared history and the bonds that connect us across time and circumstance.

Other Books by Mila Douglas

The Figs' Mysteries
The Dancer at the End of His Bed
The Wolf at Her Heels
The Truth Behind the Walls (coming soon)

www.miladouglas.com.au

Note to the Reader

My obsession with a dead man began in 2020 with a message from a stranger:

> *Our DNA tests match. I have details for your family tree. This information is too sensitive to share by email.*

Hours on the phone, and countless shared documents later, the mystery of the paternal grandfather unfolded in all its glory.

I listened to anecdotes of an amusing wheeler-dealer. Read newspaper clippings outlining criminal misdeeds, while others described touching acts of kindness. There were transcripts of interviews with men who'd shared harrowing times in a Javanese POW camp.

The one common thread? Everyone who met Sam loved him.

Sam's story seduced me, compelled me to bring him back to life the only way I knew how—on the page.

Would Sam mind me filling the gaps, adding fictional flesh to the factual bones? I hoped not. After all, Sam had enjoyed plumping a story or two.

I begged for answers. 'Which were you, Sam—a charismatic conman or a war hero?'

He slicked back his hair, voice loud and clear. 'Why do we always have to bloomin' choose?'

From the moment he answered, I began to write.

Most of what follows actually happened.

Chapter One
POW Hospital Camp, Batavia, 1942

Inside the hospital, we were all dying. Some quick-quick, some torturously slow, all smothered by the blanket of humidity and the sickly-sweet stench of gangrene and death.

Scrunching my eyes against the relentless heat and blinding light, brought only scant relief. Web-like patterns, imprinted on the underside of my eyelids, transported me momentarily to my bedroom in the Netherlands. Imagining those familiar white lace curtains filtering the tranquil morning sun was enough to bring on a half-smile. But my fevered brain could not completely block the reality of war. The drapery screening our windows was fallen palm fronds strangled by barbed-wire.

Most prisoners tried to sleep during the day, avoiding the malice of Japanese guards, who like cruel boys taunting caged creatures, wanted their captives to die but were unwilling to let them go in peace.

Almost all the POWs employed an animal survival tactic and played dead. Some in a fear-induced catatonic state were barely acting. But one man, Captain John Douglas, refused to cower. I'd heard his was an assumed name—but what was wrong with that? Everyone called me Young Dutchy.

Despite his injuries, the captain eyeballed Japanese guards and told them jokes.

"Did you hear the one about the Jap soldier and the Aussie prisoner?" Captain John slapped the mattress beside him and laughed. "The Jap asked: did you come here to die? The prisoner replied: No sir, I came here yester-die."

Like the other human inmates, I strived to stay unseen and unheard, only the orange-spotted geckos watching from the wall were brave enough to bark what passed as laughter. I was thankful to have the bed beside him. I could blend into the background while bearing witness to the stories this man twice my age whispered in the quiet of night.

Capt. John declared himself too private to talk about his own life. Instead, he spoke of Samuel Solonsch, a man he'd known when he was young. I didn't believe all the adventures, and sometimes wondered why he felt the need to talk about this other man, but nonetheless I was thankful.

Perhaps the Captain wasn't quite right in the head, but his tales pulled me through the indescribable suffering, and I clung to every word as if my salvation depended on it.

CHAPTER TWO
ORTELSBURG PRUSSIA 1912

Samuel Solonsch couldn't be sure which created most heat—the warmth of his brothers' bodies crowded into the one bed, the patch of searing sunlight from the east-facing window, or the horrible illness he'd heard his mother whispering about in the night.

"Go to the market please, Esther." His grandmother, Bubbe, handed Sam's mother a woven string bag. "Swap eggs for vegetables."

Mother shook William then grabbed Joe, her youngest son, before pulling the blanket off eleven-year-old Samuel. "Come on. Out of bed."

Samuel smothered his head with the pillow.

"You sick?"

"I don't know. Am I?" he asked.

"Don't answer a question with a question. Give Bubbe peace and come shopping."

"Please, *bitte, proszę*. Let me stay." Although he begged his mother, he secretly pleaded with his grandmother.

"It's all right," Bubbe said. "Samuel can stay, as long as he keeps out of my way."

Samuel had convinced himself he was dying. But to know for

sure, he'd have to ask Bubbe. She was incapable of hiding the truth. No matter how serious her facade, softness seeped through like spilt tea from a cracked cup. Samuel saw the truth. His older sister, Fay, claimed he'd a gift for reading people. When he'd asked how anyone could read without words, she'd explained people-readers knew when others lied. They helped police solve cases.

After waiting for his mother and brothers to leave, Samuel watched Bubbe sprinkle sugar over the dough, studying her face for signs of concern.

"Am I okay?" he asked. "If I'm not, I want you to know that even though I don't always behave, I love you."

Bubbe swept him into her sugary arms, dusting him with the granules clinging to her apron. "You're more than okay, Samuel. You're wonderful. But you'll soon grow into a man, and must learn to make careful choices."

"What if I don't grow up?" He watched her face for a hint of concern. Her expression flickered with the half-hidden amusement she always wore.

Bubbe's expression confused him. The scratchy woollen blanket covering his head last night barely muffled their voices. When boys weren't listening, grown-ups spoke about interesting, adult things.

"Why wouldn't you grow up?" Bubbe raised her sparse eyebrows. "You've more life-force than anyone. If I could bottle your energy in preserving jars, I'd spread it across my bagels."

This momentarily pleased Samuel, but he couldn't shake the feeling he might drop dead. He closed his eyes and recalled what he'd heard.

"I love you, Esther," Bubbe said to his mother during the night, "but you'll have to return to London. I don't have enough money to keep you. Besides, your home is with Solomon, not in Prussia with an old crone like me. If you stay here, who will the girls turn to for help? Your husband isn't perfect, but he's suffered much."

Sam had shuddered at the mention of Solomon. The image of that man cramped his belly. He'd concentrated, forcing the women's voices to sail away. They were almost at sea when his own name sounded like a foghorn, dragging him back from the ragged edge of sleep.

"It's not Solomon." His mother's hushed voice trembled. "I'm worried about Samuel."

He'd bitten his lip to stop himself squirming beneath the bedcovers. He didn't need to see his mother's face to recognise anguish. Fear gripped his throat like Father's angry hands, forcing an involuntarily cough, and the women stopped talking. Samuel felt the burn of their eyes through the blanket and imagined his mother holding a finger to her mouth in a silent 'Shhh'.

He'd clutched at the pain. The pain he felt at his father's anger. The pain which worsened when his mother cried. Samuel stayed unnaturally quiet.

"What's wrong with the boy?" Bubbe asked.

"It's the badness," Mother said. "He has the bad seed growing inside him."

Samuel plugged his ears with his fingers and counted in his head. Up to a hundred in different languages. By the time he'd finished, the women had gone to bed.

Eventually, he fell into a fitful sleep, dreaming of a bad seed spreading a deadly disease.

Now, in broad daylight in Bubbe's kitchen, his mother wasn't around to shush him. Despite his gut writhing, he moved around the table to face his grandmother. "Is it true I have a poisonous seed and my mother expects me to die?"

"What are you talking about?" Her green eyes held their usual twinkle, her smile crinkled the corners.

Samuel laughed and kicked his legs like a Cossack dancer. "I'm not unwell." But his foot caught the chair knocking apples from Bubbe's hands.

She righted it sharply and tapped the seat. "Sit."

He did as he was told.

"How many languages do you speak?" she asked.

"English, German, some Polish, and a little Russian."

"A lot for an eleven-year-old." Bubbe flattened Samuel's hair. "Do you know the story of Babel?"

"No, Bubbe." He leaned his elbows on the table. Her stories transported him to magical realms. He hardly thought about his parents' dreadful arguments when he was with her in Prussia. He shuddered, thinking of the times his mother had left England, taking only the three girls, leaving him and his brothers behind.

"The Babylonians built a lofty tower in the finest city. Their people tried to climb to the heavens, but God thought them too proud. He hindered their progress by giving each person a separate language, then scattering them to the corners of the earth. One who can speak different tongues, such as you, could help bring people together, but first, you must learn the language of compassion."

"What's that?"

Although Samuel refused to let his grandmother hug him in public, he didn't complain when she tucked an unruly strand of hair behind his ear.

"Compassion is difficult to explain," she said. "But I've heard from your mother about you hitting young Joe. If you care about yourself more than others, you're not on the road to kindness."

Her eyes bore deeply, burning his cheeks with shame. He believed Bubbe's stare revealed all his wicked deeds.

Samuel looked away so she wouldn't see him fighting tears, but she enveloped him in a sheltering hug. He whispered, "I will be better. For you."

And, for a few seconds, Samuel meant it. He melted into his grandmother's embrace like butter in the pastry she'd rolled ready for the *Szarlotka* pie.

He patted Bubbe's shoulder. "I love you more than *Szarlotka*." Through the gap in her arms, he spied the open container of steel ball-bearings she used to bake the pie crust flat. Reaching out slowly, he grabbed a handful to hide in his pocket. Bubbe wouldn't miss a few and he could trade them with the marble playing lads back in London. He'd declare their rarity and explain how European royalty played with nothing else. He imagined the trade. A pile of aggies and a peacock-onionskin. Or maybe he'd swap them for cash.

Bubbe pulled herself upright, her voice suddenly clipped and no-nonsense. "That's enough. Sweep the floor and straighten the beds. Show your mother the kindness inside."

Samuel took extra care shaking the worn blankets. He flattened the covers until the beds were smoother than the ice on Lake Dlugie, and glanced at his grandmother to see if she'd noticed his theft. Bubbe, her face framed by a triangular headscarf knotted beneath the chin, concentrated on peeling apples. Although she continued to peel and chop, she wore the hint of a particular smile he recognised: Bubbe was proud. Her belief overwhelmed him and his stomach ached again. This time with guilt.

Needing to act before his mother returned, Sam fumbled in his pocket, searching for a wily way to return the stolen pastry balls. He snaked his hand along the edge of the table and had almost reached the jar when his younger brother, Joseph, burst through the door, calling, "I won the race."

Samuel dropped his clenched hand into his pocket and released the balls.

He shrugged at Joe. "Not much of a victory. William lets everyone win."

When Bubbe shook her head, Samuel changed his tune. "Nice win, Joe."

Moments later, carrying a box laden with vegetables, twelve-year-old William arrived, barely puffing. "Good job. You beat me."

Samuel frowned. Instead of the bad seed William had the seed of compassion.

While their mother and grandmother unpacked the supplies, Samuel sidled up to the table again. It was now or never to make right what he considered a minor wrong.

His mother glared with don't-mess-with-me eyes. "Off!"

Samuel shrugged. She'd prevented him returning the marbles, the sin now belonged to her.

Chapter Three
POW Camp Batavia 1942

The Aussies handed out nicknames like grandmothers doled out advice. Long names were shortened, short names lengthened, and people like me with difficult to pronounce names were assigned something new. That's how I became one of the Dutchys. There was Big Dutchy, Touchy Dutchy and me—Young Dutchy. Captain John mostly called me The Kid.

There was one prisoner without a nickname. For a while the men called him Blotto because the poor sod's damaged brain made him appear permanently inebriated. But Captain John didn't think it fair to base nicknames on infirmity, so we called him Billy. I guessed that was his real name.

Maybe appearing permanently blotto wasn't so bad. Given half the chance we would have all drunk ourselves into a stupor to dull the sharp reality.

A few of us sat on the wide verandah one torpid afternoon to watch Billy risking his life yet again. Even the bedridden turned their heads. With the double doors and large window shutters propped out on a stick, the boundary between inside and out blurred.

Every now and again, something snapped inside Billy's head and he taunted the Japanese guards. His weapon, through lack of choice, was bamboo cut off the stems growing close to the compound's fence.

"Back inside." Capt. John called. He clambered out of the chair, barely masking his pain. "Over here," he yelled, waving his arms and attracting enough attention from the guard to make me break into a sweat.

None of us could decipher Billy's nonsensical slurred speech, but from his belligerent tone, I assumed he was swearing. The guard turned away from Capt. John's attempt at distraction and scowled at Billy who'd begun his drunk-like wobble-walk while brandishing the bamboo. Capt. John, wearing a gritted-teeth smile, dragged himself into position between Billy and the guard, muttering as he undid his trousers. "Look," he said. "I'm pissing blood."

John peed a red river which etched a scribbly wet track in the dry earth like a line in the sand, dividing allies from enemy.

John led Billy towards the verandah, joking as he crab-walked in pain. "Red is a great shade for most things, but not piss. I'm annoyed the communists stole my favourite colour."

Billy nodded and blinked as if he understood, or maybe because he wanted to understand. Captain John kept talking low, slow and calm, even though there were now two guards circling and eyeing them suspiciously.

"The Russian word for red is *krasnyj*, and it is no coincidence the word relates to *krasivyj*, which means beautiful." He smiled and bowed melodramatically in Japanese fashion, before escorting Billy to safety.

"What I don't understand," I asked as he resumed his usual place at the window, "is why you smile? It's almost a game. Don't you hate the Japanese?"

He shrugged. "Everyone has their place. A Japanese soldier is just a fighter like the rest of us—no more, no less."

John salvaged the bamboo he'd taken from Billy and snapped it into smaller pieces, crafting as he spoke. "Pick-pockets and martyrs both have value, but the value of each fluctuates. Value is conditional on the circumstance."

Agitated looks punctuated an intense conversation between the

Japanese guards, but John ignored them. Instead, he fashioned bamboo arms, legs and a cylindrical head which he bound together with leaves. When he pointed visibly at the guards, my innards jitter-bugged. "That one over there looks vindictive," he said with a laugh.

My fuzzy vision focussed on an officer scanning the plantation of dying men before fixing a sharp gaze on Captain John.

"Watch out!" John smirked. "He's trying to pick the prisoner with the worst posture."

"Why is that?" One of the newer men asked, not yet accustomed to the Captain's black humour or tell-tale wink.

"Who here has the worst posture?" he continued. "I don't know...I have a *hunch*... it's going to be me."

The geckos laughed as always, but the rest of us held our breath at John's lack of respect and the guard's abruptly straightened stance.

He stormed in and barked orders in Japanese, gesturing for John to wrap his arms around the veranda post.

John clung to the column, smiling as if greeting a long-lost lover, and held position as the horse-whip struck him between ribs and bony hip, the place of his damaged kidneys. His only flinch was the tightening of his fist around the tiny bamboo figurine. "Glad that part of the day is done and dusted," John said as he resumed watch from the window.

"How do you do it?" I asked.

"What? I just stood there." He shrugged.

"But you took a flogging without complaint."

"It's easier to get a whipping from one whose job it is to hate you, than a thrashing from someone you hoped would show love."

Chapter Four
London, England 1913

The trees in London were hunkering down for winter. The brothers and their sister, Fay, crossed the railway line, heading home from school. Samuel kicked a pile of fallen leaves and snapped a bare white twig which he held like a cigarette, exhaling cold breath instead of smoke. "Look at me." He pretended to smoke.

William rolled his eyes like always. "Want to skim rocks along the railway track?"

Samuel checked Fay was out of earshot and hefted the dull silver pastry balls he'd been hiding since they returned from Prussia. "Nah. I've business to do."

William spun Samuel's arm until he had the upper hand. Despite the strength from being older and taller, Samuel easily broke free.

"I'm not letting you take them." Samuel backed away. "I'm the one who took risks pinching them."

"How can you nick stuff from Bubbe?"

"Come on. She had a whole jar. I bet she's never noticed them missing." He whispered. "Listen to my plan. I'm going to call them

Prussian Steels and tell the gang of lads they've been used by royal princes. The Kaiser's sons."

"Prussian Steels? Balls of steel, more like. That's what you've got."

"Balls of steel." Samuel laughed and grasped his crotch.

William furrowed his brow. "Don't you ever feel bad about doing this stuff?"

"Why? I'll never be caught." Samuel's voice was strong and sure, but his gut twisted like a guilty mouth desperate to speak up.

"Hurry up," Fay yelled from across the track.

Samuel pushed William away, then called to Fay, "Go ahead. I'm meeting a friend."

Once they'd gone, he traced patterns across the soot-grimed walls in the laneway, intentionally lagging. Although Samuel's head could bargain with decency, his gut knew the truth. The bad seed had taken root.

He waited for the St Vincent's School boys who played marbles in the dead-end street.

They'd skitter rocks at his boots and call him a dirty Jew, but his urge to make a deal was stronger than the desire to avoid bullying. Besides, he'd spoken to the tallest of the louts, Alf, a few days before and he'd seemed mighty interested in bargaining.

It wasn't long before the Catholic gang swaggered towards Samuel. Alf striding out front, the top button of his hand-me-down jacket straining to stay fastened, knock-knees peeking out like crossed eyes from beneath his too-short pants. Like most lads around here, the only thing that fitted was his cap.

"Right-o," Alf said. "Give us a gander at these Royal Prussian steels you reckon you've got."

"Show me your money first."

"I've got sumfin' better 'an dosh. I nicked a few fings ter make a swap." Alf emptied his school bag. "How about Robin Hood? Cracker of a tale, I've heard." He sneered at his mates. "Not that I've read it. Readin's for sissies."

Although Samuel kept a straight face, his heart drummed with adrenaline. "Not interested." He wanted the book. He'd read it in the small school library, but the only book allowed at home was a Tanakh, the Hebrew Bible. Once, when he'd been sent home early, he'd caught his mother reading a tattered magazine. He never forgot her terror.

"Wot 'bout this then?" Alf held up a small tin soldier with a dented head and worn paint.

Samuel shook his head while maintaining his gaze. "Too old for toys." But as he was outwardly signalling no, he was thinking of places to hide the stash. Somewhere his father would never find them.

"Well, I doubt this is up your alley bein' a Jew-boy, but I reckon it's worth sumfin'." Alf opened his fist to reveal a necklace with an embossed silver crucifix. "The beads on Gran's rosary are made of sumfin' real." He held it towards Samuel for closer inspection.

Sam grazed his fingers across the Catholic religious piece, expecting his skin to blister, but the black-glass beads felt cool and calm.

Alf had chosen the exact items Samuel's father would never allow him to have, which made him want them more.

"I'm not wearing jewellery. If the beads were big enough, I'd break the string and use them as marbles, but they're tiny. Won't your Gran miss it?"

"Not where she's gone. Any road, yer don't wear it. After you confess yer sins ter the priest, yer use it ter say a few Hail Mary's and how's yer father." Alf laughed and his army of mates joined in.

Samuel lifted a single eyebrow and cocked his head. "Doesn't God ask you to make right with the person you've wronged?"

"Maybe yer do that in your *sinner gog*, but in a right proper church God forgives everythin'."

Samuel folded his arms across his chest, feeling lightheaded at the idea of a God who allowed people to sin, then let them off. He could benefit from such a being.

After a few deliberate seconds of silence, he considered his next move. This Alf character could come in useful for future wheeling and dealing, but only if Samuel gained the upper-hand. "No deal," he said, taking a step towards home. "My Prussian steels are worth more than your rubbish."

"I'll give yer the lot fer four Prussians?"

Samuel turned away, smiling to himself and licking his lips at the taste of victory.

"Three then," Alf said. "Me final offer."

Samuel flicked his hair, then smoothed it slowly. "Go on then. But make it quick."

Alf tendered the goods, eager for the exchange, but Samuel hesitated. "One more thing. If you throw stones at my younger brother again, you will be begging your God for mercy."

With the deal done, Samuel strutted off, head tipped back, his beaming smile lightening the melancholy sky. He now owned a book. The Merry Adventures of Robin Hood. His to read.

Rather than go straight home, he leaned against the laneway wall. He would only open the first page. Samuel became so absorbed he didn't see his father approaching.

Solomon gripped Samuel by the ear, twisting the cartilage and digging a sharpened thumbnail into the nerve-filled skin. He dragged his son along the cobbled street and threw him inside the house.

"Why were your meeting the Catholic boys?" Solomon's voice dripped venom.

Samuel lifted his head from the floor. "A game of marbl—"

A slap across the mouth cut his sentence short.

"Empty your satchel."

Samuel unfastened the buckle but slipped one hand inside as he flipped the bag upside down. The book and rosary beads toppled to the floor, but his fist grasped the toy. "The book is from school," he lied, choking on the taste of success turned sour. "A book review project. The teacher's making everyone write one."

"And these?" Solomon snorted, pointing his nose towards the rosary beads. He booted them across the floor, like he was shovelling excrement out of the house. Once the abhorrent object landed in the gutter he faced Samuel. The veins in Solomon's forehead pulsed blue.

Emotionless, Samuel watched as his father cracked whitened knuckles and seized the cane from a rusty nail behind the door. Staring into the fire, Samuel's hand tensed around the soldier and he transported himself into Bubbe's kitchen, where he was safe in her sugary arms.

Chapter Five
POW Camp Batavia 1942

My memories of rain in the Netherlands were of a softly falling dot-dash-dot of drizzle. In contrast, the Javanese downpours plunged like swords into a magician's basket, sharp and fierce from every direction. Until the monsoon arrived, I'd puzzled over the stilts that held up the huts. Why not build them straight on the ground? The deluge suddenly made sense of the architecture and the dry, dusty ground turned into a mud lake.

A few of the bedridden lifted and tilted their heads in synchronicity, following Captain John, who ignored the downpour to slosh through the mire. He moved slowly, doubly burdened by the weight of his worsening ailments and the mattress he carried from the newly vacated bed.

"What happened to the bloke who carked it?" a new fella asked, a lanky Australian with the air of someone looking for trouble. As if we didn't already have more than our share.

"We don't talk about the men dying. But there are countless possibilities." I blinked and looked away from the rusted wire bed frame, where Billy had slept. In the world before war only old men died. Death didn't stalk the young.

John struggled to sling the sodden bedding on the fence, and I swallowed hard, blocking out memories of the departed. This hut was a Petri dish, perfect for multiplying every tropical disease known to man—and then some.

"But why is *he* taking the mattress out?" The lanky one's emphasis on 'he' made my skin prickle. In my pre-war life back in Holland I would never have thought to make friends with someone old enough to be my father, but I'd grown close to John and these comments made me seethe.

"Water and sunlight are our only disinfectant." I pressed my lips together hard, hoping this new guy would take the hint and shut up. People were dying around us, but we tried not to talk about it.

The sun shone briefly and John brushed himself down on the doorway steps, his doggie-shimmy-shake scattering sparkly water droplets.

"Got me a wash at the same time." John grinned, imitating a playful soaping up of armpit and groin. "There are three kinds of people in this world. Them who bath. Them who shower. And them sleeping next to me in this stink-hole."

"No finger-pointing," I said, sniffing my underarm and pegging my nose with my fingers.

The new bloke pushed me aside and offered his hand to John. "Sergeant Jackson. Dick."

John laughed as he wiped wet hands on wet shorts before shaking Dick's hand, and I smiled in anticipation of the slew of Dick jokes I imagined brewing in John's head.

"Captain John Douglas," he said, showing his teeth, the whitest things in the room.

"Oh. You." Dick folded his arms. "I've heard about you."

John gave no reaction, but my nostrils flared.

"The Doc who patched me up at the other camp told me stuff."

John shrugged and wrung out his shirt, hanging it over the railing, casually displaying his bruises.

Dick twisted his mouth like the sole of an old boot leaving the leather and directed his comments to me. "You don't know then? He's a plant. Sides with the Japanese."

John took up his usual watch at the window and in a shameful act of cowardice, I turned away. No wonder John called me The Kid. I should have spoken up. No-one seeing John's bruises could doubt his authenticity.

For the rest of the afternoon, I glared at Dick and waited for him to start another round of insults. I wasn't sure how I'd respond, only that I would.

Once as a child, I'd left a piece of cheese near a rat hole and waited for hours. That rat didn't make an appearance. The vermin called Dick in hut 17 had the sense to stay away.

Later, when the other men were snoring and groaning, I whispered to John, "I hope Sergeant Bloody Dick doesn't move next to us. Sorry about earlier. I should have said something."

"Nope. You did the right thing."

"Why didn't you defend yourself?" I propped myself on my elbow and squinted to discern his expression in the near-dark. He lay on is bed, head on his arm, looking up at the rusty tin ceiling.

"Human judgement isn't my concern. I intend to leave the final verdict to the Almighty."

No stories were shared that night or the next. I saw Dick whispering to the others, sharing the doctor's warnings. Although John went about his day, a deluge of suspicious looks fell harder than the tropical rain, further dampening our morale.

I trusted Captain John. Traitors are cowards and a man who takes a beating to save another is a hero.

Capt. John and I played poker. For gambling chips, we used the helicopter-like seed-wings from a tall Meranti tree. Usually, a group of men surrounded us, making side bets against me. John was almost a sure thing. It was as if he wore a pair of the X-ray vision glasses advertised at the back of American comic books and could see right through my cards.

On this day we played alone. Sergeant Dick was in the far corner whispering to a raggle-taggle audience of POWs whose only entertainment was gossip.

"You little beauty!" John yelled, laying out his hand. "A royal flush."

"Stone the bloody crows, I have to hand it to you," Dick said, walking towards us with a hint of swagger despite his limp. "You've almost got the Aussie accent down pat. Not bad for a Jerry." Dick clicked his heels and rearranged his maw of a mouth, making it small and tight, then placed a finger to imitate Hitler's distinctive moustache. "German passport, you said?" Dick asked a soldier across the packed prison room. "That's right, isn't it, Cullen?"

I wanted John to deny it, but he shrugged instead. "I'm fighting for Australia. What else matters?"

"But are you? I've heard you're not even a captain."

"Another game?" John asked, reaching under the bed for a handful of betting seeds which he gave me, since I'd been cleaned out.

"Sure."

Dick hovered and watched as I dealt, but I directed my eyes firmly towards the flattened bed serving as our card table. "Watch what you say, I reckon. The ..." Dick coughed into his hand. "The Captain is feeding info to the Nips."

The hut fell silent, the only sound the pattering of rain on the metal roof. My back was turned but I felt the filthy eyes of a dozen men staring at John. I didn't want to look at him, in case he thought I was checking for signs, but his face was a magnet pulling my eyes slowly to his. There was no twitch, no ragged breath, no indication of John making ready to respond to Dick's accusation. I drew a couple of cards from the deck and placed my bet.

I couldn't sleep afterwards. Was there any truth to this? If John had denied the allegations, he would've probably looked guiltier than he did keeping quiet.

The following morning a Japanese guard came for Dick. A chain of translation passed from the guard, to a Javanese fellow who spoke some Japanese, then through Captain John who spoke Malay. "The sergeant's leg's healed enough for him to be transferred. He's off to a different camp."

CHAPTER SIX
LONDON, ENGLAND 1916

"You can't go, William. We won't give permission. I'll contact the war office if you do and they'll send you home." Mother wrung her hands, weeping between softly spoken words, until father's yelling drowned her out.

Fay herded their sisters and younger brother from the room, but Samuel stayed to watch the argument. He leaned in with the same fervour he would've given an F.A. Cup football final if they'd had one that year. All matches had been suspended because of the war, which was part of William's argument. If famous soccer players left their teams to join up and fight for King and Country, why shouldn't he leave his family?

It was devilishly compelling to see William in the firing line for a change. Their mother was obviously despairing, but Samuel read her subtler expressions. At fifteen, the face-reading had become more than habitual, it was embedded in his every interaction. This time he decided she wore what he called the double-duty-anguish. At a guess, his mother was both concerned about losing her older son and anxious about the more pressing problem of his father's brewing anger.

Samuel had no doubt if he'd asked his father about enlisting, he would have helped him pack his bags. Out of all six children, Samuel was the one most likely to trigger his father's temper. Perhaps they were mirror images because no-one in the world irritated Sam more than his dad.

He pondered the factors that shaped him: his father's bad traits and even the bloomin' names his mother had chosen for her children. He'd once flicked through a name book on a table at the Jewish clinic while his mother was seeing a doctor. There it was, William: determined guardian, ever faithful, admired for good intentions. Samuel had gagged and laughed when he'd read it, but the funny feeling in his chest had swirled in the wrong direction when he saw the meaning of his own name. Samuel: God heard. The book didn't elaborate on why God was eavesdropping. For all Samuel knew, God had heard rumours of him being untrustworthy.

"Okay, I'll stay." William stuffed his hands guiltily into his pockets and rocked lightly on his heels. "I'm sorry to cause so much trouble."

William's surrender was too quick for Sam's liking, but he was relieved when the mood of the room plummeted from fiery to cool. Mother's shoulders relaxed and Father returned to his usual spot at the table where he stared at the wall. Samuel wondered if his father was questioning his life. He doubted it. Solomon never showed remorse.

When William looked up from unpacking his rucksack, Samuel saw the truth written clear as day —William had rubbed the corner of his eye —he was going to disobey.

William knotted the laces on his shoes, then stood and patted his pockets. "Need anything from the corner shop, Ma? I'm ducking out for a bottle of Dandelion and Burdock."

A stormy look from his father warned of another turbulent conversation brewing, so Samuel pulled his shoes on and followed William. He whistled to himself until they reached the corner of Sidney Street, then threw a glance over his shoulder. "You still plan to enlist, don't you?"

"I've no idea what you're on about." William shook his head.

Samuel assessed the situation. William rarely lied, so why now?

If Sam enlisted it would be for the thrill, but William '*the determined guardian*', probably intended to save mankind. "Practise makes perfect, brother, and when it comes to deception, you're not up to snuff. Right now, your true intentions are written across your forehead clearer than the slogan on the war poster: YOUR COUNTRY NEEDS YOU!"

William stopped and shook Samuel's shoulders. "Shhh. You know nothing, so stop gabbing." William let his chin flop to his chest. "Anyway, I'm stuck now. Mum said she'll contact the authorities and have me kicked out."

"She won't be able to if you enlist under another name."

"But I have to show identification."

Samuel smoothed his hair then tapped his head. "I've an idea."

"What?"

"My mate Alf knows a geezer who's good at forgery. Just cough up some coin and pick a name."

"I wouldn't know where to start." The lacklustre tone of William's voice was unconvincing, coupled as it was with brightly curious eyes.

"My advice, considering the names politicians throw at Jews, is to go for something less foreign sounding than Solonsch. Something simple. Easy to spell, and easy to pronounce." By helping the good son enlist, the expectations set for Samuel would be lowered.

William straddled the flowing gutter, then in an almost choreographed move he crossed his feet, jumped and spun to face Sam. "You set up a meeting and I'll choose a name."

"You'll never attract a woman with your buttons fastened in the wrong hole," Samuel said, making a fuss of unfastening and refastening William's jacket while using sleight of hand to slip the awaited forged documents into an inner pocket. "Feel like some fresh air?" Sam gave the slightest of winks.

"Not a good idea. Looks like rain." Their mother pulled aside the small curtain over the kitchen sink, revealing threatening clouds.

"We're not soluble," Sam said, kissing her on the forehead. "Human skin comes with its own protective coating."

Mother cast Samuel a chastising glance for quoting such facts, trying to avert a rekindling of the heated exchange about evil found in books other than the Torah. Solomon hated books. The arguments had intensified a year ago when Samuel, in his last year of school, defied his father by openly reading an adventure novel inside the house. After throwing the offending book in the fire, Solomon had snatched the cane from its hook. Except this time, instead of disappearing to the safe place inside his head, Samuel stood his ground and spoke to Solomon deep and slow. "You can burn every page and every word I've ever read but it's too late to stop the ideas living and growing." Samuel had grabbed the poker to push the book out of the flames and into the ashes, but he didn't miss his father's flinching realization, that his son was holding a potential weapon. Solomon had grunted and hung up the cane. Samuel filed away that flinch.

"We'll be fine outside, Mum." William gave her a hug that lasted a beat longer than usual.

She bit her lip as she nodded. Her warning look at Sam was no longer necessary. Instead of beginning a tirade on the evil of words, Solomon slumped in his chair.

The brothers slapped each other's backs and whooped once safely outside. William whistled as he sloshed through the gutter, each watery step taking him closer to enlistment.

Fay interrupted their celebration. "Wait!"

They turned to find their older sister, arms akimbo, her usually smiling mouth downturned. "What are you up to?"

William launched into a nonsensical string of excuses and apologies, but Samuel put his hands calmly in his pockets. He knew Fay better. She wasn't annoyed at them planning something underhand, she was annoyed at being left out. More than once she'd told Sam how much she wished she'd been born a man because men have all the fun. She adored her boyfriend, Tom, but complained he had more choices in life simply by being born male. If she discovered William's plan, rather than running off to tell mother, she'd be working out ways to join up too, and at twenty she wouldn't need to lie about her age.

"Sorry. We can't tell you." William squeezed Fay's arm and kissed her forehead.

"But you've told Sam?" Fay pursed her lips. "If you trust him more than me you've got lumps of coal for brains."

"Thanks for your kind words, sister." Samuel cocked his head and fluttered his eyelashes as he clasped his hands to his chest. "You've missed your calling working as a dressmaker. You should move to America and go into the Valentine's Day greeting card business."

Sam got on one knee in front of Fay. "Roses are red, violets are blue, no one has more coals for brains than you do."

Fay swiped at Samuel's cap. "Thanks for illustrating my point." She growled at them both. "Spill the beans."

"Not here," Sam said. "Walk with us."

Sam checked no one was peeping over laneway walls, and waited for a boy on a bicycle to round the corner. Certain they were alone, he gave William the nod, and he retrieved the papers from his pockets and inspected them. "Look completely real."

Fay reached to take it, but William drew his hand back. "I'm not letting either of you know my new name. You can't tell Mum what you don't know."

"So, what's your escape plan?" Fay wiggled her eyebrows with amusement.

"Probably best he just nicks off," Samuel suggested.

"No. That won't work. You need to put a bit of time between disappearing and Mum setting out to find you." Hands on hips, Fay took charge. "William, when's your next film reel delivery for the picture houses?"

"Not much happening. I've a short trip coming up, but I'm only swapping with neighbouring counties." William kicked a pebble.

"Fay's onto something here," Sam said. "Tell everyone you're going away for a month. Say you got a promotion and are delivering films from Edinburgh to Timbuktu. By the time Mum realises you're gone, that ship will have sailed. Literally."

William had been gone a month when the family decided to go to the picture theatre, taking advantage of Solomon leaving on *'important business'*.

This was trouble on a stick. A big, chaotic stick.

When Fay started whistling the tune, *I'm Henery the Eighth, I Am,* Sam answered the call to action and groaned. Faking illness was the first thing that came to mind.

"Aaah!" He clutched his belly. "I've eaten something that doesn't agree."

Sam and Fay had shared the private whistle signal since they'd heard the song. An upstairs' neighbour starred in the local music hall a few years earlier and his singing practice always ended up in an argument. They'd loved the song because it had the words, won't have a Willie or a Sam, but the whistle evolved to mean *'there's trouble'*.

Sam dashed outside, heading in the direction of the shared lavatory, then doubled back to peer through the kitchen window.

"We better stay home and look after Sam," Fay said. "I've never seen anyone look so green."

Their mother sighed, took off her gloves and rested her handbag on the sideboard. "No, I'll stay. The rest of you lot can go to the matinee without me."

Fay whistled again, this time with half-relief. Samuel's ploy had almost worked. Mum just needed prodding. "What if Sam's got something contagious? Shouldn't we all stay home?"

Millie shook her head. Since she'd turned nineteen, she'd been testing the restrictions of childhood, and she grabbed Mother's gloves, while Jane picked up the handbag. The sisters hooked arms either side of their mother. "Come on," Millie said. "Fay doesn't even like the movies. She never sits still. And if Sam was really sick, he wouldn't have moved so quickly through that door."

"I agree," Jane said. "We're all dressed and ready and I've saved some of my wages to buy popcorn. Sam's fine."

Their mother weighed up her decision, looking from the front door to the back. "I suppose we'll only be gone a couple of hours."

"Mum," Millie said. "We'd better hurry or we'll miss the movie."

"20,000 Leagues Under the Sea." Jane fanned her face. "The movie star on the poster looks smashing."

Once they'd left, Fay tapped the window in an all-clear signal, and Sam came back ready to continue his star performance of a dying man.

He stood motionless when faced with an audience of one. "Where are they? This wasn't the plan."

Old Mr George at the box office surely knew William had left? What was going to happen when his mother expected free tickets and Mr George gave her bloomin bad news instead?

Fay massaged the back of her neck. "She's going to find out sometime, Sam. I don't think there's any way around it."

He closed his eyes and draped himself dramatically over the back of Father's empty chair, sure Solomon was in the locked backroom of the curio shop again, gambling his children's hard-earned money on cards. Samuel hoped this was one of his father's luckier days. The ones where he stayed out late and came home with what almost passed as a smile instead of a fight fermenting in his belly.

Sam fixed his eyes on the clock. "They'll be crossing Church Street about now." He wanted to stop his running commentary, stop predicting where they'd be on their journey, but the clock ticked too loudly for him to stop. He stared at the second hand jerkily marking off time and when, by his estimation, the family had reached the motion picture theatre, he sighed. "They'll be there."

Fay blew out a long breath and Sam's heart beat twice the speed of the ticking hand.

They sat like statues waiting for the fallout. "Mum could have had ten disagreements with the cinema's owner and returned home by now," Fay said.

They looked at each other with new hope.

"We've dodged a bullet," she said. "We deserve a calming cup of tea,"

"Too right. William, the lucky bugger has bought himself another month as the golden boy."

Sam was drinking his last mouthful when the front door burst open.

"Fay? Samuel!" Their mother's voice hit a range Sam wouldn't have thought possible. "The two of you are thick as thieves with William. What happened?"

Sam raised his eyebrows and opened his mouth in what he hoped projected a convincing expression of surprise. "What happened, Mum. We haven't seen William in a month."

"William no longer works for the cinema."

"Isn't he delivering film canisters?" Sam's voice was remarkably calm.

"Fay?" Their mother stared and waited for a different answer.

Sam crossed his fingers behind his back hoping Fay would come up with something good. She lowered her head for what Samuel considered too long for an innocent. "Didn't William talk about changing jobs? Maybe he got a promotion from one of the other theatres and wants to surprise us?"

Their mother's stare could have burned a hole through steel. Fay backed away.

Sam ignored the warning. "He's up north I—"

His mother slapped his cheek with her gloves. "The Torah prohibits lying."

"Except if changing the truth protects another." Samuel gave an imploring look. "It was an *emet shel chesed*, a kind and loving 'truth' to save you from worry."

"You can stop digging the hole for your grave, Sam," his mother said. "We know exactly where—"

Jane, pink-cheeked and puffing, cut in. "You missed the excitement. We sat near the front, they dimmed the lights, and the velvet curtains opened." She swished her arms to illustrate. "As always, they started with a newsreel. It's a wonder you didn't hear Mum scream from here! William was on the big screen. He looked so handsome in his naval uniform, smiling straight at the camera and waving as the ship departed. Our William's gone to war!"

Chapter Seven
POW Camp Batavia 1942

Although the sun had long set, I could see Captain John's face clearly. The moon cast a kindly light with gentle shadows which bathed the entire wing of our hut. A single light bulb covered with cobwebs, gave the otherwise severe room an air of tranquility.

But there was little serenity here. Most POWs were asleep while John kept a lookout, hooking fingers through his thinning hair and raking it to one side, pushing it behind his ear.

John chewed over his next words. "I feel those phantom strands," he said. "They tickle as they brush my face. Knew a good bloke once who'd lost an arm. Said he could feel his amputated fingers twitching when he wanted a cigarette. Even asked me to scratch an itch on his elbow once. So, in my books, my brain remembering overflowing locks isn't a major problem."

"I never know whether you're joking, Captain. Even the adventures you tell about your friend Samuel seem unlikely. How do you know so much about what happened?"

"Samuel was a lot like me. Loved to spin a yarn, and I enjoyed listening."

"But are the stories true?" I crossed my fingers.

John turned to look at me, then did the hair thing again. This time I was sure he was doing it as a joke. "Best I pass to you my grandmother's advice. Take everything with a pinch of salt. She was a wonderful woman, my grandmother, but she made a dreadful cup of tea."

When I closed my eyes, John twisted my ear, which made me yelp. "What?"

"That was one of my better jokes, but you didn't laugh. I had to check only your sense of humour was dead. I wasn't looking forward to reading you the last rites or whatever religious flavour you prefer."

I shrugged. "I didn't understand it."

"Of course. The Aussies and the Dutch don't have the same idioms. Take it with a grain of salt means to view everything you see or hear with scepticism."

"What's funny about that?" John was good at many things, but not at clarifying humour.

"The joke's been strangled and tortured to death. I was suggesting my grandmother put salt in her tea, but after my poor attempt at explanation, I'm crossing it off the side-splitting list."

At that, Captain John chuckled and shook. Even though what he'd said was no less confusing, his muffled laughter was contagious and I bit my knuckle as I laughed with him.

When he turned to face the window, I closed my eyes, hoping to sleep. But the nights in Hospital Camp were never silent. The older beds were stable enough, made of metal or wood, but as the need for hospital care grew, the able-bodied soldiers constructed extra beds with bamboo frames. As the wounded men turned painfully in their sleep, a rasping sound of bamboo against rope echoed off the walls.

I'd almost drifted off when an irregular clattering split the silence —a clank, click, clank accompanied by a sweet, yet unfamiliar birdcall. Wordlessly, John slipped off his bed and padded his way softly down the steps.

It was none of my business where he was going. John probably just needed to take what he referred to as 'a leak', but no sooner had he left the building, than the thudding stopped. Surely the rumours weren't true?

I shambled across the wooden floor, angling my body behind the door to get an unobstructed view across the enclosure. The moonlight exposed a figure at the boundary near a clump of pandanus, light clothing with darker cloth draped over head and shoulders. It looked so much like the nuns in the convent of Good Shepherds back in the Netherlands, that I rubbed my eyes and pinched myself to make sure I was awake.

This person, neither identifiably male nor female, was flapping a hand to beckon the captain. A barely audible buzz of hushed conversation accompanied an exchange of sorts, an object passed through gaps in the barbed-wire fence.

At the far corner of camp, a flame flared, then a pinpoint of red glowed from the tip of a cigarette. The squat silhouette of the Nipponese guard we called Widey, or Y.D. which was code for Yellow Devil, rolled his broad shoulders and cricked his neck from side to side.

Without so much as a thought, I limped as fast as a man with a leg ulcer could, not looking at John, but heading straight for Widey. "Cigarette? Cigarette?" I called.

Widey responded with his usual command, "*Kere.*"

Salute. I made a fuss of standing at ease then at attention, doing this three times while making sloppy salutes and repeating loudly, "*Kere. Kere. Kere.*"

POWs were strictly forbidden from roaming at night. The only valid excuse was a visit to the toilet and the guards would watch us.

Fortunately, Hiro our most lenient guard came outside to see what was going on. His generous mood rubbed off enough for Widey to show mercy, but not enough to share his cigarettes. I was thankful he didn't slap my face, kick my feet beneath me, or take down the dreaded whip. I dragged my leg back to the quarters, scanning the yard as I clumsily climbed the stairs. No sign of Capt. John or his visitor.

"I owe you," John whispered from his window seat.

"For what?" I shrugged dismissively, hoping he wasn't up to

something dubious. I'd rather hold on to my belief that his actions were for the good of the men.

"Thank you," John said, "for understanding that captives are like family. We look out for each other, even if it means looking the other way."

Chapter Eight
London 1916

Sam reluctantly agreed to escort his three sisters to *The Women's War Work Exhibition* in Knightsbridge. He'd argued with his mother the girls were hardly in danger of being pestered by men, especially when accompanied by Fay. She was feistier and more imposing than many men he knew, but his father started shouting about Sam being rude and his mother gave the signal to 'clear-out'.

Sensing trouble brewing, Sam decided a giant hall full of stroppy women was the lesser of two evils.

Given the same circumstances, William would have insisted on staying home, but Sam's breath pounded in his ears imagining his father losing his temper and he left as quickly as possible.

The girls took forever admiring the main entry display. They even wasted time deciding which direction to walk.

"The best exhibits are this way." Jane pointed to the right.

"Okay, let's start on the right-hand side and loop back," Millie agreed.

"No. We're not in Europe or America." Fay stood her ground.

"In this country we drive and walk on the left. We'll go the same way as everyone else."

Sam's eyes glazed when they stopped only three feet away to admire a prettied-up collection of military flags. He forced an overly loud cough, then waved his hand over a table of flowers and scented candles. "You can't half tell this is a woman's show. What a tremendous contribution to the war effort. You know what I—"

Fay delivered a sharp chop between his shoulder blades. This time he coughed for real.

"What?"

"You sounded phlegmy. I'll give you another thump if it'll help?"

She marched down the left side of the hall with the sisters at her heels while Sam lagged behind, looking at the multi-paned warehouse windows and giant ceiling beams. The architecture interested him more than the displays. Now if he could come here alone and spider crawl across the beams, soaring high above everything—that would be an incredible outing.

Fay elbowed him in the ribs again. "Stop staring upwards like you've gone all doo lally. Come on."

He immediately felt sorry for her fella, Tom. He couldn't understand why, when Fay was so bossy, Tom continued to smile at her.

"No flowers in this stall, Sam." Millie pointed to a booth for the local munitions' factory. Two women dressed in grey shirts and grey overalls were sorting and packing shells.

"Don't panic folks. Not real T.N.T," a woman with a matching grey head-scarf joked. Her co-worker, wearing lipstick the same blood red as her scarf, made direct eye-contact with Sam. Her scarf, knotted in a large pussy-cat bow, couldn't have been there for safety reasons. She caught Sam gawking at her and she winked. "Not T.N.T, love," she said, "but I go off with a bang."

When Sam blushed and loosened his collar, Fay grabbed his arm.

"You can thank me later for saving you." Fay threw daggers at the woman, then laughed once she'd dragged Sam away.

Miss T.N.T was the first woman who'd treated Sam like a man. Despite the embarrassment he was quite pleased with himself and he glanced over his shoulders, hoping the woman was still watching.

His shoulders dropped when he saw her repeating the same patter to a grey-haired gentleman.

His sisters lingered for an eternity at the Railways and Police Force exhibits. The women droned on and on about the unfairness of the world and how only the recent shortage of men allowed women to work as ticket collectors and officers of the law.

One of the women recited the doctrines of Emmeline Pankhurst, so Sam scooted off, preferring not to witness an uprising of hunger-striking suffragettes. Besides, they'd begun targeting men they decided were too cowardly to join up, and if Miss T.N.T had mistaken him for someone older, they might, too. Sam felt enough shame for leaving his mother at home with his angry father, without risking a woman handing him a white feather.

He honed in on a sign. *Every photograph in this stall is taken by Mrs Hannah Hannerton. Portrait and postcard specialist.* Instead of striding past, his eyes darted from the displayed photos, many of enlisted men, back to the stallholder herself.

This pretty woman looked familiar, but he didn't recognise the name.

Hannah Hannerton. Maybe she looked like someone he knew? Hannah Hannerton sounded musical even when spoken inside his head. The Mrs part hit a wrong note in an otherwise lovely tune.

"You must be one of the few men not away in the war." She looked him up and down as if trying to work out why.

Sam wasn't sure how to take this remark. He braced his shoulders and thrust out his chest. Another woman had called him a man. "I haven't enlisted yet, but I soon will."

He furrowed his eyebrows, trying to identify where he'd seen her before. She couldn't be much older than Fay, who'd recently turned twenty-one. He gasped. "Mabel Normand."

"Sorry?" The photographer scrunched her cute nose.

"I've been trying to place you. You look like Mabel Normand. Have you seen the Keystone Cops pictures? Mabel starred opposite Charlie Chaplin in *Tillie's Punctured Romance*."

"Is she beautiful?" Hannah tucked a strand of hair behind her ear.

"Without doubt." Sam took a step closer. "And now that I've heard you speak, whenever I see her on the screen, I'm going to imagine your lovely voice." He considered telling her how he'd begged his brother to get him one of the Mabel Normand movie posters and that he'd hidden it at home so he could look at her face, but it would make him sound like a child, a creepy one at that, and he was enjoying his moment as a respectable young man.

Hannah blushed and bit her lip. "My husband's away at war. He volunteered right after we married." She took a picture from the display. "This is his portrait. I used a medium glass plate camera."

"Where is he now?" Sam asked.

"Gallipoli, I think. 13th Division. I hope it isn't true about the number thirteen being unlucky."

"I hope not, too." He bowed his head, a rotten taste rising in his throat. Here was a young woman whose husband was risking his life to save his country, and Samuel had imagined himself playing her real-life leading man. "I'd better go."

Hannah took a postcard from the stand and wrote her address on the back. "Here." She handed it to Sam. "I don't have a High Street shopfront, but I've set up the front room as a studio. Come and see me when you're in uniform."

"Thank you." Sam accepted the postcard without taking his eyes off her, then he turned the postcard over. *Self-portrait of a War Bride*. A photograph of the beautiful Hannah Hannerton herself.

"Thank you," he said again, blushing because he'd repeated himself.

"I know," she said. "Why don't we take a photograph now. It might draw attention to the stall." Without waiting for an answer, she removed a naval uniform jacket which made up part of the display. "Put this on and sit in the chair."

Hannah turned to set up the tripod and her skirt twirled with her. Sam soaked up every movement. The slow blink of eyelashes, her shapely ankles, and the flash of calves beneath the swishing fabric. But he especially loved her rose petal lips.

"Sit up straighter." She straightened her own shoulders to

demonstrate and he needed it. He was staring at lips, lost in thought.

She now looked less like Mabel Normand. Hannah's lips were pinker and fuller, but the word swirling in Sam's mind was that her lips were naked. *Naked.* His chest tightened and for a moment he forgot how to breathe.

He sat upright, watching as Hannah adjusted the lens on her camera. A butterfly shaped clasp captured most of her wavy brown hair, holding it hostage behind her head, except for a few wayward tendrils which spiralled over her creamy complexion. He sat on his hands to stop himself reaching out and tucking the hair behind her ears.

Fortunately, she didn't seem to notice him staring. He looked around for his sisters. The last thing he needed was another doo lally remark.

Hannah set up her equipment, then barked orders about the pose she deemed looked best. She moved his limbs into a predetermined place, as if Sam were a doll. She repositioned his shoulders and tilted his head without comment. His chest sank. He was merely a photographer's prop.

On her last shutter click, she brushed down her dress. "I'm satisfied we've got an excellent shot."

He swallowed a gasp. She wasn't throwing him out.

Sam stayed in the chair, mesmerised by her every move as she packed up her camera. Her hips swayed in leisurely half-circles like a sensual dance. She reached high to return the lens boxes to the top shelf and rather than jump up to help, he stayed seated to glimpse her tightening calves.

Hannah turned to look at him unexpectedly, and his breath caught at the mere thought of her catching him spying. He faced away like a thief caught with his hand in the petty cash.

Hannah handed him a card with a session number. "I don't expect you'll want copies but I keep them for thirty days. You can take the jacket off now. It's hot in here. Like a greenhouse with all these windows."

"I'm fine," Sam said. But he wasn't. It wasn't the sun's heat causing him to smoulder. "I've enjoyed it. Why don't I stay here with it on? To attract customers." He could not risk removing the jacket and revealing how much he'd enjoyed the session.

"You're a polite young man." Hannah said. "When my Harry gets back from the war, I hope to have a well-mannered son like you."

She gave him a small smile and for the first time, Samuel cursed his ability to read faces. She wasn't interested in a stupid boy. She was missing her husband.

"Your mother must be proud of you."

Sam's throat went dry as he pictured his mother at home with his father. He felt suddenly ill. His dad wasn't angry at Sam for being rude, he'd already sent Joe to their auntie's house and suggested they all go out. Sam was old enough to know that parents enjoy time alone, but his mother had bitten her lip the way she did when she was frightened.

He handed back the jacket and excused himself with a prior appointment, then raced off in search of his sisters.

"I'm leaving," he whispered in Fay's ear.

Then he ran.

With every stride closer to home, Sam's anger burned hotter. The cold wind against his skin an ineffective balm against the seething beneath his skin. Why had his mother returned to his father so many times? Perhaps Sam was yet to understand love.

He kicked a stone at the gutter in a game he'd often played with William, but it bounced back and hurt his leg, making him incensed at himself and everyone else. Why was William the good son? He'd taken off. Yes, he was defending his country, but what if underneath he was in search of adventure?

Sam stopped to slow his breathing when he rounded the corner of his street. He'd achieve nothing good by bursting in—not in this worked-up state.

The living room was a picture of calm. A welcoming fire blazed from the fireplace, his father wore a shirt, sleeves rolled up to his elbows, and stood near his mother who was reading aloud from the family Bible. They both glanced at Sam, but his mother continued reading.

What had Sam been afraid of?

He excused himself to the bedroom he shared with Joe. This was a rare chance to compare Mrs Hannerton's picture with Mabel Normand.

It was hidden behind a substantial cupboard between the set of bunk beds and the single bed. Sam lifted one corner and slipped his blanket in the space underneath to drag it away from the wall. He retrieved his precious items from where they were jammed and shielded from inquisitive eyes.

Sam's jaw ached from clenching his teeth like a vice. It wasn't the physical lifting, but the thought of his father. He couldn't think of another teenager who needed to hide everything in print.

Before unfolding the poster from where he'd slipped it safely inside his Robin Hood book, he raked then smoothed his hair as if the movie star could see him, too. Propping Mabel Normand against his pillow, he looked from her to the postcard, comparing the face of a woman he'd admired when projected larger-than-life, to the real-sized fragility of Hannah. There was a poignancy about her eyes. The photograph captured the sentiment of a woman yearning for her man. There was no contest who was prettier.

After concealing his treasures and ensuring everything was back in place, he remembered William's cache. Surely he would've emptied it before he left? It was worth checking while he had the chance.

William kept his secrets in an envelope taped behind a heavily framed painting of Bubbe's original farm in Ortelsburg.

Sam toppled with the frame in his arms, then twisted sideways and tossed it onto the bed. After brushing himself off, he flipped it over. The envelope was still there.

A note inside was folded in the distinctly peculiar way William always folded paper. Sam's name was on the front.

Dear Sam,
  I'm expecting you to look here and I hope this finds you well. My

war wages of two shillings and 3 pence per day will be deposited into the bank by the army, and I've left my bank book here in case I do not return. If I die at war, which is not my plan, I need you to forge my signature, withdraw the money, and get everyone away from Solomon.
I refuse to use the word father anymore to describe that man because father denotes affection where I have none.
   William

Samuel's hand trembled as he replaced the note. William had enlisted in order to help the family. He wasn't abandoning them to Solomon's wrath.

At that moment, Sam considered his brother might die. No. He exhaled his worry with the next breath. The British military was the mightiest in the Empire, and they would never lose the war. But if something did befall William, Samuel would follow his instructions, exactly.

As William guaranteed, the bank book was hidden along with another smaller envelope. It contained the counterfeit identification documents Alf had provided. William left them behind.

Two brothers using the same name? Surely, no one would check such a thing with the severe shortage of fighting power?

Sam now possessed the means to escape, but he wanted to think. He slipped the forged papers into his pocket. He'd been as wrong about William as he'd been about leaving his parents at home alone. They'd just wanted time alone to read from the bible. He slumped on the bed and closed his eyes, painting a picture of a loving family in his mind. His parents bathed in the warm glow of the fire. Time together without the family noise. Sam sat up abruptly. The room was oven hot, but his mother was wearing a coat.

She wore her coat inside when she had bruises to hide.

Sam ran downstairs. "Mum, you've forgotten to take your coat off. I'll hang it up."

His father's eyes went straight to the cane on the back of the door.

"I'm fine, Sam." She gripped the table to stand.

"Sit down," his father yelled. "You will keep reading until you've learned your lesson."

When Solomon Solonsch stepped back to reach for the cane, his eyes reflected the malevolent yellow of the flames. He was coming for Sam.

There was a split second to choose. Sam could run, disappear into his bodiless state and wait for it to be over, or he could defend himself like a man.

Sam grabbed the poker beside the fire, but didn't just hold it in defence. He was ready to attack. To kill his father if necessary.

Solomon backed away when his mother's screams pulled Sam out of his enraged trance. When she looked at him, with tears in her eyes, Sam knew she was seeing him just like his father. Like father, like son. A bad seed.

Sam ran the London streets until well past dark. He would follow in William's footsteps, but he had an additional reason to leave. He needed to get away from Solomon before he killed him. He used his pay from the factory to buy the photographs taken at the exhibition, then he marched to the enlistment office.

Like William before him, he deposited his bank book in the cache behind the frame. If both brothers died, he wanted his family to have the means to escape. No more cries in the night. No more 'clumsy-me-running-into-doors'. No more flinching at the cane on the back of the hook. No more living with Solomon.

He wrote a quick letter to Fay, which he pushed under the girls' bedroom door.

Dear sister Fay,
 I enclose two pictures, one for you and one for Mum. Please break the news to her gently. We will make a new life when I get home, and I promise to return in good health. There are letters from me and William hidden behind the painting of Bubbe's farm, to be opened if you receive bad news.
 Your loving brother, Sam.

Chapter Nine
POW Camp Batavia 1942

A feeding frenzy of black flies covered the open sore on my left leg like a vibrating scab. No matter how many times I waved my right foot over the injured calf, the unsatisfactory outcome was a moment's respite for the leg while they hovered around my eyes and mouth. The constant buzzing grated on my nerves and juddered my back teeth.

"This is shit," I said. "I'm a steaming pile of stinking shit and the flies know it." I rolled onto my side and whispered to no one in particular, although perhaps I intended my message for God. "I would prefer to die." I don't think God was listening, but Captain John heard.

"You'll be fine." John put out his cigarette then lifted my leg. He reached under the bed for my spare shirt and rolled it up under my knee. "To elevate the wound," he said as if he knew what he was doing. Maybe he'd had medical training in Australia, before fighting had changed the world.

"The flies are bastards, but if you end up with maggots they'll do more good than harm. It doesn't matter how often the Red Cross drop in medical supplies, there's never enough." John shooed the flies and looked at the rubbish pile right outside the door. "I'll ask

Hiro if we can get some able-bodied men to bury and burn our rotten waste. With luck, the flies will search for stinking pickings elsewhere."

I lifted my head as John marched over to the guard near the gate. He wildly saluted and bowed crookedly from the waist. Hiro spoke a hodgepodge of Malayan and English, while John seemed to have found common ground using a mélange of Malayan and Japanese. After much pointing, nodding and Hiro gesturing for a cigarette, the amicable bartering appeared successful. John had demanded something in return, but nothing obvious came about.

That night and the next, the click-clank-click of pebbles fell outside the hut again. John crept out into the dark. His outside source was back to bargain, but the spasms in my leg prevented me from sitting up and seeing who it was. In honesty, it was more than pain that stopped me. I wasn't sure I wanted to check on John's dealings. My stomach twisted as I remembered Sergeant Dick. He'd been abruptly and mysteriously moved out after accusing John of skullduggery. Usually, men are transferred to the working part of the camp or their bodies removed to the cemetery under the banyan tree. Having Captain John beside me was the one thing that made this place tolerable. I looked away.

The following morning, he skulked beside my bed. "When's your birthday?" I knew he was talking to me, but I kept my eyes shut. The throbbing rippled up my body and sounded in my head. If I was about to die, maybe it was better not to associate with a possible enemy. If only I could be sure which side of the war God was on.

"I've a present for you," he said.

Birthday presents did not fit my mental image of a traitor, so I lifted myself up on my elbows and watched John use a splinter of bamboo to cut open a plump, ripe papaya. I salivated. I must have lost twenty pounds since the war began, and I was always, always hungry. But John bypassed my mouth, using slivers of cool papaya flesh to dress the festering wound.

"While I was on the loose out there in the rainforest—" He nodded towards the green wilderness. "I met a local who practised jungle medicine. He swore by this fruit. Said it had ten times the healing power of sulphur powder. Not that we have any of that at hand."

I stared in disbelief. John wasn't on the straight and narrow, but I hadn't expected him to risk himself for me.

"One more thing," John said as he reached under his shirt, producing a length of fabric like a torn section of mozzie netting. Facing a chair away from my bed, he draped the net from the seat-back and over my leg. "That should keep the buzzing bastards at bay. But if it doesn't, we're in luck, we can pluck out the maggots and have meat with our rice."

"Always the jokes." I laughed.

"I've got another," he said. "What do you call a fly without wings?"

I shook my head from side to side smiling in readiness for another corny gag. "No idea."

"A walk." John slapped his thigh. "I could probably dig out a few more from the old memory bank if it makes you feel better?"

"I'd rather you distracted me. Tell me whether your friend Samuel met up with the photographer woman."

"Darn good idea." John settled on his bed, and rested his head on his hands, positioning himself for storytelling. "Proverb 10:12 tells us how hatred stirreth up strife, but love covereth all transgressions."

Chapter Ten
London, 1916

Samuel gave silent thanks to the weather gods as they trained outdoors. Synchronous sets of star jumps, push-ups and drills completed, it hit him how humans were a small subset of the greater animal world. He compared these men, dressed uniformly in white, to the schools of silvery fish which mesmerised him on the boat-trips across the Channel to Bubbe's house. When one fish signalled to change direction, the others instantly followed. All a connected part of a whole. Now he belonged to such a group. Along with hundreds of men, he blindly followed barked commands from the warrant officer.

"At ease men. All members of the Royal Navy must hold a P.S.T." The commanding officer spat words like bullets, but at the initials P.S.T. the recruits looked to their neighbour for enlightenment. "P.S.T," he said again. "Passed Swimming Test. Men, fetch your swimming trunks and towel. We'll meet at the Public Baths at 1300 hours."

The indoor pool reeked of chlorine and stale body odour. Sam lined along the edge with the others, clenching and unclenching his fists. Again, he imagined the school of fish, darting through the water, except one poor sucker floundering.

Once, on a birthday outing for his sister Millie, Samuel and the family had visited a public bathhouse. He and his siblings had splashed in the shallow end, afraid to venture out of their depth. Samuel had barely dared to lift his feet from the bottom, his curious combination of cycling and bobbing hardly classed as a recognised stroke. Two years on, under watchful eyes, he prayed he'd improved.

The instructor's voice echoed against the hard tiled-walls. "First, the basics. Do I have any competent volunteers?"

Several young men raised an arm and were immediately dispatched to various points in the pool to demonstrate. Sam concentrated on the strokes, the breathing, and the floating. Although from the outside his body seemed still, his muscles flexed and tensed, as he rehearsed each movement.

"Those who feel confident jump in on my command. If you are not sure, stay on the edge. Sending a bad-news-telegram to families about the demise of poor chaps who've never even set foot out of the country is not my favourite job."

Bert, a skinny redheaded fellow who shared the same barracks, nudged Sam and whispered, "I'm not keen. I've never even sat in a bath, let alone soaked myself in something head deep."

"Why'd you choose the Navy then?"

"The Naval Enlistment Office was the closest. One of them suffragettes handed me a bloomin' white feather. Couldn't sign my name, Bert Errol Harris, fast enough."

"Right." The instructor yelled. "Those inexperienced men on the perimeter, if you fall into trouble, do not grab your fellow sailors. I repeat. Do not grab your fellow sailor. Wave your arm and I'll throw you a life-buoy. The only thing worse than a bad-news-telegram for a dead man is breaking the news about a sailor being drowned by someone on the same bloody side."

It didn't take long for Bert and Sam to end up clutching life buoys, but they made a competition of pushing the floats in front of them, increasing their swimming distances with support.

Bert cocked his head flippantly towards the cadets swimming laps across the deep end of the pool. "Bet they're not having as much fun as us."

"You actually believe that?" Sam wasn't having fun. He felt like the class dunce, wearing a buoy instead of a coned hat.

"Course, I do. New skills. I'm the first in my family to swim."

The instructor barked an order at Sam, "Jump out as far you can, then get yourself to safety any way you know how."

As Sam dog paddled to the edge and lifted himself out, Bert whooped.

Bert thought everything was amusing.

"Last exercise for today," The instructor yelled. "If the ship goes down, there could be burning debris on the surface. You need to practice holding your breath so you can swim away from danger."

At first Sam was terrified of holding his head under water, but he transported himself elsewhere, like he'd done many times when his father held the cane. By the end of the session, Sam was as calm as a meditating monk and could hold his breath longer than anyone.

He'd dried and dressed when Bert joined him. "We passed the first test. More importantly; I flamin' well survived, and you were the underwater champion."

Bert's teeth had such wide gaps, that he whistled when he exhaled. "How d'ya do it?"

"What?"

"Stay under the flippin water."

"I pretended I was reading my favourite book; The Merry Adventures of Robin Hood."

"What d'ya mean, reading it?"

Sam smiled. "*IN MERRY ENGLAND in the time of old, when good King Henry the Second ruled the land, there lived within the green glades of Sherwood Forest, near Nottingham Town, a famous outlaw whose name was Robin Hood.*"

"D'ya read the whole flippin book? Underwater?" Bert looked incredulous.

"Only the first page. I would have bloomin' drowned if I'd done that." Sam tipped his head to get water out of his ear.

Bert laughed and slapped Sam's head for him. "I was impressed with you holding your breath. Reading as well? That's incredible. I'm sticking with you from now on."

The barracks was a hive of activity as the men packed up and made their beds taut enough to bounce a coin.

"I want those boots polished as well," yelled the officer in charge. "Shiny enough to get a glimpse up a woman's skirt. But don't go doing it. You'll likely get yourself a right slap."

He walked up and down the dorm, checking everything was ship-shape. "Right fellas. Today, us in charge are crossing the *T*s and dotting the *I*s on your paperwork. That gives you all a day off. We sail in a week so if I was in your shoes, I'd hit the road."

"A day off," Sam said to Bert. "Will you go see your family? Say another goodbye?"

"Not on your Nelly. My old man would twist my bloody ear off. He's already said goodbye which was more like good riddance. And for a great gollumpus, he moves right quick when he's inflicting pain on others." Bert's laughter had a hollowness that Sam felt rather than heard.

"Let's get big fat greasy chips," Sam said. "It's gonna be ages before we have anything good to eat. I'm already sick of Navy rations."

"Want to splash out and buy battered fish?" Bert raised his eyebrows in hope. "I've never had the dosh to buy chips. Only scraps."

Although Samuel had sometimes asked the woman at the chippy for the leftover deep-fried fish-batter called scraps, here was Bert who'd never tried the real thing. "Come on. We'll eat so many chips we'll sink to the bottom of the pool."

"What an adventure," Bert said, smiling as he tested his long-legged pace in a rush towards the food.

Sam needed something more thrill-seeking than buying fish and chips to get his heart pumping. But his turn was coming soon—one more day and they'd set off on a real-life adventure.

Back at the barracks Sam, Bert and three other young men were singled out.

"Right, you lot, the paperwork doesn't match your physical appearance. Either you're small for your age or you've lied. Lying is an offence, but because you did it for a noble cause, you have choices. Prove your age. Go home and wait until you're older. Or, we can transfer you to the merchant navy where you'll learn seamen skills. When you're old for the Royal Navy proper we'll transfer you back."

Sam and Bert caved when pressed for birth certificates, and were promptly dispatched to the Mercantile Marines.

Chapter Eleven
The North Sea, 1916

The merchant ship had been stationary in the North Sea for a month, transferring supplies to naval ships engaged in the combat. Other seamen were sheltering below deck, and for good reason. The grey water of the North Sea blurred into grey skies and the darker grey of the ship matched Sam's mood.

He turned up his collar and rested his rugged-up arms on the ship's railing. Not even layered clothing protected him from the gnawing cold of the arctic driven wind. His daydreams of regaling everyone with tales of bravery and weaponry were replaced with this bleak scenario. Grey upon grey days of boredom. Sam pulled his hood off in an attempt to freeze out thoughts of William, weighed down by medals while surrounded by swooning female fans. Sam lurking in the background, swathed in grey, having nothing colourful to tell.

"An important job," the commanding officer had said. "You will be part of the naval reserve. Every war machine needs support. You'll join a merchant ship sweeping for mines, searching for submarines, and transporting vital supplies."

Sam must have shown his disappointment more than Bert because the officer slapped his back. "If it's danger you're looking for, there's plenty to be had. Quite a few merchant seamen have gone to watery graves."

"Aren't you pissed off, too?" Sam had asked Bert as they packed up their belongings.

"What for? I don't care about being too young. Nope. I'm still getting away from home, I'm getting well paid, and I'm not in the flamin' line of fire."

Sam had shrugged. "The war better not be bloody well over before we join up proper."

At least Bert and Sam were on the same ship.

William was no doubt closer to action on a ship flying the white ensign—a symbol of the British Royal Navy. Sam squinted his eyes against the cold and stared at the red ensign flapping in the wind. He was marking time under the wrong flag.

"Boo!"

Sam jumped when Bert joined him on deck. "Anything out there?"

"Not while I've been here, but we're ten nautical miles from the Jutland battle zone."

Sam ignored a rumbling under foot but it jolted Bert into life. "Did you feel that? An explosion?"

"Yep." Sam couldn't be bothered faking excitement. The Navy were blockading the exit and only U-Boats were getting out. They never saw those because they were under the sea.

"Hope that was an allied bomb sinking an enemy ship." Bert pumped a fist into the air.

"It doesn't matter to the war effort whether the sunken vessel is friend or foe, as long as it blocks the German fleet, and stops them sailing into the open ocean."

"Course it matters. If it's an enemy ship, we're not losing our men. At least we have God and King on our side."

"Surely God is losing men no matter which side wins—" Sam cut his speech short at Bert's confusion. "Anyhow, the explosion has likely just muddied up the ocean floor."

"Let's see if they got any news in the signal room, I can add to my map." Bert skittered ahead, eager for information.

Sam knew the drill. Bert would ask, then forget the name of any ship involved. Sam would write it down then listen to Bert for evenings on end, reading the names or moving them from his 'live' map to his 'dead' map.

"Was the last explosion a hit?" Bert asked the warrant officer receiving telegraphed messages.

"Negative to a bullseye," the warrant officer said.

Bert nudged Sam with his elbow. "You were right. Blown up the sea floor again."

Sam was baffled by Bert's enthusiasm. Some war. He'd seen more military action playing with toy soldiers in the laneway. "There'll be hundreds of fish with headaches and a school of dead ones *floundering* about."

Bert laughed, and the warrant officer rolled his eyes. Life was so predictable.

When the radio burst into German chatter, the warrant officer called for an interpreter, and Sam cocked his head, listening intently to the news. The operator stared at him with distrust. He'd have to be more careful. He read others easily. Now, he must make sure his own face didn't telegraph secrets. Letting on he spoke fluent German would not be seen as a positive. The British viewed all foreigners with suspicion. Sam shuddered at the thought of being interrogated. A German speaking man with falsified documents could be charged as a traitor.

He dragged Bert down to the sleeping quarters to get ready for the night's show. He might not be helping the war effort in the way he'd hoped, but he was determined to put on a good performance for the nearby ship. His vessel was about to boost the morale of sailors anchored in the area. The ships' crews took turns putting on pantomimes and Sam had been one of the first to volunteer for this one. Their audience tonight, a ship's worth of rowdy Australians.

Having watched many silent movies, some several times, Sam had easily come up with an idea for a skit. Poor, reluctant Bert shanghaied into playing the part of Mabel Normand against Sam's Charlie Chaplin.

"Before we start, what was the name of that ship that just sank?"

"The *Lützow*."

Bert recorded it in his journal, then began pinning a bed sheet together to create a barely plausible dress. "Why do I have to be the girl?" Bert complained.

"You have sexier legs," Sam said as he punched a black bucket hat into a rounder form. "Hopefully the men will be drunk enough to visualise this as a bowler hat and believe you're a real woman." He chuckled to himself as he painted on a short dark moustache and grabbed the cane he'd improvised using a broken umbrella.

Sam was ready for this—he and William had spent hours practising the Charlie Chaplin walk. Feet turned out like penguins, clumsy waddling steps, then a high swing of the right leg before spinning to step in the opposite direction. All done while twirling a cane. While not a duplicate of Charlie Chaplin, he would be recognisable enough to entertain desperate men.

"The Aussies are stamping their feet," Bert said. "We'd better hurry and appease this boisterous bunch."

They crept onto the stage and peeked through the make-shift curtain at men clanging tin mugs together. "I don't think they're drinking tea," Sam said. "I'm looking forward to making them laugh, but don't be so convincing as a woman that I'm forced to fend off sex-starved sailors and defend your bloomin' honour."

"What if we aren't funny enough?" Bert whispered. "I've seen sailors chuck random objects at poor performers. I'd rather my family not receive a telegram saying their son's war injury was inflicted by an Aussie wielding a stinkin' mackerel."

"Come on. You look just like my Mabel Normand poster. They're going to looooove you."

Bert elbowed Sam in the ribs, then called through the curtain in a loud high voice. "Cut it out. There's a lady in the house."

When the curtain was drawn, the pair sidled onto the stage.

The audience cheered at the peek-a-boo of Bert's slender legs. Once the background music started, Bert swooned, sighed and fanned himself as instructed by Sam. He gave a horrified gasp when Chaplin-Sam lifted his hat, scratched his head and swung his cane right between Mabel-Bert's trembling knees.

"Nice legs. What time do they open?" yelled one Aussie.

Chaplin-Sam continued his silent movie routine, pretending to pluck a hair from Mabel's head and balance it on his nose while twirling the cane.

"Enough of that. Pucker up and give your girl a smoocheroonie."

Bert's eyes widened, which added to the air of helpless female in distress. Sam enjoyed the audience attention, and mimicked a love-struck man. Eyes closed, lips pouted and fist a-thump-thump-thump at his chest to show the pounding of his heart.

Bert tried to leave, so Sam pulled him back. He toppled and Sam's arms were waiting. He placed a hand over Bert's lower face and pressed his lips on Bert's covered mouth. The audience stamped and whooped at the fake kiss.

Bert curtsied and made his escape. Sam bowed then penguin walked off stage.

"They loved us," Sam shouted above the raucous applause.

"You didn't stick to the bloody script." Bert's brown eyes looked black. "We're a laughing stock."

"That's what comedy is, Bert. Getting people to laugh at you so they don't have to laugh at themselves." Sam cupped his ear. "Listen. They're calling for you."

The chants of *Bring back the woman,* morphed into *Bring back the floosy and her boyfriend.*

"See?" Bert said.

"It's a joke," Sam said while Bert almost tore off his skin removing his make-up. "I don't fancy you one bit, but I did find you funny."

Sam was considering other ways to tease Bert when the ship's Captain interrupted. "You! I want a word."

The Captain spoke in two volumes, loud and deafening. This order was issued at the earsplitting maximum.

Sam knew why he'd been summoned. From the moment he'd been caught listening in to the German broadcast, followed by the radio operator's intense stare, his pulse thrummed a warning beat. If only he'd swung his Charlie Chaplin legs high enough to kick his own arse instead of doing an equally flexible move to shove his foot in his mouth.

The Captain's cabin was merchant navy-issue grey with the exception of a timber desk and bookshelf with steel rods to prevent books flying across the room in rough weather. Against the background of heartless steel, the Captain projected warmth. If Sam could talk his way out of this, he'd have a story to tell after the war.

"A most serious matter has come to my attention."

Sam cocked his head from side to side, weighing up his options, deciding on offensive rather than defensive. "I know exactly what I'm here for, Sir. It wasn't Bert's fault at all that we destroyed the ship's property. The ruined bed sheet is entirely on me, as are the modifications of the bucket hat. I fully understand the consequences and am ready for you to dock my pay."

"That isn't why you are here." The Captain steepled his hands and tapped the finger tips as he considered his wording.

"Was it the show, then?" Sam asked. "I know it was lewd. Shoving that cane between Bert's legs wasn't rehearsed, Sir. The sailors called for something more, and that was the first thing that came to mind. Poor Bert is as shocked as you."

Although the Captain didn't smile, Sam noted a subtle attitude shift. He'd dropped his hands and relaxed. Enough of a signal for Sam to know the Captain wanted to be on his side.

"An officer has reported that on multiple occasions you have listened to German radio transmissions and appeared to understand."

Sam's pulse thumped in his tightening throat, but he commanded his heart to slow down. Since no question had been asked, Sam waited. A moment of silence was the best tactic at this point of the game. He'd studied his own siblings when accused of a minor wrongdoing. They'd jumped in too quickly to defend themselves when they were guilty. Instead of a simple, no, they'd say, 'no, no, not me, I wouldn't do that, I wasn't even home.' An obvious sign of guilt.

The Captain leaned over his desk and squinted at Sam. "How much German do you speak?"

"Sorry, Sir? Do you want me to learn?"

Performing the pantomime had required balls, but this conversation was the performance of his life. Sam's eyes wandered over the bookshelf behind the captain. He imagined how someone innocent would react. He rearranged his face— lifted his eyebrows as if interested in what the Captain was asking, while giving his best impression of being distracted by the books.

Under the Captain's continued critical gaze, Sam took a shallow breath through his nose and incline his head to read the titles on each book's spine. "I love the word spine. A wonderful word. You could use it for someone with strength and substance. Books contain both. I've never known someone with their own library. My father banned all books from our house. Well, except for the bible."

The Captain shifted uncomfortably in his seat. "Do you like to read?"

Sam wasn't intentionally playing the sympathy card, but it worked so effectively, he filed it away as a killer card for future use.

"Whenever I get the chance." Sam sensed he was almost out of danger, but knew the language issue needed putting to rest. "If you have a book on German, I could try to learn. That's if it would be of use to the war effort. I am a quick learner, Sir."

"That won't be necessary." The Captain stood and pointed to the exit, then gestured for Sam to wait. "If you would like to borrow a book, you may, but I expect you to take good care of it."

Chapter Twelve
POW Camp, Batavia, 1942

Captain John's stories were like a nightly episode of a dramatic radio play and if I closed my eyes, I could imagine myself back in Holland crowded around the large timber wireless, watching Dad tune in to the *Inner Sanctum Mysteries*.

The only thing amiss about Captain John's instalments were the confusing sound effects. His stories about Sam at sea, were sometimes interspersed with Japs yelling orders or the sharp whistly bursts of the cuckooshrikes.

I'd watched a short film once, 'Back of the Mike' which revealed the secret sound effects of radio plays. John's stories didn't need help; whatever he missed with words, he made up for with his delivery and my own imagination supplied the rest.

Except this day, I had questions. I stewed for a while. Questioning John might put an end to his tales, and I desperately needed the stories to keep going. But once things played on my mind like the annoying sound of a dripping tap, I had to make them stop.

"Captain?" I asked over a meal he called 'meat and rice'. It was a Malayan vegetable rice dish, but John reckoned it had enough cooked maggots to count as meat.

"I'm not sharing." He smiled in such a way that instead of a POW in his forties, I saw the younger, handsome man he would have been before the Japanese beatings took their toll.

"May I ask about Sam?"

"Sure. Although I knew him well, there were things he did that I never understood."

"You still call him Sam. What name did he use in the Great War?"

John swallowed his mouthful of food "Jack. But he was always Sam to me." He continued sweeping rice into little balls with his fingers and eating without so much as a twitch.

This lack of reaction emboldened me to push my luck further. "Was Sam trying to listen in to the military secrets?"

"Yes and no. He was eavesdropping but didn't think about why. Impulsive youth."

"What would have happened if he hadn't convinced his commander?" I scooped some rice, my eyes fixed on Captain John.

He stroked his chin. "Probably would have jumped overboard, and stowed away on the Aussie ship." John laughed, then gasped before clutching his back. After a few steadying breaths, he regained his composure. "Like many young men, Sam searched for meaning. Adventure filled the void for a while, but it took him longer than most to find out what he needed."

"I bet he was terrified of being caught spying."

"Maybe, but he was young. It's not until we're older that we realise how frightening the world is."

"Well, you're never frightened." I lifted my chin, imitating John's strength even though I felt none of it. "I've watched you closely and have never seen the fear the rest of us feel."

"That reminds me of a story." John stretched an easy smile across his face. "I was staring at a woman in a restaurant once. She was swigging drink after drink. My wife noticed me staring, and asked who she was. 'An old girlfriend,' I said. 'I broke up with her before I met you. My mates told me she started drinking the night I left and has rarely been sober since. Now I see it's true.'"

'My God,' my wife said, 'I've never heard of anyone celebrating that long.'

John was avoiding my question, but his laugh was contagious. We quietened when a guard called out a threat, but even subdued, our chuckles still brightened the hell hole.

"How do you remember all these jokes," I whispered.

John tilted his head upwards. "When whoever hands out traits gave me mine, they gave me too good a memory."

"How can a memory be too good?"

The Captain focussed on his maggoty rice, the two lines between his eyebrows deepening. "The effort some people put into remembering, is the effort I spend forgetting."

Chapter Thirteen
At sea 1918

"Ah've 'ad me eye on you, lad."

Sam knew who the voice belonged to without looking up. There was no chance of mistaking able seaman Wilko's broad north-country accent.

"Yer a reet grand worker."

"Thanks." Sam continued stocktaking, marking off each box of supplies and moving them to a pallet ready for re-stocking a neighbouring vessel. Wilko's stare bored hotly into the back of his head. This wasn't a casual visit.

"Easy on it, cock. I'll park myself 'ere a bit, if yer don't mind."

Sam prepared the stock until he'd finished a complete page of the order. What did Wilko want? He didn't work in this section. Sam broadened his shoulders like a posturing bird. If Wilko thought Sam was lower on the pecking order, he was sadly mistaken. "Out with it," Sam said.

"'ang abewt. You mightn't know this, but thar's allus extra provisions."

"And?" Sam kept his expression disinterested.

"Them lot won't notice nowt missin'. If you put spares ter one side, thar's a profitable market."

Sam ticked off the next batch of items. "Get lost." He put his head down and rechecked his work.

Wilko waited patiently at first, then he stood and tipped his cap. "Ta-ra then. Ah'll visit you again in't morning."

"Don't bother."

Once Wilko left, Sam prised open a wooden crate filled with packs of cigarettes. He checked the inventory. Wilko was right, there was more in the delivery than on the list.

His Bubbe's voice whispered across the ocean, '*Be good, Sam. William would never be led into temptation.*' An uneasiness ran up Sam's arm and tingled in his fingers, but he kept exploring.

He wouldn't be caught. Sam wasn't teaming up with bloomin' Wilko. The fewer people involved, the less chance of being found out.

To limit water damage, each crate had a base layer of lining material. As Sam removed a layer of cigarettes, he imagined his father removing his belt and wrapping it in his fist. '*You're the bad seed.*'

Sam cursed and spat. He wasn't listening to that man.

He emptied the crate, shoving three sheets of cardboard under the base layer, and repacking it. Unless someone counted the individual packs, the box appeared untouched.

Desperate to unload the goods he'd stashed in his nap sack, he nipped down to the quarters he shared with Bert, best to go when the cabin was empty.

"Hey," Bert called from the bunk.

"Why are you here? You okay?"

"Was about to the ask the same thing. You look like you've seen a ghost."

That's exactly how Sam felt.

"Sorry, this is me cogitating face." Sam forced a laugh.

"Sounds bloody painful." Bert clutched his belly. "Talk about painful, I have to dash to the heads."

Sam waited for Bert to leave before he hid the cigarettes in a laundry sack at the bottom of his locker.

He could have returned the empty bag to the storeroom before

Burt returned, but a personal war fought inside his head. *'Why did you steal the cigarettes?'* One voice asked. Another voice answered. *'Not such a bad thing. No one got hurt.'*

He was sitting cross-legged on the floor when Bert returned.

"That's better... for now," Bert groaned, hobbling clenched-buttocked to his bunk.

"I've been wondering," Sam said, "is everything in the world black or white?"

"Well, obviously bloody not. Trees are green, the sky's blue, and your hair is brown as shite."

"I'm thinking about subjects like God? Why isn't there one religion? It would cut back the wars."

"Too hard a problem for me at the best of times. And at the minute, my concentration is on my arse, not my head."

Sam hesitated a moment. "What about stealing then? Is that always bad?" He kept his voice light and curious.

"Not if you're stealing to keep someone alive."

"Like Robin Hood?"

Bert chuckled. "Isn't he the bald bloke shovelling coal in the furnace?"

Sam was too tense for a witty come-back. Bert knew exactly who Robin Hood was, he'd made him tell him the story more than once. He picked up the duffel bag. "I'll leave you in peace."

Sam navigated a complex route from his quarters to the storeroom, each step more reluctant than the last. Wilko might have given him the idea, but it was Sam who'd taken action. He imagined selling contraband smokes to the next ship they encountered. He tried convincing himself the profits would go to his beloved mother who never spent money on herself, but he knew the story of Robin Hood word for word, and there'd been no wiggle room where Robin kept the money for himself.

"What brings you around this end of the ship?" barked the Captain.

Sam transferred the duffel bag from one shoulder to the other. An empty bag seemed a strange thing to carry and could be tricky to explain. Sam's brain went into over-drive, his throat tightening.

"Looking for you, Captain. An able seaman told me I might find you 'round here."

"You brought me something?" The Captain pointed at the bag.

"Err… sorry… no. It's empty… but I hope to change that." He threw the Captain his best smile and waited for him to return it. "I was wondering… would you possibly trust me with a book from your library? My chums spend most of their spare time playing cards, but I'd rather read."

The Captain grunted, immediately reminding Sam of his grandmother who made a similar sound when she wanted to appear strict. He suspected every gruff idiosyncrasy: the voice, the stance, and the forced seriousness; made up a protective shell to hide the Captain's gentler core.

Sam employed a similar technique in reverse, coated himself in sugar to mask the rot.

The Captain set off in a methodical march with Sam as his shadow. Both stood 'at ease' in his cabin. Sam feeling anything but.

"You expressed an interest in learning languages. Here are my old Latin text books." He dropped them into the bag. "Now, this one's interesting reading, but again it's non-fiction." He showed Sam the woven fabric cover of a book by Francis Galton.

"*Hereditary Genius,*" Sam read aloud. "*An Inquiry Into Its Laws and Consequences.*"

"Yep. This fellow is smart." The Captain tapped the cover. "He has riveting theories about men. A cousin of Charles Darwin." The Captain searched Sam's face for understanding. He ran his finger across a shelf of books. "If you haven't heard of Darwin, you'd better take this one, too."

"What does it all mean?" Sam hadn't heard of Darwin, Galton or whatever 'hereditary' was.

"In a nutshell: Dalton studied identical twins separated at birth to find out what traits are inherited and which are the product of upbringing."

"What did he find?" Sam wasn't sure he wanted an answer. Not if it meant bad seeds were unchangeable.

"Intelligence, it seems, is either there or not. You can't put in what God left out. You've an unusual cleverness, lad, who do think you got that from?"

Sam's ears turned pink. "My mother."

"Good. Now, the other strongly inherited trait is criminality. A tendency to walk on the wrong side of the law."

An image of Solomon surfaced and he blinked it away. "Can't be undone then?"

"This is only the theory of Nature versus Nurture. A clever man would try to control his urges and choose a wife with positive tendencies which counteract his faults. That's what I did and I'm right proud of my children." The Captain tapped his desk like an auctioneer closing a bid. "Time for me to get on with my inspection. Take care of my property."

Sam walked away with a full bag, but a hollowness in the pit of his gut. He intended to read the books, hoping to disprove his mother's belief.

As he strode back to his sleeping compartment, he thought about the Captain's children. How lucky to have a father who read books and cared about his family.

The Captain's words instilled hope for a less bleak alternative. The inevitability of bad-seed destiny may not hold true. Sam's brain might be an impetuous beast, but if he could rein in those impulses, he could set his own direction. Sam tapped his head as he walked. "I am not my father. I decide my own future."

He'd return the cigarettes immediately.

He opened the cabin hatch and was relieved to find it empty. With dizzy optimism, he collected the contraband and returned it to the stores. As he held the hammer to nail the crate shut, his brain pleaded to make a compromise. Wouldn't putting half the cigarettes back be satisfactory? Sam hesitated, then crammed them in, striking the hammer with such force the nail ricocheted across the storeroom deck.

He readjusted the slatted lid, intending to seal it, but he thought of Wilko. If, as Wilko claimed, there were surplus supplies, it wasn't as if anyone was gonna miss out.

He was doing the merchant navy a favour by not taking an entire case.

He carefully rearranged the layers and took a few packets for himself. "Here you go, boy," Sam said, tapping his head. "A harmless reward for doing the right thing."

Chapter Fourteen
London, 1919

Sam hunched his shoulders as he walked the London streets in civilian clothing. He'd felt exposed from the moment he'd handed in his uniform. Only three years had passed since he left, but he looked at his home town through a stranger's eyes.

London was worn-out and battle-weary. Before the Great War, Sam never paused to study the buildings, such was the haste of youth. While the grandest old buildings still shone with former glory, many crammed in-betweens needed repair and a coat of paint. Had these streets always looked tired, or had the shortage of manpower sped up decay?

He entered the back laneway to home, then debated whether he should knock on the front door like a visitor. Guilt hit about the infrequency of his postcards. His mother knew he was alive, but only because she hadn't received a telegram telling her otherwise.

Were Fay and Tom married? He hoped Joe and Jane and Millie had survived unscathed.

Clouds darkened the sky and reflected Sam's murky thoughts. If one person had to be missing, he wanted it to be his father.

He unlatched the back gate then hesitated, but Fay caught sight of him through the kitchen window and ran outside, wrapping her arms firmly around him.

"You're taller than me now." She bopped Sam playfully on the head and smiled, but her voice was drawn, the attempted teasing forced.

"Are you angry at me for not saying goodbye?" he asked.

Fay blinked back tears. "No. I'm relieved you've returned." She twisted her engagement ring and tears spilled down her cheeks. "Tom was stationed in Gallipoli..." She sniffed and wiped her face with the back of her hand.

Without another word, Sam knew Tom was one of the many who never made it home.

He pushed away an awful thought before it took hold. William would be waiting. A war hero, no doubt. No right-thinking God would keep Sam alive and let his brother die.

Fay pulled him into the living room which hadn't changed, the same worn upholstery and frayed curtains draped against chipped-paint.

Fay squealed, "Look what the cat's dragged in."

William stood at attention and Sam expected his brother to make a joke or salute, but he simply nodded.

Sam dropped his bag to embrace Millie and Jane, then went to hug Joe. Joe pulled back to shake Sam's hand, and William stepped forward to shake hands, too. Although the handshakes were firm, and the smiles warm, they were men now, and men share neither hugs nor feelings. The change in his brothers spread an emptiness from his gut to his throat, making speaking difficult. Later, he recognised it as loss.

He hugged Jane and Millie again, pausing to inspect them. Either they'd grown prettier or he'd forgotten. Family members have a beauty you don't always recognise until you've been apart.

Sam nodded at Solomon who glared from his place at the head of the table. Sam's pulse raced as he searched the room for the person he'd missed the most. His mother.

"What's going on?" She called down the stairs, stopping, mouth open, on the bottom tread. Her face was drawn and more lined. Like the uncared-for buildings, Sam's mother had deteriorated in his absence. He raced to lift her off her feet. She gripped him tightly, her body trembling as she sobbed into his chest.

His father snarled what could have been generously interpreted as hello, but was more likely a complaint. No wonder his mother looked downtrodden. While he was at sea, Sam had studied the Captain's book on nurture versus nature and he understood the value of a supportive atmosphere for children, yet nowhere did it mention the negative effects of constant criticism towards adults. His loving mother was withering.

Their father stood, his chair scraping the kitchen floor, the sound like a screeched '*good riddance*'. He scowled at Sam's mother. "I'm off to work. The rest of you carry on time wasting."

They all knew the boot-maker's factory was closed on Saturday. Things had stayed the same; Solomon was gambling and blaming everyone else for his failure. But no one would ask him to stay at home. Like the magic of electric lamp-light throwing night-time sunshine, Solomon brought light to a room by departing.

"Sit," Sam's mother said, giving him a start. "If it hadn't been for the one measly postcard you sent, I would've been beside myself. If you find a woman crazy enough to marry you, then you better not do this to her. You shouldn't leave your loved ones worrying themselves sick."

"Mum. You knew I was okay. Bad news travels fast." His smile pleaded. Back with his mother, he became a boy trying to avoid trouble.

"And how would they have let me know? I looked for you. Army. Navy. Everywhere. No record." She leaned against her armchair.

Sam wriggled uncomfortably under his mother's icy glare. He dropped to the ground by her feet, steepled hands in front of his face to avoid eye-contact. "I used a different name. I had to; I was underage. Besides, I didn't want anyone thinking I was Russian or German. William did the same."

"And William sent me a long explanatory letter. All you sent was a stingy postcard. *Safe, thinking of you.*"

Sam relaxed against the arm of her chair. She could get as angry as she liked. Bottling up resentment couldn't be good for her headaches. If only she'd direct it at his father.

She reached down and stroked Sam's hair, with a look he interpreted as resignation. He preferred the anger. The worst thing he could imagine was a mother resigned to being disappointed by her son.

"I'm really, really sorry, Mum. I wanted to fight for our country and I didn't think about anyone else."

"So, did you fight?" His mother gave him the truth-telling stare.

"Nothing bloomin' glamorous. Once the Royal Navy discovered my real age, they transferred me to the Mercantile Marine. I never carried a gun, but I learned a lot about ships and sailing…And it was dangerous…"

Millie jumped to Sam's rescue. "You should tell us some stories like William has. He fought alongside Australian soldiers in Gallipoli, but we're mostly getting the silly nicknames they gave each other. William's not a storyteller like you."

William shrugged. "War shouldn't be an exciting story. The fighting men were big-hearted and scared, but they looked after their mates. War was mostly dirty and wet with lots of waiting. There were hours and days of willing something to happen while dreading it at the same time."

"We had blokes with nicknames, too," Sam said, trying to lighten the mood and get everyone laughing. He winked at his sisters and smiled at his mother. "This one bloke I met broke his wrist as a kid. Even though the bone mended, his hand never grew properly. The sailors called him The Clock."

"Why?" asked Millie.

"Because he'd one long hand and one short hand."

Only Millie laughed. The rest knew it wasn't funny to laugh at another's misfortune.

Chapter Fifteen
London, 1921

Sam didn't mind unloading cargoes of grain, meat, tobacco and vegetables at the Royal dockyards. He watched the passenger ships with interest. So many places he'd yet to visit. The work was constant and he liked the physicality, but it was boring. The most satisfying parts of each day were the short sharp whistles letting them know of meal breaks and the drawn-out triumphant *phweeeeet* signalling knock off.

One Friday the whistle blew early. Rumour had it that someone important was inspecting the wharves. The secrecy and lack of notice suggested it was King George V himself, but Sam wasn't interested enough to hang about. He wasn't anti-Royal, in fact he felt kinship to the King who'd dropped his German name Saxe-Coburg for the English sounding Windsor. But Sam had something better to do. He'd finished his library book, and seized the unexpected opportunity to borrow another.

He raced the cobbled streets from the docklands to Whitechapel, almost skipping through the back door at home, but he stopped in his tracks at the sight of his mother resting her head in her hands, elbows on the kitchen table. Lately, Sam worried about leaving the house and abandoning her to his father. There was a growing weakness in her manner and his mother was giving up on many things she'd once insisted on. There she was, elbows on table—something she'd never allowed.

"You all right Mum?" His fingers shook as he touched the warm teapot then stared at the unused cup. "You've made a pot of tea and not poured it."

She nodded, but didn't lift her head.

Sam swirled the teapot and poured two cuppas. "I'll join ya, Mum. You sick?"

She looked at Sam through red-rimmed eyes. "No. A little sad, but sadness can be worse than sickness."

"What's happened?"

"A bit of everything. I received a package today from my sister in Prussia. Your Bubbe passed away. There's a trinket for each of you."

She reached under her chair to retrieve a brown paper parcel, then began sorting through the contents. She traced her finger over the raised pattern of angels on a silver dresser set of hairbrush, clothes brush, and embellished mirror. "These are for the girls. Bubbe always said the faces of the three winged-messengers were modelled on your sisters."

She took slow stuttering breaths to control her tears, then unwrapped a piece of fabric with S scrawled in ink. "This is yours." She turned a coin in her fingers. "When I wrote to Bubbe telling her I couldn't find what country you were fighting in, or what name you had used, she begged me not to worry. She wrote how she imagined you as one of the concealed, the *Nistarim*. Said you were a special man disguised as a naughty boy." His mother looked up with a teary smile. "The coin is dated 1836. Thirty-six—the number of the *Nistarim*." Sam's mother took his hand and wrapped it around the money. "You were Bubbe's favourite. You're everyone's favourite, Sam, but your grandmother only believed in the good."

His mother stared into space, then spoke Yiddish. "*Lamed Vav Tzadikim*. The thirty-six righteous men lie in concealment until a time of great need. Then and only then do they know their true destiny. At that time, they are called to step out from the shadows."

Sam leaned his head against his mother's shoulder and cried. His beautiful grandmother had gone. In some way his tears were of relief. Now, Bubbe would never be disappointed. She wouldn't see him unworthy of her devotion.

"Come now," she said. "We'll be okay. But it's time for a change. When you and William came back from war, this house felt different, more hopeful. I thought Fay might have picked up a bit, but she hasn't."

Sam watched confused as she scooped her teaspoon through the sugar bowl, absentmindedly breaking up lumps. Teary-eyed she looked at him. "I don't know what happened while you were away, but you came back full. I don't know what you were full of, but I believed it to be hope. It's less than a year since you came home, and that energy is leaking away."

"I don't know what you mean?"

"I've written to my sister in Melbourne, and she says it's a splendid place to live. You've watched passenger ships sail to new lands. Find out how much money we would need to move to Australia. But please, don't mention this to your father."

Sam rubbed the coin between his fingers as he walked to the library. He inspected it again. NEDERL? INDIE? Where did his grandmother get it? His fingertip traced the outline of a swan, a crown, and six-pointed stars. Not the Jewish Stars of David with their interlocking triangles Bubbe had taught him to draw as a small boy.

He felt Bubbe standing beside him, cradling him in her warm arms and chanting the significance of each of the six points. Soft arms that would never embrace him again, Samuel whispered the attributes of God in time with his footsteps. "Power. Wisdom. Majesty. Love. Mercy. Justice."

He didn't stop until he pushed through the double library doors.

"Excuse me," he asked the librarian. "Do you have coin books?"

She slid her glasses down and peered over them. "Coin books?" She touched the tip of her nose thoughtfully, then flicked through the index card catalogue with frightening efficiency. "Numismatic section: 737, or for other information about coins, stamps and medals you should go to 332."

"That's the Dewey Decimal system isn't it?" Sam felt compelled to prove he wasn't a complete idiot, although the librarian didn't look the sort of woman who was ever impressed.

"Or you could search by country," she suggested.

Sam hesitated before admitting further ignorance. "Sorry, Miss. I don't know where the coin's from."

"It is Mrs. Thank you. Can you show me?"

He held out his open palm, and she picked up the money, turning it like a dead cockroach. "Nederl and Indie? Somewhere in the Dutch colonies. The East Indies, I believe." She returned the coin and Sam interpreted her nod as a snooty dismissal.

He climbed the stairs to the upper level, and pressed the cold metal to his lips. His grandmother had never left Prussia, and the Dutch East Indies wasn't a place on his wish list. 1836? More than eighty years old? It could be worth a couple of bob.

Chapter Sixteen
POW Camp, Batavia, 1942

When John finished his story, instead of rolling over to catch a moment's sleep, he smiled to himself, appearing drunk, intoxicated by the memories.

I took advantage to ask a question.

"Sam didn't sell the coin, did he? It'd be heartless to sell a memento from someone you love."

I would never trade the Saint Christopher medal my mother gave me.

"We can't sell the most precious things people give us. The coin was only a reminder that his Bubbe believed in him, he didn't need the physical object."

"So, he got rid of it, then?" I shook my head.

"If my memory serves me correctly, and it usually does, he swapped it for cash in a curio shop and added the money to a well-hidden jar labelled *Solonsch Australian Travel Fund*."

"It's obvious why the two of you got along. Some are sentimental and others…not so."

"Anything else on your mind?" he asked.

"Do you enjoy reading as much as this Sam?"

"Yes."

"I've never been one for novels," I said. "Too many words. Comic books are better. It's the pictures that tell a thousand words, isn't it?"

"Not for me." John sat up, twisting from side to side as he rubbed his back. "I get more than enjoyment out of reading. I have a theory that every person who's ever lived solves a miniature part of life's puzzle."

I tilted my head to one side, checking John's eyes hadn't taken on the scatty glazed look of men who'd finally lost the plot. "There's no puzzle," I said. "We're animals. We live, we breathe, and we die. There's nothing better than war to prove that theory."

"I know what you're thinking, mate. Old John is blabbering about the meaning of life. Don't worry, I don't have the words to explain what I mean."

"I'm not going anywhere soon." I indicated my wounded leg. "This blasted thing's incapable of taking me anywhere."

"Don't say I didn't warn you." Captain John relaxed into his story telling position. "Whenever I want to know how things work, say an internal combustion engine or an aeroplane in flight, I find an expert to explain. Experts know what they're talking about because objects can be taken apart, inspected, then put together again. Even the dullest of people can become an expert in things with enough practice.

But we humans are far more complicated. That's when I turn to reading. In every novel the author inserts a little of themselves. A good writer sheds light on humanity, conveying the truths they've discovered about life and love and death. They disguise it as fiction, but it's real—and I consider these insights new puzzle pieces. I've been collecting as many truths as I can. Now, I'm trying to put them together."

"Surely there's only one truth?" I asked.

"I don't believe so." John pointed to the Japanese guard pacing the perimeter. "When *Rikugun Taishō* is around, *Makoto* becomes a tyrant, too. He goes beyond the commands, outdoing the cruelty of his General. But when *Makoto* is here alone, he gives extra rations to the weaker prisoners. Can you be both a harsh, cruelly-compliant soldier and a kind human being? Which is the true *Makoto*?"

The Captain paused, smiling. I waited for a punch line, but there was no sign of the joker I'd come to know.

Perhaps this man was more than he seemed. I would have sworn on a Bible he was travelling through this life for a lark, yet on this day he displayed something deep and unrecognisable.

"You could be onto something," I said, trying to lighten the atmosphere. "I've found no secret messages in my comic books, but you know what? I'd like to find one. Maybe it would explain why this world is in such a mess."

CHAPTER SEVENTEEN
MELBOURNE, AUSTRALIA 1923

Sam inhaled the warm Melburnian air to discriminate which smells made this city different. It wasn't one particular scent, but the effect of heat. The flowers outside the florist shop had a headier aroma, but equally intensified were the stenches of rubbish and hot bodies clad in clothing too heavy for such a blistering day.

He'd happily put up with the stink if it meant not crowding around an English fire to catch chilblains—or being chilled by Solomon's presence. That man could freeze the balls off a brass monkey with a glance.

He and William walked the length of Chapel Street, which was wider than the streets of London. The sunny weather offered a warm welcome after the long ocean voyage, and the closer they got to the Yarra River, the more Sam liked this place, Australia. They'd left in Winter and as if by magic arrived in Summer. Imagine every Melbourne day being this glorious?

"They've got everything here—and more." Sam pointed to cinemas, dance halls, tobacconists and milliners. "I expected Australia to be rougher and a bit eccentric, like the Aussie sailors. Thought there'd be things we'd miss, but it's got the lot. Rather cultivated, actually. I can't wait for the others to get here."

"Hold your horses, Sam. we've a hundred things to do first." William shifted the heavy bag to his other shoulder. "We can't lug these around on a sightseeing tour. We need a boarding house or somewhere inexpensive."

Sam caught his reflection in a window. He hadn't needed a mirror to realise he needed a wash and a shave. He fancied people would mistake him for a bushranger. "Plenty of time." He gave William a lopsided grin.

"I'm serious. We need to find jobs."

"Let's have a wager." Sam nudged William's ribs almost causing him to drop the luggage. "See who's the first to find suitable accommodation and the first to land a job."

The voyage had dampened William's mood. "Not everything's a gamble. Turning it into game won't get things done faster."

Sam laughed it off. He wasn't set on a journey that went from A to B. He preferred life as a discovery tour. He rested his hand on the bonnet of a black car, then made a show of blowing his fingers cool. "Cor! Feel this, William. There's steam. I reckon we could fry an egg on that metal."

"Forget the eggs." William parked his bag on the pavement next to a newsstand. "Over here. We might have more luck with newspaper advertisements than walking the city and hoping something jumps out."

William handed over the two-pence to buy a copy of *The Age*. Sam bought *The Argus*. Sam had no idea whether these publications were reputable or frivolous. There was a lot to learn.

"Can we at least bloomin' sit by the river to read?" Sam started down the hill towards a watery glimpse.

"Okay, we'll make a competition of it," William called after him. "I'll scour this rag for places of suitable lodging, and you check out the 'situations vacant'."

Sam spun around with a glint in his eye. "What's the prize?"

"Somewhere comfortable to bloomin' sleep and enough coin to buy an egg that we don't have to cook on a bloomin' car."

Sam reached a low stone wall near the river bank without stopping for a breath. They both sat and flicked through the pages.

The bet was on.

"Listen to this." Sam nudged his brother. "An article about wool prices." He adopted what he hoped was an Australian gentleman farmer's accent. *"Robbery, the farmer declared with vigour and adjectival trimmings, it's downright robbery."* He laughed and shoved the paper under William's nose. "Can't imagine the farming section publishing this in London's Daily Herald, can you?"

"Have you found any jobs?" William's eyes were heavy and his tetchiness returned.

"I've marked the appropriate pages."

Under William's narrowed-eyed gaze, Samuel sighed and flipped open to the Situations Vacant. He read aloud. *"Man. Tall.* That's you, Will, you're the tall one. *For inquiry work.* No idea what that's about, but I reckon you could do it—"

"We need serious job prospects."

"Wait. There's more. *Salary no object for a shrewd live-wire."*

This time William laughed, too. "That job sounds real dodgy. Is live-wire some kind of code. What on earth kind of job is this?"

"Don't know. I gather you're not interested, then." Sam fanned his neck with the paper.

"Sounds more up your alley. You're the live-wire. And if shrewd means conman then all you need is folded newspaper in your boots to give you the extra height."

Sam thumped William's arm. "Shrewd means astute and intelligent."

"Not the job for you then… keep looking."

"Man, for horse washing. Lapton Bros training sheds, Flemington Racecourse. Good for this heat. Working with water would cool us down."

William wasn't convinced. "Any others?"

"Man. Driver. Ford delivery van. 109 Lonsdale Street."

"I can't drive."

"No. But I can." Sam tipped his hat and smiled.

After circling more jobs and accommodation prospects, the brothers traipsed towards the city centre, stopping for directions to Essendon.

Eventually they found the advertised accommodation. Rather than a cheap part of town, the house was in a leafy tree-lined street with expensive homes set well back from the road.

"You've made a mistake, Will. This is a bloomin' mansion." Sam waggled his finger as he counted. "Sixteen windows on one side!"

"The advertiser was very particular. Clean, well-spoken, refined lodgers only. It's rented out room by room."

"Well, that describes me to a tee." Sam winked and tipped his hat. "But I've no idea where *you* are going to sleep."

"Come on. Try to behave."

A long path led to wide verandah stairs. William removed his hat at the front door, smoothing his hair, then raising an insistent eyebrow at Sam—an unmistakable command ..

"You're two years older than me, not twenty." Sam took his hat off while he argued. "Stop being so bossy."

William forced a smile, took a deep breath and knocked with slow, even raps, as if it was the polite way to do it.

While they waited, Sam stared at the perfect red bricks, white painted arched fanlights and wavy glassed French doors.

A woman in her fifties with shimmering white hair and matching pearls looked the brothers up and down. Stepping back cautiously, she asked, "How can I help you?"

William unfolded the newspaper he'd tucked under his arm. "We're answering the advertisement, Ma'am. Room and board?"

Behind her in the hallway, an ornate hall table displayed silver candlesticks, a bowl of white lilies, and a marble Virgin Mary cradling baby Jesus.

"I'm thankful we've discovered a fine lady with religious beliefs." Sam said, ignoring William's muted cough. "We only arrived in your country today, and so far, we are most impressed."

"You're Catholic lads, then?" A hint of smile escaped.

Deciding not to lie, Sam moved the conversation along. "Your house is unbelievable. Finer than any I've seen in London. Don't you agree, William?"

William nodded, his ears turning red. Sam willed him not to tell her they were Jewish.

"At the turn of the century, Melbourne was considered the richest city in the entire world," she said without inviting them in. "Gold, you know. Everyone had money back then. Not anymore."

William froze and Sam took the lead, providing the English names they'd adopted during the war. He indicated his scruffy beard and clothing with a wave of his hands. "Apologies about this. I can guarantee we both scrub up well. At least our mother thinks we do."

"Brothers? Okay." She opened the door slightly wider.

"Our mother made us promise to stay somewhere respectable."

Her shoulders relaxed and she ushered the brothers inside, lifting her chin as she spoke. "My name is Mrs Wilson-Peck and I keep strict house-rules. They are posted in the breakfast nook. Money must be paid a week in advance. If you agree with the rules and the price, I'll show you to your room."

On their first night in their manor-house flat, William rolled over and sunk into the overstuffed mattress and down filled pillows. Sam imagined him burrowing underground like a wombat. Sam hadn't yet seen one, but William looked right at home. Born to live the good life.

Sam however, tossed and turned, staring at the gilt-framed paintings and wood-panelled walls, eventually falling into a fitful sleep where he dreamed of his family. He was making cups of tea and adding mounds of sweet sugar to his own, but spooning salt into everyone else's cup.

He considered getting up in the dark, but waited. It wouldn't do to have Mrs Wilson-Peck speculating about strangers wandering her house in the night.

"Wake up," Sam called to William at first light, pulling on his boots with fierce determination. "If anyone'll have me I'm taking on two jobs. We need to buy the family tickets quickly."

William rubbed his eyes and tutted. "Give me a minute. Is this another one of your bets?"

"Could be if you're up to it."

While William brushed his teeth, Sam thought about this new

land. It would be easy to enjoy this life, the abundance Australia offered, and ignore his family back home. With ample distractions to push their memory aside, life in Australia could be too good and too easy. He changed his soft cotton singlet to an itchy woollen vest, vowing to keep himself in mild discomfort.

When Sam returned from his first day of job hunting, Mrs Wilson-Peck was relaxed and friendly, sitting opposite William at the four-seater table in the breakfast nook. Will certainly looked like a young man every mother wanted their daughter to marry.

"Thank you kindly for your note, Sam. I was just telling your brother how thoughtful you both were. You saved me from cooking unnecessary breakfasts." She sounded as if she was talking around a mouthful of marbles. Not unlike the people in London who are brought up on the right side of the tracks. "But if you chaps are going to make a habit of early rising, it might be easier for me to pack crib boxes the night before." Colour flowed into the deep lines radiating from her lipsticked mouth, giving her lips the look of a pink centipede.

Sam did his best to hide a shudder. "You are very kind, Mrs Wilson-Peck."

She pulled a bowl of apples towards her, and began peeling. "My name is too long and formal. You can call me Mrs Cora."

"Can we help with dinner?" William asked. "I often chopped potatoes at home."

Sam regarded his brother with surprise. Had William helped in the kitchen? He'd never thought to offer.

"Your mother must miss you both," Mrs Cora whispered. "I was never blessed with children. If I had been, I might have been able to keep the house as it was when my husband passed away," She brushed down her floral dress and cleared the fleeting air of sadness with the creases. "I would appreciate a hand in the kitchen. My roast pork is almost done. While you're helping, you can tell me about your job search."

William glared wide-eyed at Sam while Mrs Cora donned a starched white apron.

Sam winked and stifled a laugh at William's horror. Pork.

Solomon would be furious to imagine his sons eating pig. Sam's smile broadened and he added that to his mental to-do-list—he'd noted everything that sent Solomon into a rage.

"I won't have any pork," William said. "Meat is so expensive and you should save it for your other lodgers."

"No. I insist. Besides, you're my only tenants at present. I had a full house last week when the farmers and their families came into Melbourne for The Cup. They brought beef, pork and lamb, so we will be eating well for weeks." She paused to look at the brothers from head to toe. "Well, this week at least."

Sam chatted with Mrs Cora, while William busied himself around the kitchen; peeling potatoes, and setting the table. William was the good son.

To see William squirm more, Sam asked Mrs Cora, . "Did you use pork fat for this crisp skin and over the potatoes." He checked to see if William was fully-fledged retching, but the only change was his colour from pink to green.

Sam had no problem with the meal. He savoured the taste of pork for the first time, revelling not only its flavour, but in the image of his father's red face, raging at the transgression. He relished the pork, indeed.

Mrs Cora continued chatting during the meal. "What with two regular house guests and farming families every now and again, things are working out nicely. I don't want to take in just anyone."

In between mouthfuls of pork, Sam muffled his laughter and watched William push food around his plate.

"Come on, William, don't be shy," Mrs Cora said. "It's a wonderful thing watching young men enjoy their food, knowing how strong they'll grow getting what they need. Especially if you're employed in physical labour." With every sip from her sherry, the pink-tinged centipede bred smudgy offspring on the rim of her glass.

"I've snagged myself a delivery driver's job." Sam smiled. "There's some lifting but I'm no longer a bludger. Is bludger the right word for someone who doesn't work? I heard someone say it today, and I'm intent on sounding like a true-blue Aussie before my next birthday."

Mrs Cora smacked her lips in distaste. "Many would say bludger, but never about hard-working men like you two."

"I'll be delivering goods from four shops in Footscray. First up in the morning, I visit the Queen Victoria Market to pick up fruit and vegetables for Gordon's Fruit Palace. Then I collect stock for the other shops. After that, it's home deliveries from the grocery, the butchery and the fruiterer."

"Well done." Mrs Cora raised her glass, as if suitably impressed.

"I'm relieved the Aussie shop keepers agreed I've got the right *koala-fications.*" Sam winked at Mrs Cora, who chuckled behind her napkin.

"How did you go?" Her smiling eyes settled on William.

"The jobs I'd circled in the papers were already gone. I've bought today's editions to see if there's anything new, and I'll buy new papers in the morning. My back-up plan is to hand out my details at building sites." William glanced at the black telephone in the dining room. "Would you mind if I used your number for any messages, Mrs Cora? Otherwise, I could give your address and ask them to slip a note under the door?"

"No. No. No. I don't want just anybody at my doorstep. Make it the telephone and get them to call around dinner time."

"Thank you." William pushed his chair under the table. "Thanks for a delicious dinner. If you don't mind, I'd like to excuse myself and scour the job advertisements before bed."

"I'll help you look, brother." Sam bowed good evening.

Mrs Cora was midway through a sip of sherry; she waved at Sam. He paused. The pink centipede had lost all its body colour, leaving only the 'legs' behind as her face folded into a smile. "You could stay and talk to me if you like?"

He clutched his chest in mock regret. He wouldn't mind talking to the old dear, but not if William was leaving. "I'd love to, some other time, but I'd better help my brother."

William checked Mrs Cora wasn't within earshot as he closed the bedroom door. He cast a stony-eyed glare at Sam. "Why do you always do that?"

"Do what?" Sam held his hands palm-up in confusion.

"Smooth-talk people, say whatever you think they want to hear. Making them like you, making them think you care."

"It made her happy. She's lonely."

"But you don't care, do you?"

"Come on, brother." Sam rested a hand on William's shoulder, but he shrugged it off.

"Now, she thinks we're good Catholic boys and the hardest of workers from perfect loving families. We ate pork for dinner. For goodness' sake."

"How does any of that hurt? We live with the woman so we may as well get on."

"Did you see the look on her face when she talked to you, Sam? She was licking her bloomin' lips like a cat about to steal the cream."

Sam tugged his ear. He'd seen none of that and not much got past him. "What are you on about?"

William raised his eyebrows, then gave a wink, wink, say no more.

Sam shook his head at Will's insinuation. "That's ridiculous. She's older than our mother." He dropped onto the bed, jittery with confusion and stared at the patterned floor rug, shaking his head as he replayed the conversation. He considered Mrs Cora's words and actions until certain William was wrong.

Sam slapped his thigh and laughed. "You had me there. You're not usually a trickster."

William frowned. "See? That's exactly what I mean. You would think it funny if a lonely widow took a liking to you. It's wrong. Not everyone in this world has been put here for your entertainment."

"Come on. Admit you're wrong. At least I don't make life miserable for everyone…" Sam bit his lip to stop, but he blurted the rest. "I don't want to be anything like Solomon."

William's jaw relaxed and he perched on Sam's bed. "You're

nothing like him. You're your own man. Not perfect but you have a unique set of faults." He laughed and punched Sam's arm. "Don't waste your life trying to be the opposite of someone hateful. I'm never giving that man another thought."

Chapter Eighteen
POW Camp, Batavia, 1942

Few POWs attempted escape. Thousands of miles of shark-infested ocean divided us from the closest allied land, and horrific tales of those who'd failed, were enough to put anyone off.

There was, however, movement between the camps. Men were transferred depending on work skills or physical fitness. You could leave a hospital camp like ours in one of two ways: be deemed fit to re-join the work gangs, or get sicker and die. Most transfers were of the latter—our camp a mere stop-over on the final journey.

The day Silent-G, an Aussie whose real name was Hugh, and the Welshman, known simply as Welshman arrived in Hospital camp, it got me thinking how many homelands we POWs represented. The Netherlands had posted soldiers to protect Dutch businesses and the wealth of the colony long before the Japanese invaded.

Along with Indo-Europeans and handful of Americans, there were soldiers from the countries making up the United Kingdom.

Welshman, and Silent-G, had been transferred from *Sukabumi* for medical treatment. Silent-G claimed his busted fingers were inflicted by an angry Jap testing the butt of his rifle. Both watched the Captain and me playing poker for several days, neither speaking to us directly beyond the introduction. I'm sure John noticed their inordinate interest—there was barely a moment when Silent-G wasn't whispering and throwing glances our way.

Not much escaped Captain John, but he didn't dwell, instead he continued his light-hearted quips. I preferred this happy-go-lucky phase over his recent period of serious reflection. Perhaps under different circumstances, I would have enjoyed philosophical discussions, but my energy in Batavia was reserved for blocking out pain.

During one of our card games, Silent-G wandered over, bandaged hands at his side, to stand behind John.

John tipped his cards to hide them.

"Play your cards close to your chest, don't you?" Silent-G laughed then winked at his Welsh mate.

John didn't smile as he drew another card from the pack. "Looks like you've already lost a couple of hands."

"Cut the bullshit. I heard about you from another POW camp. You talk nothing but shit, they reckon. And here you are in the middle of a flippin' crisis making stupid flippin' jokes at one of your own countryman's expense."

"Sorry if humour offends you, mate. I'm making the best of a crook situation. It's the only thing in my control."

"You don't play by the rules, do you?" Silent-G let out a half-whistle then looked at me. "The rest of us are tied in bloody knots, but this whole war is nothin' to Captain John. I'm not sure whether he's off his bloomin' noggin or whether he thinks playin' with people's lives is a flippin' game. Not even sure which side of this war he's on. Are you, mate?"

I ignored him and picked up a handful of seed-pod chips and bet on my cards, waiting for John to continue our game.

"We're all tied in knots," The Captain said with a shrug. "A joke here and there relaxes the stranglehold. Who knows? A good laugh might loosen you up, Silent-G. Cos the way you're picking arguments where none exist, seems to be tightening the knot enough to cut your air-supply. It's a wonder your face isn't turning blue."

"Come on." The Welshman tugged on Silent-G's torn sleeve.

"Let's take a walk round. See if we can catch one of them fancy feathered birds. They'd make a grand meal."

Silent-G paused and stared at me from the doorway. "I hope you haven't passed on any Dutch military secrets during your little chats. Or perhaps you've revealed all while talking in your sleep. This shonky character will have sold them to the enemy by now."

"I don't speak English in my dreams." I forced a laugh to hide my splintering voice. At that moment I needed Captain John to be the man I believed he was.

Silent-G's eyes bore into mine. "How do you know he doesn't speak Dutch?"

Once the pair were out of earshot, I turned to John. "Why did he say that? This isn't the first time someone's suggested you're a spy. Do you speak Dutch?"

"So, you're going with 'where there's smoke, there's fire' are you?" John was deadly calm. "I've never asked details of any missions, and I never will. That'd make me a failure in the spy business, I reckon. You'd expect me to at least try."

I cleared the cards off the bed and slumped towards the wall. Two geckos, which the locals called *Tjik tjaks*, stopped their noise-making to stare. Probably judging me for being a bad friend and a fool. My throat burned with shame. John was right, he'd never attempted to pry information from me or anyone. He went out of his way to help us and make us laugh. Yet, I'd all but accused him of being a traitor.

"Wanna smoke?" John handed me a lit cigarette.

This peace offering made me feel worse.

"I'm sorry." I took it from his hand.

"Don't be. We're in the middle of a bloody war. Wariness is a matter of survival."

I moved over so John could sit next to me, then he dealt out the cards as if nothing had happened. "Look at that pair," he said, pointing to Silent-G and the Welshman aimlessly searching ground and sky as if they didn't know what a bird looked like. I leaned back on my elbow, preferring not to see them at all.

"That man couldn't find his cock if he used both bandaged hands." John made a dismissive throaty grunt.

We played in a subdued yet companionable manner for a while. John ignored Silent-G and the Welshman when they slunk in empty handed, but a few minutes later something alerted Captain John's finely tuned nose for trouble.

He sat at attention, craning his neck to smile at something outside, then jumped to his feet, flourishing his arms and framing the window which faced the guards' house.

"Roll up! Roll up! Get ready for the greatest show on earth, folks, and for one unique performance it is playing outside at a special price ..." He drummed his fingers against the sill. "...for... free."

I suspected there'd be nothing much to see, but Captain John could sell ice to Eskimos and any spectacle was better than boredom. Like the time John pointed out a cloud and claimed it had been painted by the spirit of Michelangelo because the brush strokes matched those on the Sistine Chapel. John had apparently seen a photograph of it in a book.

Whatever show was on offer, I was in for the ride. A ticket for the small price of hobbling to get a front-row seat. It was worth the pain. John conjured the smell of imaginary sawdust.

"Here we have the three monkeys. None of them awfully wise."

There were indeed three monkeys in a tree, and all of them were industriously plucking seedpods off branches and aiming their ammunition at the guard on patrol. Although Widey had no facial hair, it was easy to imagine him dressed in top hat and twirling an evilly curled moustache, billed as the villain of the show.

A bunch of us gathered around to watch, hands over mouths to hide the splutters of laughter. No one wished unspeakable repercussions from Widey, but I also didn't want to miss the Captain's commentary. Somehow, John turned the real and potentially awful into something make-believe.

Widey swore, cursed and shouted what I imagined to be Japanese threats. They came thick and fast but did nothing to deter the monkeys who continued their monkeying-around.

"His ultimatums have been lost in translation, so let me be of service." John bowed. "Ladies, Gentleman, and vagabonds, I'm receiving a radio signal." He cupped his ear with both hands waggling his eyebrows while opening his mouth in exaggerated curiosity. "Our esteemed guard, Widey, is arguing with the monkeys, *'Your juggling acts are below par, and your trapeze work is frightfully sloppy. I am terminating your contracts.'*"

As if on cue the smallest monkey swung low, unwinding his tail as if taunting Widey, but it lost grip and tumbled to the ground at the guard's feet.

We held our collective breaths when Widey wielded the bayonet. The baby monkey screamed and reached its arms to the mother dangling above.

John's yell was thunderclap loud, and Widey stopped to look. A sardonic sneer before he turned back to the target of his cruelty.

"And for our next performer...," John boomed. "We have Bozo the clown."

Widey yelled towards the barracks in Japanese before resuming his taunts towards the monkey he'd trapped with his foot.

"Did you hear about the cannibals who cooked up a circus troop stew?" John's hollering attracted Widey's attention, again. "One cannibal asked, *'Does this clown taste funny to you?'*" John started a slap-happy penguin walk down the stilted veranda's steps. "My father was a clown. He left me big shoes to fill..."

Widey ignored the Captain, grabbing the little monkey's arm and throwing it up in the air—aiming his bayonet ready for the fall.

"Noooo." I tried to close my eyes, but they wouldn't obey.

This time, Captain John's voice almost burst my eardrum. "Stop. *Yamero.*"

Widey stopped. Then John bellowed another direction in Japanese.

The mother monkey leapt from the tree, knocking her baby sideways and they tumble-rolled away until the little one could climb safely on her back.

I wanted to cheer. John had saved her. But the other POWs eyes were fixated on John. He had spoken Japanese.

No-one mentioned the Japanese speaking incident, not even Silent-G. It was two weeks before the Captain could say another word—in English, Japanese or any language, for that matter.

Whispers and gossip ran amok amongst our group—heavy with worry that John wouldn't recover. Widey had viciously beaten John's lower back with the butt of his rifle, bashing his already damaged kidneys until he'd left more bruises than skin. The horrific swelling was the only bulk on John's emaciated frame.

Silent-G took me aside. "Look. I feel bad for saying that shit about your mate. I'm still not convinced he's dinky-di, or everything he claims to be, but he challenged the enemy and risked his life for a helpless animal. I believe he'd do the same for all of us. Him using that Nippon lingo surprised us all, including Widey, I reckon. John's probably picked up a few Japanese words while living in this shit-hole. Anyway, if he was a double-agent, those bastards would protect him instead of bashing the shit out of him."

When John eventually got out of bed and hobbled through the compound, the men cheered. Widey spat on the ground as John passed, but the Captain bowed through his pain, saluted, and greeted Widey like nothing had happened.

It seemed incredible that anyone could be beaten senseless and not hold a grudge. Perhaps the Japs had in fact beaten him senseless.

I considered the idea that trauma had caused amnesia. But as soon as John regained enough strength to sit by the window, he resumed our evening story-hour and not even the smallest details were blurred or forgotten.

Listening to John relate his tales about Sam was a much-needed escape, and I was happy to block the whole ugly incident. There was no escape from this hell, but John helped me survive. I could pretend I was free, out there with Sam, starting his new life in Australia.

Chapter Nineteen
Melbourne 1924

Frequenting the morning fruit markets for six months had advantages. Sam became friendly with the stall holders and sometimes things just 'fell from the back of a truck'. All Sam had to do was transport them to where he was pointed, getting a 'tip' for additional services. On other occasions, the windfalls had no-strings-attached.

"Wanna take some of these?" Old Sparra, the cocky fruit vendor, heaved a crate of Tasmanian pears, offering them to Sam. "Rough trip across the Strait. Bruised. The lot of em. Your missus might wanna make 'em into preserves."

"Single man. Playing the field." Sam flicked, then slicked down his hair, before nodding yes. "But my landlady likes to chop, boil and bottle."

"Is that what you young uns call it? We called it canoodling." Sparra winked at a couple of his offsiders who chortled like kookaburras.

"Knock it off, blokes. She's not just a landlady she's a lady." Sam sighed, playing up the dramatic effect. "You fellas have found your women. Marriage is more than just a word—at least to me." He winked to himself and loaded the pears onto his trolley.

"You're not going all philosophical on us?" Sparra asked. "I thought you were fun."

"Yep," Sam's usual lip kicked in. "Marriage is more than a word...it's a bloomin' sentence."

Sparra laughed enough for a joke worth three times the value. "You're all right," he said. "Come and see me when I'm not flat out. I might have a side job for a bloke like you."

After a full day of deliveries, Sam parked the van up the long driveway and carried the crate of pears inside. Mrs Cora and William were drinking tall glasses of lemonade in the breakfast room.

"Here's a present."

"Thank you so much," Mrs Cora beamed at Sam's gift, admiring the damaged fruit as if it were a bouquet of roses.

William raised an eyebrow, but Sam shook his head. This was legit.

Sam felt slightly guilty not telling Mrs Cora he'd gotten them for free. Now he knew her better, the mildly ill-tempered expression she'd worn at rest, had disappeared and her whole face had softened.

She pointed through the window to a large timber table under a grapevine-covered pergola. "Best done out there. Can you carry the pears for me? I'll be out in a minute."

Sam and William took a handle each and carted the crate over the lush lawn, setting it on the table.

"We've done well in only six months. I picked up the vouchers from Thomas Cook and Sons," William said. "Jane and Millie can book their steamship tickets as soon as they're ready."

"Two down. Two to go." Sam flicked at fruit flies hovering around the pears. "I don't know why Mum can't be the first sail. She needs the break more than the girls."

"And leave her daughters behind with the monster?" William threw a look that made Sam shiver. "What sort of mother would do that?"

Sam bit the inside of his cheek. He'd be glad once he'd never have to think of Solomon again. He checked over his shoulder, ensuring Mrs Cora was still inside. "I suppose we'll have to find a new place to live."

"We wouldn't have had this problem, if you hadn't led Mrs Cora to believe we're bloomin' Catholic. There's no way Jane or Millie would go along with that lie. Fortunately, they've written to say they've going to stay with Mum's cousin—"

Sam directed a sharp kick at William's shins, then called towards the house. "Do you need a hand?"

"Here you go, boys." She put a bowl and a paring knife in front of each brother and pushed an old washing tub under the table with her foot. "Ready to start?"

Sam and William stared blankly.

"We were lucky to see a pear in England, let alone do anything fancy with one." Sam said.

"Peel them, but don't take too much off, except for the places where the fruit is bruised. Pile the newspapers on the table and the food scraps straight in the bin." She tapped her toe against the metal tub. "I'll get one of you strong men to throw those in the garden when we've finished."

William unwrapped a pear and flattened a sheet of old newspaper. "Are these Tasmanian pears?"

Sam was impressed. "How horti-cultural of you."

"It's the paper. A Tasmanian Advocate from June." William held it up to show him, then started to read. "Refined and well-positioned gent in his late forties, seeks a refined and sensible wife."

"Are you blushing, Mrs Cora?" Sam asked. "This refined gent sounds all right, doesn't he? I bet he'd find you a good catch, too. You could put an advertisement in the matrimonial section."

Mrs Cora looked aghast. "A refined woman's name only appears in the newspaper three times in her life. Birth, marriage and death. I would never advertise myself. Your second mistake is assuming a man would consider a woman my age." She sighed deeply. "Tens, maybe hundreds of thousands of men were killed or maimed by the war, and the Spanish flu buried an awful lot more. Many young women are left with the choice of marrying an older gentleman or remaining a spinster." She chucked the scraps in the bin. "No man with his choice of fine-feathered chickees, would court an old bird."

A lump formed in Sam's throat at the thought of Mrs Cora settling for a life alone. At least she'd experienced love once in her lifetime. His sisters were arriving soon, hoping Australia would deliver all their promises. Maybe they'd have to rethink some of their dreams.

Sam peeled a pear carefully, trying to imitate Mrs Cora's lethal movements with a blade. As he licked the dripping pear juice off his arm, he looked at William, similarly clumsy. If this was typical of female weaponry skills, women should have fought in wars and left the men behind.

Mrs Cora found a newspaper article of her own. "*Eugenics,*" she read. "*The betterment in mind and body of the human breed.* What's that?"

"Read it, please," Sam said, making an immediate connection to this article and Francis Dalton's study on nature versus nurture. "It's about breeding out bad traits."

Mrs Cora read aloud, her rounded vowels making her sound like a well-mannered head mistress. "*We look for rams and asses of good stock, but a man minds not to wed the daughter of an evil sire...*"

"What on the earth is that about?" William screwed up his face.

"Let Mrs Cora finish." Sam smiled encouragingly.

"*When a young man's fancy turns to thoughts of love, the eugenist would have him first consult a eugenic expert who is to select or reject the proposed life-partner.*" She put the newspaper down. "You're more attentive to this than I'd expected, Sam. Are you thinking about employing someone to choose you a bride?"

William stabbed a rotten pear, tossing it under the table. "I doubt he'll be offered much choice. He should marry the first woman silly enough to take him. His only chance of success will be with a female of feeble mind. No woman with a brain would fall for his antics."

Mrs Cora tutted at William before turning to Sam. "Well, I can offer you my advice until your mother arrives. Neither of you want to be taking up with those flapper women who wear too much makeup. They show their arms and knees and… their…neckline. Those dresses are more suited to the beach."

In bed, Sam reflected on the evening's conversation. The Eugenics article planted an idea. He could choose a woman intellectually, one who strengthened the good and diluted his undesirable traits. He wasn't convinced about the bad seed, but it wouldn't hurt to avoid rolling it in manure.

When he heard William snoring, he removed his writing compendium from the nightstand drawer. An unsubtle present from his mother. He hadn't used it, but William wrote letters regularly, so no point repeating news. He planned instead to make a 'wife' list.

He got stuck choosing a title. He rejected 'Breeding Stock' and 'The Perfect Woman', deeming them unsuitable. Starting with the woman instead of himself, was arse about.

A farmer would assess his stock before choosing breeding mates. Unless he recognised the deficits, he'd have no idea how to counteract them. Sam needed to identify all his shortcomings.

He fell asleep with the compendium open. The page still blank. His thoughts a painful reminder of Solomon.

"What part of Italy do your family come from?" Sam asked Sparra while they shared a smoke during a break.

"Italy? Where in the bloody blazes d'ya get that idea from? Look at me. Look at my hands. I can carry on a conversation without flamin' well flappin' 'em. Well… unless you count me draggin' on my ciggie, but I could probably smoke without lifting my fingers if I tried hard enough." Sparra hunched his shoulders, leaning in until his lips reached the cigarette in his hand. He succeeded, but coughed up smoke with his laughter.

"Sorry, mate, my mistake. Australians seem to shorten everything. It was your name, Sparra" Sam said. "When I was in the Navy,

I worked alongside a bloke called Sparano. I thought Sparra might have been the Aussie shortening for something similar."

"Strewth, I've had the name Sparra most o' me life. It's short for sparrow. My brother reckoned I was born a pest. Dull and grubby, too."

Sam laughed, then laughed more when he noticed Sparra's nose resembled a beak. "I'll never be a real Aussie until I get a nickname." Sam leaned against the van and took a thoughtful drag of his ciggie. "What about sword? Get it? Sam? Samurai?"

"The first rule about nicknames is you don't give 'em to yourself." Sparra lowered his voice. "I want to talk to you about a couple of jobs I've got on the side. How about I chuck some specially marked boxes right up the back of your van? Later today when everything else is done, you can drop 'em off? No questions. No trouble. I'll pay you Mund'y mornin'." Sparra tapped the side of his nose.

"What's in the boxes?" Sam asked.

"No questions. No trouble."

Sam leaned against the windowsill, looking from his watch to Mrs Cora's back garden. He did this several times, wiping his sweaty palms on his trousers after checking the van was still parked where he'd left it. He couldn't miss this delivery run.

William cycled up the driveway and made a gravelly-spin-stop right next to the vehicle, Sam raced down the stairs, almost crashing into Mrs Cora.

"Between you and your brother I'm living with a pair of Whirling Dervishes," she said. "Did you see William on that bicycle? He was a blur."

"I saw him all right. I'm not sure what a Whirling Dervish is, but William did put on a whirl." Sam kept moving as he spoke, planning to stop William snooping.

He wasn't regretting his decision to take up Sparra's offer. Sam hadn't done it entirely for the money. The flutter of excitement at taking risks coursed through his veins. He'd felt a similar tingling on his scalp when a female barber had cradled his head and shaved his beard. Her touch made Sam feel doubly alive and he'd thought of going back a week later. This *'No questions. No trouble'* deal gave him the barber-shop sensation.

"Hey!" he called to William. "I've a late delivery to make in a few minutes, but we could go walking in town tonight to see if there's anything on."

"You're eating dinner first, I hope?" Sam was surprised to find Mrs Cora behind him. Hands were firmly on her hips.

"I'll be an hour, no more." Sam bowed and tipped his hat which made her smile.

"I'm feeling rather jealous," she said. "Sam with his four wheels and William on two. Here I am reliant on my own feet, and they don't take me too far."

Sam lifted his hat again. "You, my dear Mrs Cora, could be a Whirling Dervish on a bicycle."

"Don't be daft. Ladies do not ride."

"Why not?" William threw his hands in the air and laughed. "I'm sure our sisters will, once they get here, and they'd probably beat us in a race."

Mrs Cora tutted. "It might be different for women in England, but in Australia it's frowned upon. One of the ladies at bridge told me the story of a friend whose sister's niece had started riding a bicycle and… became aggressive…in a most peculiar way?"

"Peculiar? Aggressive? What on earth did she do?" Sam wore a sassy smile. "Peck people while doing duck impressions?"

"No." Mrs Cora's centipede lips thinned and she fanned her blushing face. "A… personal assault. On a man."

William turned away to hide his laughter, but Sam opened his eyes and mouth in mock horror. "Did she attack this man in the street? In broad daylight?" He winked so she'd know he was joking. "Give me the address and I'll loiter near her house."

Mrs Cora rolled her eyes. "You are quite wicked. Now off with you. I'll make dinner while you run your errands. Thanks to you, we're having cinnamon baked pears for dessert."

Sam unfolded the Melbourne map, and memorised a route to

the address Sparra had supplied. He chose a safe path along back streets and lesser-used minor roads. Best to avoid police patrols.

As he turned into Cromwell Street, a young woman was getting quite the pedal up on her shiny red bicycle. She ducked and weaved to avoid potholes, while a yapping dog snapped inches from her bare ankles.

He slowed right down. A fine pair of ankles they were! Smooth and shapely.

With every turn of the pedal, Sam caught a peek of her knees from beneath her hitched-up navy skirt. She raced into the breeze and strands of hair floated above her head like a wispy halo of golden grass.

Sam took his foot off the accelerator to get a closer look at this particular breed of woman. If Mrs Cora's theory about female cyclists was to be given any credence, she may or may not be of the temperament to take charge in the bedroom. He'd be interested to find out.

Upon hearing the motor, the girl turned her head and made immediate eye contact. They held the gaze for a moment then continued travelling at a leisurely pace. She didn't appear to be the woman Mrs Cora gossiped about. There were no black-outlined eyes or red-painted Flapper girl lips on this beauty. Just a healthy glow and a mouth like a freshly picked rose blossom.

The delay gave the dog an opportunity to catch her. He seized his chance and sank his bared teeth into her leg.

As if in slow motion Sam watched the bicycle wheel wobble. She veered from the edge of the gutter almost colliding with his van, and he slammed his foot on the brake. The stalling motor jerked Sam's hands off the steering wheel and the van careened, knocking her off balance.

He grabbed the wheel one-handed and desperately thrust his arm through the open window to grab hold. But she fell, slowly, slowly, her arms thrown out in helplessness until she hit her head on the road. He felt the thud in his chest.

Sam leapt from the driver's seat. "Are you okay?" He slapped her cheek lightly. Her eyelids opened, but unseeing eyes rolled back in her head.

A middle-aged man appeared, tying a leash to the mongrel dog. "I was chasing Nipper, and I saw all of it. You knocked her off her bike. Poor woman."

"Fetch a doctor," Sam pleaded, raising her head and blowing air on her face as his grandmother had once done when his sister had fainted.

"I'm more inclined to call a policeman. You've committed a crime."

Sam caught his breath, then crouched and lifted the woman in his arms. Her mumbles were barely audible, but they got louder until she cried out in pain. The sound was music to his ears, at least she was alive.

Once he'd wrestled her into the passenger seat, he threw the bicycle in the back. "I'm taking her to The Alfred Hospital."

The man shook his fist. "This is kidnapping. I've taken your number plate and I'm reporting you to the nearest policeman."

Sam raced full throttle for the hospital.

Hospital administration moved with deliberate precision and Sam was helpless among the professionals. He was relieved when the injured young woman was wheeled away on a stretcher. He pushed his scribbled details across the information desk to a duty nurse.

"Here's my name and the phone number of my landlady. I'll be back shortly, to find out how the patient is doing."

His initial excitement at the goings-on of illicit dealings, was replaced with sickness. His heart beat so loudly in his ears he couldn't think, but instinct screamed for him to get rid of the boxes in the back of his van straight away.

He made the delivery in a blur then dashed back to the Alfred Hospital, where he tethered the young woman's bicycle to a tree.

A policeman marched over to intercept him.

"Is this the young man who kidnapped a girl?" the officer asked the dog owner from the accident scene.

"Yes, he's the scoundrel. And that's her bicycle. The one he mowed down."

"Is she okay?" Sam asked softly, scared to look the policeman in case the answer was no.

"Let's take this somewhere private." The policeman folded his notebook and addressed the man. "And you sir, go tie up your dog."

Sam was holding open the hospital front door, when they were interrupted by William's dramatic arrival. A feet-down bicycle-skidding affair, with a breathless Mrs Cora seated on the handlebars bedecked in pearls, gloves, and an unbecoming feathered hat which resembled parrots fighting to the death.

Her face blushed pinker than her lips, "My apologies about the transport, Officer, but we needed to get here quickly." She threw her hands in the air when she spotted Sam, right as rain. She patted his arms then checked his temperature with the back of her hand on his forehead. "The phone line was scratchy but I was under the impression you'd been injured."

"Not me." Sam took short, quick breaths. "A young woman—through there." His hand trembled as he indicated the entrance.

Striding towards them, a nurse in a blue gown and starched white veil reminded Sam of Mrs Cora's statue of the Virgin Mary, making him doubly uncomfortable. She marched and stood with military deportment. "The young lady's family wish to speak to you." The nurse pointed at a middle-aged man comforting his wife.

"Can we get a first-hand account of the incident? From the patient?" The officer asked her.

She nodded. "I'll be right back."

As they approached, the mother stopped dabbing her eyes with a lace handkerchief. "We're not sure what happened. Our Cecelia is a capable rider. Mr Lakeman and I are relieved our only daughter isn't permanently damaged."

Sam opened his mouth to speak, but Mrs Cora was faster.

"Sam probably saved your daughter's life, bringing her in as promptly as he did. He's a quick thinker and a kind Catholic boy. Both brothers are wonderful. They're saving all their money to bring their poor mother and sisters out from England. Finer examples of youth would be hard to come by."

Although Mrs Cora was addressing the girl's parents, she paused several times to eye-ball the policeman and check he was recording her glowing reference.

"Excuse me, officer." said the nurse on her return. "Dr Faulkner would like a word with the Lakemans. He's treating Cecelia for minor concussion, but also had to stitch a nasty bite on her ankle. According to Dr Faulkner, our patient gave a clear account of being chased by a vicious dog, which she'd been fending off for more than half a mile. It was the dog attack which caused her to veer into the van."

She looked from William to Sam and back again. "From her description, one of you two must be the Good Samaritan. If you are free tomorrow, visiting hours are between ten and twelve. Ask for Cecelia Lakeman."

Questions and answers bounced between Sam, the complainant, the officer and Mrs Cora until eventually, the policeman addressed the dog man. "I'll need your details, sir. The young lady might wish to press charges regarding the dog bite. I suggest you keep that dog on a lead." His demeanour relaxed when he turned to Sam. "Young man, it was very lucky you came along and delivered the injured woman to hospital."

Sam sighed with relief for himself, but his heart beat erratically, pounding with concern for the girl with the fly-away hair.

The policeman jotted new details in his notebook, then thrust his jaw at the dog owner. "Since everything confirms the young man's version of events, you can accompany me to the station where your dog will be locked in the pound until I decide on an appropriate fine."

Sam woke the following day, eager to visit the bicycle girl in hospital. Over breakfast, he tried to recall the colour of her eyes, but he wasn't even sure he'd recognise her in a line-up. He'd caught her shocked expression in that split-second before she fell, then was almost too afraid to look when she hung limp in his arms. He feared she would die.

William had left earlier, so Sam helped Mrs Cora clear away. While she washed, he wiped, staring at his van, safely parked near the garden wall— black against the riot of colour.

Flowers? Should he take flowers to the hospital?

"Mrs Cora," he said softly.

She wiped her hands on her apron. "What is it, pet?"

"Being a weekend and all, the shops are closed. So, I'm wondering if... perhaps you could sell me some of your flowers. It wouldn't have to be a large bunch, just an apologetic offering to take to the hospital."

"You didn't do anything wrong. Even the policeman said you were in the clear."

"I've been thinking... maybe... if only I had driven to the other side of the road, maybe I wouldn't have startled her. It's possible she wouldn't have fallen."

"There are too many '*maybes*', and '*only ifs*' there. To me that suggests you've done nothing wrong. Come on, we'll pick some flowers. You grab the bucket and a wet rag from the laundry, while I fetch the secateurs."

Mrs Cora marched up and down the garden bed inspecting her floral troop. "The peonies, I think," she said emphatically. "Do you agree?"

Sam didn't know the difference between a peony, a daffodil or a daisy, but he nodded agreement.

"Pity the roses are out of season. Yellow roses are the perfect flower. Yellow is for get-well wishes. It is so very cheery and positive."

Sam shook his head in disbelief. "Here I was struggling to remember which flower was which, and now you're telling me the colours have distinct meanings?"

"Oh yes. You would never give a girl purple flowers unless you were serious. They are a clear symbol of adoration. And red? Well, red is for..." Mrs Cora side-whispered the next word. "Passion."

Sam blushed with her. "Peonies it is then. What would I do

without you? I'd be declaring all sorts of things in secret flower-code, and I'd find myself in hot water. "

Mrs Cora smiled and took the dampened rag from his hand. "This will keep them fresh." She wrapped the cut ends and tied them with a piece of string that magically appeared from her pocket. "Take the cloth off when you arrive at the hospital. I'll find you a pretty piece of paper to wrap them with."

Mrs Cora sat on a painted wooden bench and patted the seat beside her. "Sit with me for a minute, Sam. It's none of my business but I'd like to talk."

She was so serious Sam turned on his extra sensitive people reading skills. If she'd found out about his illegal black-market trading, he'd need to come up with a good explanation.

"You're entering tricky territory. This young woman will have imagined you as a hero. A knight in shining armour. And you… your heart will be at its most tender. She will appear fragile and in need of protection. A true damsel in distress is a dangerous thing to a brave young man like you."

Sam held the bouquet in front of his face to hide both the relief and smile. Mrs Cora was a romantic soul, but this was the stuff of girly novels. Not something that happened to men. Not in real life.

"Sam! Listen!" she said. "I know you think me a fool. Go and enjoy the young woman's company by all means, but guard your heart until you get to know her."

Sam stopped in the hospital corridor, looking at the flowers, then hesitated by a rubbish bin. Were flowers the right choice? He continued to the ward a nurse had directed him to. Of the five beds, two were empty and two had their curtains firmly drawn, but the middle bed had her name above it: Cecelia Lakeman. She was a sleeping angel, her light brown hair strewn across the pillow.

Sam slowed his breathing, not wanting to make a sound. Neither Hannah Hannerton nor Mabel Normand made his heart beat so fast.

He stood near the bed for a few minutes then moved away. If Cecelia awoke to find a strange man standing over her, she'd scream.

An open book lay just beyond her reach. He reached and turned it over. Agatha Christie: *The Man in the Brown Suit*. He brushed off his navy-blue jacket, suddenly wishing he'd worn brown. Miss Lakeman enjoyed books. She wasn't just lovely to look at. He was already smitten.

Her long eyelashes fluttered and a half-smile formed as she floated in what appeared to be a pleasant dream. His hand trembled as it inched over the linen sheet closer to her pale, smooth skin. He wrenched his hand away and grasped the peonies tight enough to tear the wrapping paper. No matter how much he wanted to check whether her skin was as soft as it looked, it was wrong to touch a woman without permission.

Pin-pricks tingled on the nape of Sam's neck as he checked there was no one else in the ward. He moved his fingertips within a hair's breadth of Cecelia's wrist. Although they weren't touching, a jolt of energy bridged the gap.

Sam couldn't see the other entity in the room. Circling above, armed with an enchanted bow, Cupid loosed his deadly arrows.

Chapter Twenty
POW Camp, Batavia, 1942

Immobilised by my infected leg. I was stir-crazy. Walking sticks were considered weapons, but in all honesty, we could've made more effective weapons if we'd wanted to. The idea of overpowering guards was tempting, but then what? There was nowhere to run. With my complexion, I would hardly blend in with the locals and most of them hated the Dutch more than they hated the Japanese.

"Can you do an errand?" I asked John. "Find a spare chair in one of the other huts? Something to hold me up?"

John lifted a leg over his knee and stubbed a cigarette on the underside of his boot. He carefully pinched off the remaining embers then brought it close to his eyes, like a child inspecting a bug. "Let me look at you, little one. Yep. You're all right. I'll put you away safely 'cos I'm off on a secret mission. I'll rescue you later."

He tucked the cigarette butt into his sock, gave it a pat, then saluted. "Be back in a tic."

John returned minutes later, holding a chair in front and lunging around like a bullfighter. He wore his usual broad smile. There were days I felt ashamed I couldn't return the favour.

I marvelled at how he found the energy to keep up the jollity, day-in, day-out. The soul-sucking surroundings into which men disappeared in the middle of the night and were spat out with injuries worse than my leg, had robbed me of optimism.

He parked the chair next to my bed, then spread his open hand across his face. The smile vanished and he took on a dramatically serious expression. A quick wink signalled his oncoming yarn. "My friend Sam invented these," he said, twirling his hand around the chair. "He showed me the very first chair he'd made and I asked him what it was? He said, '*John, it might take a bit to explain. You'd better sit down*'."

And there it was. Another successful trick. John, the powerful magician, had conjured a smile on my face. He wasn't always funny, but his energy was wizardry.

"Not your finest joke," I said, laughing. "But you get points for trying. I'm not gonna sit on it. I'm going to use it like the walking-frame my great-grandmother had. She got around okay at ninety. Swore fresh air cured all ailments."

"Fancy some company?" He gestured towards the yard.

I shook my head. There are times a man needs to find himself and can only do that alone.

"I'll help you down the steps. The rest is up to you."

The chair worked wonderfully as an aid. The pain overwhelmed me after shuffling a few steps, but since I had nowhere particular to go, I sat down until I'd recovered enough to move on.

The outside world had bloomed since my last visit. Our compound was surrounded by flowers. Tropical rain was so revitalising, a chair could sprout leaves and roots if left outside long enough.

I didn't know the flower names. My memory was slippery with details. Do girls really understand a secret floral code, like Mrs Cora suggested in Sam's story? Maybe one day I'd get to know women and the many facets of their minds.

A funny shaped tree over the fence was a frangipanni—I remembered the name because one of the blokes nicknamed it Randy-Fanny and the Aussie POWs said it over and over again biting their knuckles to keep down the laughter.

I snapped a blossom laden twig and milky sap dripped onto my arm. With it tucked between my chin and chest, I pushed the chair in front and hobbled up the steps, breathing in the sweet-old-lady fragrance. My brother, Pieter, would have loved the smell and the yellow tips of white petals dipped in sunshine.

I remembered the tense exchanges whenever Pieter danced or fussed with flowers. He could have stopped doing what he loved, instead he brushed off my father's annoyance.

The Captain reached for the branch once I made the landing. "You bewdy." He buried his nose in the blooms.

"My brother used to pick flowers," I said. "To brighten the kitchen. My mother loved it. My father not so much. It made him angry."

"He was a brave man then, your brother," John said.

I was stunned. Pieter brave? John was the sort of man one would call brave. Mum and Dad had congratulated my courage when I enlisted, but neither had a clue how frightened I was. I was terrified the first time I picked up a gun. Enlisting was a tough decision, but I only faced that once while Pieter continued picking flowers in the face of contempt. "Yes. He was far braver than me."

John held out a cigarette. "Want one? It's a home-made job. The paper doesn't burn well and for all I know they've used dried frangipani leaves to cut the tobacco. I don't care, it fills the yearning to do something familiar."

"No, thanks." I sat on the bed. "Are you afraid of anything?"

He leaned against the wall and blew imperfect smoke rings. "Yes. Plenty. I'm afraid I've let many people down. And more afraid I might not get out of here and have the chance to make it up to them."

"I worry about dying," I said—the words swirling acrid inside my mouth. Even speaking them risked attracting bad luck, and every man here had plenty of that. "Not just dying. Dying here, so far away from home."

"That would give weight to there being a better place to die. Nah. We're all in this together, and out of it, too. When your time's up, it's up."

"Hitler thinks some people are unworthy. People like my brother."

"Hitler hates anyone who doesn't fit his warped ideals." John clenched his fist until the knuckles turned white. "But he's nothing but an evil arsehole and we won't waste time dwelling on his views." He settled back to finish the remnant of his cigarette. "Pity he and his minions took over what I once thought a sensible idea. Eugenics. Great for animals but deadly for humans. Having larger cows to provide more food, or woolier sheep to knit more flamin' jumpers, made perfect sense. But applied to humans, eugenics is wrong. There's a place on this earth for everyone."

Chapter Twenty-One
Melbourne 1925

Sam loitered at the edge of the hectic market, watching Sparra, the champion haggler. When the hullabaloo settled, he whistled for Sparra to join him under the smoker's tree.

"I've come to apologise. I don't want to let you down, but I can't be doing any more runs on-the-side."

Sparra mumbled something to his offsider then turned to Sam. "Come for a drive, mate. A load of vehicles arrived in the dockyards yesterday and I could use a hand to check out the bargains. We can talk as we drive."

Sparra didn't wait for an answer, he didn't stop until he reached his old Ford lorry. "Get in. Light us both a cigarette. Tell old Sparra what you're thinkin'."

While Sam stared blankly at the city of Melbourne, he ran through everything that had happened. He didn't mind working for Sparra, but he wasn't comfortable discussing Cecelia.

"I don't know where to start. A few weeks back you teased me about grinning like a Cheshire Cat. I lied when I said it wasn't a woman."

"I knew that. The only reason men go around with that ridiculous smirk on their mugs is a girl. Don't worry, more time with the same woman wipes the smile right off. Looks like you're back to normal."

Sam didn't think he'd ever be back to normal. Nor did he want to be. "I didn't tell you what happened a couple of months ago, but I should've. I almost stuffed up on that first job you sent me to. I ran into a girl who was riding a bicycle."

Sparra coughed on his cigarette. "You what? You had a bingle and killed a kid?"

"No, no, nothing like that. A minor collision. A young woman rode into me, well actually into the van. But the police were called."

Sparra pulled the steering wheel to the left and parked at the curb. "Gawd almighty, this is serious. You got questioned about the goods?"

"No. I dropped her at the hospital, delivered the boxes, then raced back again. A policeman questioned me at The Alfred Hospital. He wondered why I'd taken off. Fortunately, I'd left my landlady's phone number and she turned up to speak on my behalf. Turned out it wasn't either of our faults. It was a dog."

"Sam, you bloomin larrikin, I have no idea what you're on about." As Sparra laughed, he jiggled from his boots up. "Next you'll be telling me you let the hairy bloody mutt drive ya van."

"There were no circus tricks involved. Just me and a lovely young woman. The dog bit her leg, and I knocked her off her bike."

Sparra burst into laughter. "Geez, mate. I didn't imagine a good-looking bloke like you being that desperate. There are other ways to meet women you know? Could have gone to a dance and asked a tamer specimen out on a date. Instead, you seek 'em out in the wild and run 'em down."

Sparra cackled again before restarting the lorry. "And now, what was you telling me? Your story had bugger all to do with givin' up 'bonus' runs."

Instead of answering, Sam stared at the stacked containers lining the road into the Melbourne shipyards.

He whistled, but after too many repeats of the same tune, Sparra punched his arm.

"Stop playin' silly buggers. You're acting like you've got a secret stash of gold. Cough up."

Sam's heart said, '*We have found gold. Her name is Cecelia and she's perfect and beautiful and I don't want to ruin it. She thinks I saved her life and sees only the good in me. I've been given a chance to become the man she believes I am.*'

Instead, Sam's head spoke for him, "Look, I'm just not that interested in the 'extra' jobs. Maybe I'm growing up and don't need the adrenaline rush."

Sparra scratched his head, then pulled into the loading area at the dock. He perched on an old crate and flipped a gold sovereign into the air.

"You don't know much about Sheilas, do you? You're a good bloke and you're paying for your family to live in Australia. But you can't court a girl without spondoolies. For a while you can ply her with kisses and cheap outings, but before you know it kisses won't be enough. You'll find yourself staring through a jeweller's window in Collins Street, clutching your chest at the hefty price tags on sparkle-arkly rocks. Unless you buy the ring that's the key to her heart, she might never unlock what's hidden by clothing." He tugged playfully at Sam's shirt sleeve.

"It isn't like that." Sam pulled his arm away. And it wasn't. There'd been no subtle progression. He'd wanted more since he'd watched her fall off her bike, and although Sam was concerned for Cecelia's health when he carried her into the hospital, his other senses were firing, too. He couldn't help but be seduced by the scent of her hair or the softness of her breast pressed against his arm. And when her skirt caressed her calf, he wanted all of her. Her kisses, her body, and her heart.

"Come on, let's look at the kind of gift men wish women would buy them. Murray, a bloke I know, stopped in yesterday. Told me there was an unloading mishap. Two brand-spanking-new Opel vans arrived from Germany and got banged-up. A slight lifting and shifting accident, he reckoned. Minor dents on the outer and nothing wrong with the workings, but Melbourne Motors Trading refused them. Damaged goods and all that. The vans are stuck here waiting for owners."

Walking along the boardwalk at the water's edge, the whiff of diesel reminded Sam of his old merchant ship. Rainbows slicked the dark water where oily spills had left their trace.

Sparra strode towards a man wearing a knotted handkerchief as a hat. "Murray, this is Sam. Yeah, where is them vans you told me about? Anything sorted?"

"I've tried me darnedest, but it's a losing battle. The bloke in charge of cargo speaks barely enough English to order a bloody beer at the bar. Even then he'd have to use actions and draw in the sand with a stick."

"No price for me, then?"

"He wrote something. Useless to me. It was either bloody German money or his weight in ounces. Could have been his birthday for all I bloody know."

"Show me where he is and I'll give it a go." Sparra puffed out his chest and winked at Sam. "What have I got to lose? A bargain is worth a spot of charades. Watch and learn, Sam. Watch and bloody learn."

Sam tried not to smile as Sparra spat broken English at the bewildered German sailor. He spoke in a normal volume at first, then progressed to a voice loud enough to reach from bow to stern. The third attempt was a yell that traversed the seven seas. "We. Can. Do. A. Deal. How. Bloody. Much? In. Quid? Understand? Mate? Give us your best price. No. Bullshit."

"Speaking only small bit English." The German sailor shook his head, then shrugged.

Sam whispered to Sparra, "How much is your best price? Quick?"

"New? Australian car 700 quid. New foreign car about 400. I'll pay 250. Not a penny more."

"What will you do with your old lorry?" Sam asked.

"Sell it. Hundred quid."

Sam marched up the gangplank, his strides triple the length of the sailor's. "Wait!" he yelled. "*Warte*! We need to discuss. *Sprich mit mir.*"

Sparra's mouth hung open wide enough to swallow one of the seagulls squawking overhead. He stared as Sam and the sailor bartered, taking turns to shake their heads and throw their hands in the air. Eventually Sam yelled, "*Nein.*" cursed in German, racing back to solid land.

Sam pulled Sparra close and led him away. "Do you have the cash with you?"

"Course. You'd be a mug to trust them banks."

"Good. Keep walking."

Sparra had his hand on the car door handle when the German yelled. "*Wartet.*"

"Looks like we have a deal," Sam whispered. He rubbed his thumb over his fingertips. "Give me your money."

Sam waved at the German then made the international hand symbol for O.K.

Minutes later, Sparra was holding new car keys, an importation license and a handwritten certificate of sale. "These are yours. The van you wanted at the price you wanted."

Sam leaned smugly against a shipping container. *I'm a man going places*. He handed over some large pound notes. "This *was* my commission. Take it as a down-payment on your lorry." Then, he lit up a cigarette, feeling like a king. His own vehicle. He'd keep his day job, work weekends for himself, and accept only the safest of fishy deals.

Now, he could take his beautiful lady to wherever and whenever she pleased. He was raring to show Cecelia the van, but first, he'd stop at the florist to buy a huge bouquet of red and purple; blooming adoration and flourishing desire.

Chapter Twenty-Two
Melbourne, 1925

Sam pulled up in front of Cecelia's house, revving the lorry to hear the engine purr. He cut the motor quickly when he thought about her father. Unwise to get on the wrong side of the man with most influence on the woman he was courting. When the front curtain shimmered and blinked before moving aside, his chest purred instead of the engine. Cecelia was watching, waiting for him.

He couldn't wipe the smile off his face when she skipped outside, her eyes widening as she took in the details of his gleaming vehicle. Sam had furiously scrubbed, tyre blacked and polished it, then done the same to his boots. He wanted the whole world to shine for this woman.

Cecelia ran towards him and he jumped out, marvelling at the swish and swirl of her skirt, at the way she leapt, limbs all a tangle—straight into his open arms.

"Oh, Sam!"

He tingled at her unbridled kiss. It was fully on the lips, right in the middle of the street. Mrs Cora would disapprove and suggest it came from bicycle riding.

The curtain moved again, this time a jerky twitch. Sam put his sweetheart down, straightening his jacket.

"Cecelia!" Mr. Lakeman called; arms folded.

Sam offered his hand. "Good evening, Sir. Do I have permission to take your daughter for a spin in my new motor?"

Cecelia squeezed Sam's elbow.

"Inside for a moment, dear." Mr Lakeman jerked his chin towards the door.

Sam gazed at the pathway beneath his feet, shuffling to avoid the cracks between the paving stones. Wasn't it bad luck? He didn't want to risk ruining the luck he'd been sent so far. Jane and Millie had arrived safely, he and William had bought tickets for his mother and Fay, and they'd almost convinced Joe to leave England, too. But best of all—the most exquisite woman in the world seemed to like him. A lot.

"Is something wrong, Sir?" Sam raked his fingers through his hair, as Mr. Lakeman closed the door behind Cecelia.

"Kissing a respectable young woman in public does nothing to reassure me of your intentions. Your landlady said you were Catholic, yet I've asked at the local parishes and no-one has any recollection of a man fitting your description."

Sam's ears burned. There was no stated warning but it wasn't difficult to read between the lines. He couldn't risk being caught in a lie, but carefully arranged words can convey a different story. "I haven't been to church since arriving in Australia. Sorry. My brother and I aren't practising Catholics."

"Are your parents God-fearing folk?" Mr Lakeman adjusted his rolled-up sleeves like Sam had seen in the hospital when he was concerned for his daughter. A straight-thinking honest man.

Sam stared him in the eye. "Oh, yes. Absolutely."

"Then you may take Cecelia for a drive, but I want a word with her first."

The sun hung low on the horizon, giving a warm glow to the earth, and Sam smiled. Hopscotching his way around the pavement as he waited, the weight of his half-lie floated away.

When she came out, she winked at Sam and took his proffered

elbow, appearing pleased at being escorted to the car. If there'd been a puddle on the ground, Sam would have happily thrown down his jacket, but instead, he tapped his forehead, locking in the idea. A chivalrous act to impress her on another occasion.

Cecelia waved to her parents, then turned to Sam. "So, there must be one of your famous stories in this purchase. You may entertain me while you drive."

He tripped over his words telling her about the cargo ship and the deal he'd made for Sparra. Cecelia squeezed his arm when he repeated the conversations in both German and English. "I wrangled myself a lorry at a bargain price," he explained. "My plan is to build my own business, then give up the delivery job and keep all the profits for myself."

"Father will be impressed." When she lifted her glossy hair on top of her head, Sam had to force his eyes off her neck and onto the road. "He asked all manner of questions before letting me out. Wanted to know your prospects and financials. It was difficult for me to hold in the laughter."

"Why is that funny?"

"As I told Dad—it's not as if we've made plans to marry. We're just young people getting to know each other and enjoying the company."

"So where would you like to go to get to know me?" Sam's voice fell flat. He'd been under the impression that by twenty, women were eager to marry. Was there something wrong with him?

"The St Kilda pier," she whispered in his ear. "Years ago, rumours circulated at school, about the pier at night. It will be dark when we get there and full of hot-blooded men and amorous women willing to let their beaus steal kisses."

"I can't imagine you discussed this with your father."

"Don't be so stuffy." She pushed Sam's shoulder. "I'm not without morals. But, the one time a handsome man literally swept me off my feet, I was unconscious. You can't blame a girl for wanting to experience something spectacularly romantic."

"I think I can oblige."

A smile crept over his face when she leaned her head on his

shoulder. He inhaled the rose petal fragrance of her hair, absorbed the comforting weight of her body against his side. She was a deliciously surprising package—part angel, part imp. A lively spirit dwelled inside Cecelia.

St Kilda pier didn't live up to their seedy expectations. Other than a fisherman, an old man with a dog, and a couple of youths, they were the only ones around.

"Don't be disappointed." Sam wrapped his arm around Cecelia's waist to walk her along the sandy white beach. "There is one ardent young man around here with impure intentions."

"Where?" She winked and turned to look behind, but Sam pulled her towards him, and swung her around as the sun set.

Once the sun lost its battle with night, Sam lost his battle to restrain passion's hunger. He kissed her quickly. Then he kissed her slowly, pressing himself hard against her body, making her gasp. But she didn't push him away. It was Sam who eventually found the strength to break their breathless embrace.

"Cecelia," he said. "I want to get to know you more. Much more. Your father would aim a shotgun at my head if he could read minds."

"If that was the case, he'd be shooting me, too." She lifted his hand and proceeded to kiss each of his fingers while looking him in the eye.

Sam stepped back to catch his breath, but he couldn't catch his thoughts or put them back in order. He had spent a life reading people, yet he couldn't tell whether Cecelia was serious about him.

She crouched like a child at the damp sand near the edge of the shore and giggled while building wonky sandcastles. He sat beside her, legs outstretched, watching her play. She was a woman who'd hung on to the magic of childhood.

"Smell the ocean," she said. The salt-smelling breeze whipped her hair across her face and his.

He scraped his fingers through the sand, picking out a shell to hold to her ear. "What can you hear?"

"A question you want to ask, by the look on your face."

Sam was so stunned, his cheeks burned and he was thankful for the dark. Cecelia was reading him. He shook his head in denial.

Although often impetuous, Sam wanted to follow a more sensible path when it came to love. He'd imagined waiting for his mother to arrive, introducing Cecelia, seeking his mother's approval, then asking advice on what to do about the Catholic and Jewish incompatibility. But Cecelia's energy spun his plans off kilter.

"What sort of man do you plan to marry?" he asked.

She traced lazy figure-eights with her toes in the sand. "I haven't made a list. I know many girls who've drawn wedding dresses and imagined themselves as brides they'll never be, not with the shortage of men since the war So, what good is a plan if there's no guarantee?" She took the shell and pressed it onto the sandcastle, jumping as a wave crept too close. "Did your childhood dreams include planning a wedding day?" she asked.

"Of course not. I dreamt of being either a character from my favourite book, or one of the leading men from films."

"Which characters? Which movies?" Her breath warmed his cheek. "Tell me everything. You must be honest if you want me to know who you are."

"Some days I dreamt of becoming a pirate, some days Robin Hood."

"Ooh. I think you would look devilishly handsome with an eye patch." She covered one of Sam's eyes.

"That's not what I spend my nights wishing for, now." He took her hand and pulled her up the beach to where the sand was dry and hadn't lost the sun's warmth. This time they sat closer than before.

"What about a wooden leg?" She knocked on his ankle making a click with her tongue as she moved slowly upwards.

When she drew circles all over his thigh, he breathed faster and got to his feet. "You're getting seriously close to danger." He took a step back and brandished an imaginary sword. "I'd rather be a handsome pirate, like in a movie I once saw. I'd fill my pockets with valuables from the treasure chest."

"Of course. Yes! Then, you would take the money and hand it out to the poor."

"Not all of it," he said. "A dashing pirate would keep a gemstone for the woman he loves."

Cecilia laughed and leaned against him, then pointed at the night sky. "Look! A shooting star."

He drank in her perfect silhouette and wanted all of it.

When the tide came in and washed her sandcastle away, Sam swayed with unease.

He didn't care any more about his mother's opinion, what Cecelia's father thought, or what anyone said. Sam desired this woman more than adventure, success, or the answers to the mysteries of the universe. He wasn't about to let her slip away.

He lowered himself to one knee. "Cecelia Lakeman, will you do me the honour of becoming my wife?"

Sam followed her gaze towards the mound of sand where the sandcastle once stood.

"I'll give it serious consideration, Sam. There's much about you I love, but I need more time. Please don't ask me to answer until I'm ready."

He wrapped his arms across his chest, and briefly considered shrugging it off as a joke. But for once in his life, Sam couldn't think of anything remotely funny to say.

Mrs Cora drank her last mouthful of tea. "There you go again, Sam," She leaned across the dining table to collect his breakfast plates. "Another interesting tale. My bridge friends loved the story of how you met. Now I've got the next instalment. The ladies will be delighted."

After she left for the kitchen, William sat slack-jawed until Sam prompted him for a response. "Well, brother? What do you think?"

"I'm not sure why you told this story or your reasons for excitement. She said no. Cecelia's smarter than I expected."

"She will say yes." Sam clutched his heart with one hand and his groin with the other. "I can feel it."

William drummed his knuckle against Sam's skull. "This might be a better time to use your head. How well do you know each other? More to the point how much does she know about you?"

"Like what?"

William watched the door, then held up his fist, his voice barely a whisper as he unfurled his fingers. "One... It might be important for her to know you're Jewish, not Catholic. Two...The marriage certificate? What name do you plan on using?"

"The name we're both using, now. Don't act so high and mighty. I'll tell the priest my birth certificate was destroyed during the Great War."

"I'll ignore that lie and move on. Three...You've been involved in some dodgy deals lately—"

"How can you even—"

"Don't deny it. You're lucky not to have been caught. And although Cecelia seems sweet and kind, criminal activity is hard to forgive." William's face was judge and jury rolled into one.

"None of your points are insurmountable. I'm a risk-taking entrepreneur, not a murderer."

Mrs Cora's footsteps echoed off the wooden hall floor and William kicked Sam under the table. But Sam didn't shut up. "Surely, the God who created the world is one and the same in Judaism and Christianity and many others. The original holy books are almost identical."

Mrs Cora clapped her hands. "You men never cease to amaze me. Such interesting discussions have never taken place under this roof before. I was having a chuckle to myself in the kitchen. Remember the time, Samuel, when you argued it wasn't a grey cloudy sky. William and I tried to point out the obvious, until you asked me cheekily if I'd consider myself a wild furry animal because I wore a bearskin coat. 'No, you wouldn't,' you'd said. Because you'd still be a person. It's what's underneath that counts. Every cloudy day from then on, I've reminded myself the sky is still blue underneath. It's only a cloudy coat." She bent to kiss Sam's head, then William's. "I hope you boys stay for a long time." Then, Mrs Cora wiped her eyes with the apron.

William gave her an affectionate smile then frowned at Sam.

"Thanks again, Mrs Cora. As usual, you do a wonderful hearty breakfast." Sam jumped to his feet. "I better dash if I want to make good time. The markets are impossibly busy when I'm late."

Sam pushed his trolley through narrow gaps between market stalls, bending to pick up loose cabbage leaves and onion skins strewn across the ground. When he had his own stall, he would keep it scrupulously clean. He brushed the dust off his jacket sleeves and tipped his hat to a passerby. Once he'd made the right connections, he would have his own business and Cecelia would jump right into his arms. What William didn't understand about life was that everything is a gamble. Sam stopped at the familiar echo of his thoughts. He was like Solomon. Obsessive. Gambling. Believing only he was right. He had many of his father's traits. Except he was doing this out of love, not selfishness.

"Here you go Mate," Sam said to Sparra, handing over his first monthly repayment for the lorry. "I was just thinking—"

"Did it hurt?" Sparra smiled broader than usual, showing gaps where teeth used to live.

"Now I've got my own transport, I'm trying to build up extra business. I'm available evenings and weekends, even if I don't sleep. The shiniest girl in the world might agree to marry me if I play my cards right."

"Shiny, you say? Doesn't sound too bright to me. Not if she's considering your proposal."

Sparra's offsider guffawed, but nothing could dampen Sam's mood.

"If you can wrangle a Monday off, I've got a three-dayer. It's a long drive. Adelaide and back."

Sam stroked his chin. If this was lucrative enough, it could be the last time he followed Solomon's footsteps. He'd get the girl, and then he'd behave like William. The good son. "Never been to Adelaide. A trip through the middle of nowhere will be good for me. I like uncharted territory."

"Well, if that's what you're looking for, I can give you a name." Sparra tapped the side of nose. "What do you think?"

"Tell me more."

Sparra lowered his voice. "This fella owns a tobacco shop; his brother has a crayfishing boat. It's illegal to transport crays across the border, but the top-notch restaurants in Melbourne pay a pretty penny."

Sam's smile widened as he imagined Solomon listening in to this conversation and turning purple. To Solomon, shellfish eating was an abomination worse than wife-beating. Much worse. "Give me the bloke's name. I can do a run next weekend."

Chapter Twenty-Three
POW Camp, Batavia, 1942

I stared glassy-eyed, but the gap through the open hut door showed an inky nothingness. Eventually, my vision adjusted to reveal the silhouette of fan palm leaves like grasping hands caught in barbed wire talons. No shadows or murky shapes belonged to Captain John or the soldiers who'd taken him away.

It wasn't unusual for Japanese guards to drag POWs outside; sometimes in the name of routine questioning, other times, a punishment for breaking a pointless rule or for what the Japs considered disrespect. One poor sod, who didn't bow low enough—an impossible manoeuvre for an injured man, was beaten until he couldn't bend at all. Another collected fallen papaya fruit and shared it with his mates instead of handing it in. The soldiers tied his hands for days as a lesson.

Previously, we knew the 'guilty' backstory of the event, and witnessed an intentionally public removal. We all got to 'look, listen and learn.'

This made the Captain's disappearance more unusual.

Collecting a soldier in the middle of the night? This had never happened before.

The following morning, I ignored the men speculating and

glancing at John's empty bed. Eventually, Cullen, a known rumour-monger, and Tubby, the skeletally thin cook, huddled over my bed like ravenous predators.

"So mate, you know the Captain best. Why'd they take him?" Cullen asked.

"I don't know. They crept in and marched him out. John didn't resist."

"Well, that's dodgy to start with," Cullen said. "This so-called Captain John Douglas has gotten himself on the wrong side of the Nips so many times it should be impossible to pick his nose."

There were many Australianisms that didn't translate and I'd learned to ignore them, but an edge to Cullen's voice scraped my nerves. "What does that even mean?"

"If they'd tortured him as often as they questioned him, you'd bloody well expect permanent bamboo slivers jammed under his fingernails."

I snorted in dismissal and kept the rest of what had happened to myself. I'd been drowsing and almost missed John saluting me. He'd whispered, 'No worries mate, she'll be right.'

He didn't sound scared.

Where had they taken him?

No one was assigned the job of making sure everyone woke up each morning, but John and I often scanned the beds; studying those who slept too still, checking for signs of breathing. To keep busy, I checked twice.

Tubby and Cullen watched me hobble to the window. The yard was empty.

"No sign of John," I said, mostly to myself. "What's going on?"

Tubby scowled at Cullen. "Stop putting bloody ideas into Young Dutchy's head. The Japanese don't trust the Captain more than the rest of us—but they do respect him."

"Respect?" I asked. "I've seen the Japs laugh at him like they consider him a curiosity."

"You're both getting fanciful about the bloke," Cullen said, leaning in too close.

136

His breath had the acrid chemical smell of starvation. I pulled away, but he continued talking.

"None of your theories explain why the Japs took him. I've me own idea and it fits with stuff I've heard. Many reckon your mate, Douglas, is a spy."

"Seems unlikely." I lowered my voice so the men in the corner couldn't hear. "If he's a plant, he's not a good one. They've left him in this camp for ages. Surely, longer than necessary to gather any information."

"Maybe that's it. He's finished the job and now they've moved him out!" Cullen clicked his fingers sharply to emphasise the point.

"I don't believe it... John would have slipped up. Left at least a clue. Nope... your theory doesn't sit right."

Tubby slapped my back. "Go for it, Young Dutchy. Trust your flamin' gut. Cullen's not the only one who hears things. The Nips have a reason for respecting the Captain. It's part of their bloody culture. Unlike us lot, John didn't surrender. Months after the Allies capitulated, he was out there playing lone trooper in the flamin' jungle. Still fighting. The Japanese despise cowards. They're indoctri-bloody-nated about real men refusing to give up. Those who keep fighting are warriors, and only warriors earn their respect."

"If there was booze in this joint, I'd suspect you of being drunk." Cullen kicked Tubby's boot. "Come on. Back to the others."

Beady eyes watched them cross the long, narrow hut, eager for scraps of fresh gossip.

John believed there were more rumours than truths circulating in POW camps. Although a bond existed between those in the gossip-circle, John advised me to stay well out. He claimed rumours damage morale—giving rise either to panic or false hope. Both were insidious diseases.

He ignored the loose talk and I followed suit. Except this time, there was a kernel of truth. During our nighttime chats, he'd told of roaming the wilds of Java after the rest of his army mates had turned themselves in.

. . .

Two days passed and my gut twisted in the same wretched goodbye as it had when I'd left the Netherlands. I wasn't sure whether I'd see John or my family again.

On the third morning, after emptying his piss tin outside, Tubby shook me awake and pointed outside. Guards were dragging John through the barbed-wire gates.

"The Captain's not looking too good," he whispered.

When there's trouble, the wise get out the way. But instead of avoiding the Nips, I pushed past the growing assembly of spectators and hobbled down the steps. If it hadn't been John out there, I would have kept my head down.

The Japs could be a vicious bunch, especially when the commandant was brutal. I thought they were all malicious, but John reckoned it depended on the man in charge. A cruel leader's actions trickled down to his subordinates.

All humans are capable of evil. Soldiers are trained killers, but one survival tactic was apportioning all acts of cruelty to the enemy. Seeing ourselves as the good guys.

I steadied myself on the railing and took a deep breath as they threw John on the ground like a broken toy. Other than army shorts, John was bare. His lower torso was a purple over-ripe plum, with splits in the skin on his back. I half hid behind a post, praying to remain invisible to the Japs. Yet hoping John would sense my presence and support.

A trio of guards stood watch. How long had they kept him awake? Every time John nodded his head in exhaustion and let his chin nudge his chest, a guard struck him with a length of bamboo.

These soldiers were an unfamiliar lot. A slightly built, boy-like officer was in charge. He barked orders and the other two grabbed John's arms, tying his hands behind his back. Another yell from the commander and his offsiders tightened the bindings until the fine rope cut into John's wrists. I winced. I couldn't tell what disturbed me most—the drops of blood seeping down his hands, or his lack of reaction. Somehow, silence was more difficult to bear than screams. The Japanese had a strange way of honouring warriors.

A guard toed his boot into the back of John's knee, felling him. I bit my knuckle to stop myself from calling out. Guilt overcame me. If our roles were reversed, John would have thought up the perfect distraction. But had an idea come to me, I wasn't brave enough to carry it out.

The boy-commander split bamboo lengthwise, then strapped the spear like slivers to John's calves. The boy-commander grinned as he anticipated exhaustion, waiting for John to slump back on his heels and slice his own thighs.

Tubby sidled up to me, pleading for me to come inside.

I waved him away, morbidly transfixed. Every time John sagged with fatigue; I clenched my fists hard enough for my fingernails to puncture my palms. Only when John righted himself, could I relax.

Tubby took my arm and pulled me off balance. "Come on. There's nothing you can do, and it won't help the Captain if you're knackered and useless. When they release him, he'll need your help."

I couldn't leave. If it were me out there, John would stay and I'd hook into his strength. I forced myself to be a man.

When night fell, the Japs left him. Presumably, to eat a decent meal and compare torture tactics. Maybe they gave each other points?

After Widey finished his rounds, I crept outside—the only light a dim glow from the guard house at the corner of the compound. I edged towards John, dragging my bad leg, steadying my hand so I wouldn't spill a drop of water from John's mug. A folded shirt draped over my shoulder protected his legs so he could rest for a minute while I held the cup to his mouth.

"Thank you." John's voice was so gravelly and low I had to place my ear near his mouth. "Now, stay away."

"I must come back again with water, or you'll die."

"No such luck," he whispered. "They need me alive."

Back in the barracks, except for a mosquito's buzz, it was silent. I rolled around the bed, but couldn't find sleep.

To comfort myself, I replayed the story John had told before he was taken.

Chapter Twenty-Four
Melbourne 1925

On the Dukes Highway, an hour out of Melbourne, a young man waved a hand-written sign in front of the lorry. *LIFT NEEDED. ADELAIDE.* Company on a trip this long wouldn't hurt, might even help time pass quickly, so Sam beeped the horn and pulled over, watching through his rear-vision mirror. The fella waved and ran to the truck.

"Shove your bags under the canvas in the back amongst the boxes, then hop in." Sam cleared the passenger side by moving a bottle of water and bag of Mrs Cora's special sandwiches onto the floor.

"Thanks, cobber. Fred's the name."

"Sam. What business do you have in Adelaide?"

"Looking for work. My brother reckons he can get me on at his place."

Sam glanced from the road to Fred, studying his face in small glimpses. He was about the same age as Sam and although rough around the edges, not a bad looking bloke. "I picked it wrong. I was expecting a woman to be involved. Well, there you go. I need more practice working out the Australian facial expressions."

Fred played piano on his knees. "There is a young lady. I met her when I visited my brother. We've exchanged a few letters. Won't hurt to see her again once I'm there."

"What's she like?"

"She'll do." Fred half-shrugged and stared through the stands of eucalyptus trees.

"She'll do? You're going a long way for she'll-do. You could at least call her pretty or witty, even if she's not beautiful."

"You're not an Aussie so you don't get it." Fred tilted his head, showing the same swagger Sparra used when he 'knew' something. "No bloke in his right mind would describe his woman as beautiful or show too much interest. That would come across as either soppy or big-noting."

"You're joking. I've been getting the hang of the accent and unfamiliar words, now you're telling me it's a whole new culture."

As they travelled through what seemed a never-ending repeat of the same film reel: red dust, rocks and the occasional tree, Fred dozed off. Sam drove on, his open window letting in fine red dust along with the breeze. As he reached into his pocket for a handkerchief, a kangaroo bounded onto the road and Sam swerved one-handed, missing the animal by less than the length of its tail.

"Strewth. Bloody strewth." Fred pushed himself upright from where he'd been thrown onto the dashboard. "What the flamin' heck happened?"

"A kangaroo came from nowhere. Lucky I missed it."

"You shouldn't have veered off the road. Especially not this side of the black stump. We could have been stuck here for days if you'd collected a tree. Wood does more damage than a roo."

Sam shook off the shock and dissolved into laughter. "This side of the black stump." He reached over to tap the glove box. "There's a pencil and notebook inside. We're on the road a few hours together yet. If you don't mind, I'll get you to write some of these sayings down. I'll be a true-blue Aussie by the time I get to Adelaide."

Fred started writing. "I had a Scottish friend once, and he was always asking what things meant. Here are a few that might not come up while we're yakking." Fred wrote for ages then read them to Sam. "You'll like this one—Pull the wool over your eyes, or spinning a yarn, both mean having a lend of someone or taking the piss."

"Gawd." Sam's body shook as he chuckled. "I'm going to need a translator to translate your translations."

"You have a catchy laugh, Sam. I suspect you're poking fun at me, but I can't help joining in."

"Am I allowed to say thanks for the compliment? I don't want to big-note myself." Sam winked at Fred, then chuckled again.

"You catch on so flamin' quick it could be dangerous."

"I'm reinforcing use of all the new words."

Mentally, Sam went through Fred's list of Aussie phrases, then one by one he said them out loud along with the accompanying meaning.

"Strewth. In flamin' order, as well! How d'ya do it?"

Sam shrugged. "I've a good memory."

"Must come in handy."

"Most of the time, but unfortunately I remember the bad more than the good." Sam swallowed hard. Here he was lying to the woman he loved and up to the same tricks as when his mother had called him the bad-seed. Sam stopped himself spilling this to a stranger. It's easy to forget acts of kindness but bad deeds always take root. And, the hardest mistakes to forgive are your own.

"Well, I reckon your blood's worth bloody bottlin'." Fred raised his hand. "Don't tell me. I know. Write it in the flamin' notebook."

Except for parking briefly under a shady tree for food, they continued for hundreds of miles through a patchwork of farmland, then an even longer stretch through red dust and low scrub. There was little conversation, but Fred played piano on his knees and whistled along, providing background music. They were all the latest songs, one a pleasant tune Sam remembered from the dance hall where he'd taken Cecelia a month ago. Her eyes had sparkled as he spun her around, then pulled her close to tell her how beautiful she was. He hadn't been lying, Cecelia was a good-looking woman, and the more Sam got to know her the more beautiful she became.

He was determined to give Cecelia the love she deserved. His stomach churned when he thought of Solomon. He doubted the awful man had ever been generous enough to pay his wife a compliment. But had Sam ever paid his mother a compliment? Probably not. Guilt and sandwiches sat in his gut like stones.

"Fred?"

"Yes?" He stopped whistling and raised his eyebrows questioningly.

"I get how it's not done to go around telling your mates you have a gorgeous girl, but I reckon what you say in private is a different matter. Even soppy talk is okay as long as it's the truth."

"Maybe."

"Do yourself and your girl a favour. Tell her how much you've been dreaming of her beautiful face."

Fred blushed and went back to whistling.

Sam hoped his advice was good. Who was he to know about women?

As they approached the hills on the outskirts of Adelaide, Fred grew quiet and wrung his hands instead of playing his tunes.

"Is this where you wanted to be let out?" Sam asked, slowing down.

Fred looked him straight in the eye. "Thanks for the ride… I've been thinking about what you said. I'll say something nice to Daisy."

"No worries." Sam winked. "I'm sure she'll be apples."

Sam circled Adelaide's city blocks until his headlights shone on an abandoned motor repair shop. He parked the lorry safely off the street, then rolled up a pullover for a pillow. With his head against the passenger door and feet up on the steering wheel, he settled in for the night He was meeting Sparra's contact early. He chuckled to himself at Fred's saying for getting up at dawn. *Up at sparrow's-fart*. As he drifted into a half-sleep, he thought up ways to throw *sparra's fart* into his next conversation with Sparra.

Before light, Sam awoke to a murder of crows screeching their raucous song. He checked his watch, then reread the address. Not only were the birds annoying, but crows-fart didn't have the same ring.

Despite his icy hands, sweat beaded on his forehead. In an hour he had to be at Halifax Street to meet his contact: Jacob Feldt.

He filled in time by eating the rest of Mrs Cora's sandwiches and familiarising himself with the city. Countless places of worship crowned the streets—the bigger churches towering over blocky new buildings lining the wide streets. An imposing synagogue, in the aptly named Synagogue Place, called to him. He slowed down, wondering if he should have a quick word with The Lord about his dilemma with Cecelia. No. The trip home would be perfect for lengthy conversations with God. Sam cranked the throttle and raced off. Once he got back to Melbourne, he'd acquaint himself with the nearest Catholic church.

It was time to meet Mr. Feldt.

Although Sam hadn't given much thought to the man he planned to do business with, the fella who answered the door didn't look at all shady. Jacob Feldt was tall and friendly and Sam relaxed as he handed over the note of introduction.

"Pleased to meet you," Mr Feldt said, after reading the card. He stepped onto the front verandah, closing the door behind him. "We've a big day ahead of us. First down to the docks to make a deal with the fishing boat captain, then you'll need to learn to pack the crayfish in newspaper and water so they don't die on the way home. I hope you're a quick learner because you'll need to do this without me on your next trip. The less we're seen together, the safer we'll be." He opened the door to go back inside. "I'll meet you out here in a minute."

Mr Feldt called out a goodbye to his family in Yiddish and a warmth replaced the tingling cold in Sam's hands. He was on familiar ground.

"Right then, Sam," Jacob said after they'd completed the morning part of the crayfish smuggling routine; where they'd readied the tanks and paid for the catch. "We've hours before the boat sails back with a catch. Good job, you worked well. *Gezunt vi a ferd.*"

Sam smiled at the praise. He wasn't as strong as a horse at all.

The older man had made it look easy and Sam had worked hard to keep up. "*A sheynem dank.*"

Jacob raised his eyebrow. "You know Yiddish?"

"*Farshtay.* Yes, I understand."

"What are you doing for the rest of the day?"

"I've boxes of broad beans to deliver and sacks of flour to backload."

"Flour?" Jacob shook his head. "Don't they grow their own wheat in Victoria?"

"They do, and I won't make any profit on it, but it's easier to hide crayfish in a fully loaded truck than have it sitting out in the open. If the police make a routine stop and do a cursory check, I'll have less trouble getting through the border."

"*Der mensch trakht un Got lahkt.*"

Men plan and God laughs at them? Sam raised his eyebrows. "You don't think it will work?"

"I reckon you could sell ice to Eskimos and you definitely know how to keep out of trouble. I'm off to the racetrack, forget what I said about not being seen together. I've taken a shine to you, so I reckon it's worth the gamble. I'd be grateful for the company if you want to join me."

At the track, Jacob placed bets on several horses, and when any of his nags managed to get out of the gate, he grinned like a kid who'd been gifted a giant ice-cream cone. Sam didn't want to overstep the mark with his new business contact, but his experience with a gambling man had been totally different. Gambling had been a vicious beast that incited his father to violence. Yet here was another Jewish man, similar aged, throwing away money with a smile.

Sam couldn't wrap his head around it. "Please don't take offence, but do you usually win?"

Jacob laughed. "No. Of course not. I'm addicted to the thrill, not the end result."

Sam pictured Solomon's temper and his mother cowering after a gambling loss. His voice trembled as he asked, "What about your family?"

"What about them?"

"Does your wife mind?"

Jacob offered his palms to the sky. "The missus and I have an agreement. Since this is a hobby and hobbies aren't necessary, gambling can't be my priority. But I work hard enough for cream to float on top of the milk, every now and again. Before I skim it off, I ask her, 'Anything you need or want this money for?' If she wants it, the cream is hers. If not, I indulge in a hobby that occasionally pays for itself."

As Sam took in this new way of thinking, the needle on his inner-scale of morality wavered indecisively. Maybe vices weren't entirely black or white: The pointer settled on a comfortable grey and Sam smiled. Regular trips between Melbourne and Adelaide had grown considerably more appealing.

Driving one-handed gave Sam the liberty to smoke and tap cigarette ash out the open window. He relaxed and leaned back for the long return drive to Melbourne.

An overzealous knock on the cigarette sent the entire burning tip flying with the wind and into the hot, dry scrub. Sam screeched to a stop and ran faster than he'd run in his life. He back-tracked along the road, but when he couldn't find the cigarette, he lost another half hour waiting for the bushfire that didn't eventuate.

"Stone the crows. This place is a flamin' tinder box. It would have been a disaster. There should be a law against smoking." Sam climbed back into the lorry, glad there were no passengers to listen to his rants.

When the crayfish in the back fought against their watery prison tubs, he yelled over his shoulder. "Oi! Stop the bloomin' rattlin' back there. You're an inconsiderate lot. If only you'd agreed to swim through the Southern Ocean, I would have been bloody happy to pick you in Port Philip Bay."

The journey passed quickly and Sam forgot to have the serious conversations with God.

He recognised the changing countryside. It wouldn't be long

until he passed through the border and the police checkpoint. What a ridiculous rule. Can't transport Rock Lobster between states, but you can throw out your cigarette butts and set the whole flamin' country ablaze.

His part-time business partner, Jacob, gambled for gambling's sake, so maybe Sam could find enjoyment when gambling with the law? His tongue tingled and he tasted the thrill. He was ravenous.

If the police questioned him, he'd be prepared. If they discovered his smuggled cargo, he'd plead ignorance or shell-shock from The Great War. He'd tell the policeman how he found some laws as confusing as the Ten Commandments. That might work. If the policeman was religious, he'd see an opportunity to set Sam on the right road. If he wasn't, he'd surely agree and have a laugh.

Mr Feldt had called Sam a *bren*, a charismatic livewire. "It would be sinful of you not to use this charisma to your advantage. You disarm people before they realise they need to be armed."

Sam took a slow, steadying breath when the border patrol officer waved him down. He leapt out of the driver's seat wearing his broadest smile. It wasn't a cover; he'd switched himself to full *bren* mode. He casually untied the ropes of the canvas flap and reached for the crate of soft drink Mr Feldt had given him for the road. "Good afternoon, Sir. Bloomin' hot out here. Want to share a drink while you're doing such an important service?" He hit the bottle tops on the wheel arch to open them and read the label, "Passiona."

The policeman took a swig. "What is this? It's sweet."

"Made in New South Wales from home-grown passion fruit. The bloke who gave them to me didn't like them either. Said they were a kiddie's drink. But the manufacturer reckons they stay the rapidly increasing plague of cancer. You can never have too much fruity goodness."

Sam patted the flour sacks as the policeman finished his drink. "Best flour is from South Australia. My sisters make sponge cakes so light they have to be weighed down with leaden strawberries."

The policeman helped Sam refasten the cover. "Next time you do a trip for flour, don't bring me this Passiona stuff. Bring me a Coopers' beer."

Chapter Twenty-Five
Melbourne 1925

If only Sam could persuade Cecelia he'd make a good husband.

He didn't know exactly what *would* convince her, but he was smart enough not to model himself after his father.

At the end of each shift, Solomon had polished his boots and placed them on the hearth with military precision before leaning back in his chair. To a casual observer, he might have appeared relaxed, but the family knew better. His eyes darted as he maintained a suspicious watch. Sam's mother often flinched under his critical eye. Solomon never once helped her in the kitchen.

Armed with a plan to become the exact opposite, Sam knocked off work early to catch Mrs Cora during the early afternoon when she was preparing dinner. As expected, she was in her much-loved spot, enjoying the breeze under the pergola. Bunches of ripened grapes hung from the rafters like a fresco from ancient Rome. Other than splatters where dropped fruit had stained the old table, it was a picture of paradise.

Mrs Cora smiled as Sam approached. She paused from shelling peas and wiped her hands on the tea cloth. "Hello, my dear. You're home early."

"I have a favour to ask." He pulled out a chair and picked up a handful of pods. "Could you teach me how to cook?"

"Is this about impressing your young lady?"

"Not really." He attempted to hide his surprise. Mrs Cora was more intuitive than she seemed. "It's just a useful skill," he said. "And who better to teach me than the best cook this side of the equator."

She smiled and one-handedly popped the peas out of the pod. When Sam imitated the move, she beamed. Not just her usual pleased-to-have-company grin of delight, but a cheeky I know-what-you're-up-to. "We could invite your sweetheart to dinner this Saturday. I'll search out simple recipes to show off your culinary talents. It will be perfect. You'll need my supervision, of course, and I expect an invitation for myself and William."

That Saturday, Mrs Cora's kitchen smelled of beef pie and vegetables. Sam had set the table with a finely-pressed cloth, and folded the napkins as Mrs Cora had taught him. Now, he sat opposite Cecilia, clad in a deep-red dress that revealed just enough collarbone to keep him guessing.

William and Mrs Cora chatted about nothing. The atmosphere was delectable—but nowhere as delicious as Cecelia's approving smile.

"What other talents do you have?" She winked and he melted like the home-made peach ice-cream he was serving.

"Well, on my trip to Adelaide I mastered the art of swearing like an Aussie trooper. Like, when something bad happens—"

Mrs Cora slapped his hand with her napkin. "Don't you dare ruin a lovely meal."

Cecelia laughed. "Perhaps another time."

"I've almost perfected my Australian accent. I've worked out the difference between Cockney and Australian. They're close, but there are a few tells."

William rolled his eyes, but Cecelia grabbed Sam's arm. "Go on. Tell us."

"It's mostly the vowels. Imagine the Cockney *O* being a circle, Listen. *Not. Drop. Off.* Well, the Aussie *O* is squashed like an oval. *Not. Drop. Off.*"

"Don't encourage him," William said. "He loves attention and he's making this up."

"But I can hear the difference." Mrs Cora was wide-eyed and eager.

"Also," Sam said, raising a triumphant eyebrow. "Rather than choppy breaks between words, Australian is kind of mellow and stretched out like caramel taffy."

Sam illustrated the difference by making compliments to Cecelia and Mrs Cora. They were both blushing when the phone rang.

"I'd better answer that," Mrs Cora said.

"Wait here." William got to his feet. "I'll get it for you."

Cecelia had removed her shoe and was tickling a strip of bare ankle under Sam's trousers with her toe, when William yelled from the back door. "Quick. It's a trunk call. From Fay."

Fay had never phoned before. She would have needed to wait at one of the few government offices in London armed with more money than any of them could spare.

The brothers hurried into the hallway, pressing their heads together to share the earpiece.

"It's Mum." Fay's voice was shaky. "She passed away last night."

"How? She's only fifty-four." William shook his head in disbelief.

Blood pulsed in Sam's head making it difficult to hear Fay speak. She was apologising about sharing William's letter. He had no idea what she was on about. At her end, banging and yelling in the background stopped her mid-sentence.

"Are you okay?" Sam asked. "What's that noise?"

"It's Dad hitting the door. He's really angry, I'm worried the officials will drag him away. He's demanding to talk to you, Sam, but I won't let him. Don't listen to Dad. Mum died of a brain aneurysm. The letter had nothing to do with it."

The banging was replaced by the last voice either brother wanted to hear. "You did this, both of you. You killed your mother. Leaving her for the war without a word. Finding out Sam plans to marry a Catholic girl—that was the last straw."

Sam dropped the phone and ran into the street. Although his legs threatened to crumple, he put one foot in front of the other, juggling emotions as he ran, keeping all of them in the air. *Grief. Hate. Guilt.* He whispered the words with each strangled breath but kept running. He would never see his mother again. She wouldn't meet Cecelia and understand why the religious difference didn't matter to him. Why couldn't his father have dropped dead instead? What kind of God would allow this to happen? He should have written to his mother. He should have waited in England and brought her to Australia with him. *Grief. Hate. Guilt.*

When Sam returned, William was waiting outside, his cheeks wet with tears. "I shouldn't have written the letter. I'm sorry. I was staring at a blank page with nothing to share, so I told Fay about you and Cecelia. I didn't know Mum would read it."

"You're not to blame. I should have told her myself."

For the first time since he was five, Sam cried. He and William lay on the large front lawn staring at the sky until dark.

Sam caught a glimpse of Cecelia and Mrs Cora edging around the corner before disappearing inside. He hoped Cecelia wouldn't think him less of a man for crying.

He wished he could explain, he wished she could mend him—but he feared his heart was irreparably broken.

Chapter Twenty-Six
POW Camp, Batavia, 1942

When John finished telling me of Sam's mother's death, he climbed out of bed and crooked his elbows on the verandah rail. In the low light, the tip of his cigarette betrayed his trembling fingers and his silhouetted shoulders heaved under soundless sobs.

Was he crying for Sam? Or his own mother? Ever since the gossip-gang planted suspicion about John not being whom he claimed, I'd wondered if John and Sam were the same man. But asking this simple question would be as disrespectful and unthinkable as asking my father how much money he had in the bank. Despite the vulgarity of war, there were lines of civility I never wished to cross.

If John was Sam, his sorrow made sense. Even if he wasn't, I felt the transferred sadness, and my thoughts went to my own mother. The letters I hadn't written. It seemed pointless, given the strict limits on content. Yet, other POWs wrote often, knowing their letters might never reach their families.

I waited for the familiar creaking of his return to whisper his name.

He tilted his head. "What is it, Kid?"

"I've been thinking about Sam. About the guilt for his mother. Except for a postcard to let mine know I'm alive, I've sent no words of comfort."

"Don't be hard on yourself. You've done your best. Beating yourself up will do your bloomin' head in."

"But I haven't done my best." My voice broke. "I'm as bad as Sam."

"What about I help you?"

I buried my face in the makeshift pillow. "Yes, please. You always know what to say."

"If only that were true. My mother passed away long ago, Kid, but it's high time I wrote to my loved ones. Not tonight, though. Provided I don't get invited to any high-class dinner parties or fancy shin-digs, we'll have a writing session tomorrow."

The early morning served up a disturbance instead of breakfast. Tubby, the cook, shouting at the guards.

John and I watched through the window.

"More flour, we've run out." Tubby pointed to his copy of the meagre rations-chart provided by The Red Cross. He held sections from the Geneva Convention regarding the treatment of prisoners. "You Japanese barely bloody pretend to care." He waved the papers as if swatting killer wasps. "I can't make damper without flour and the men need food. Look at us, we're starving."

When the Japs ignored him, he yelled again. "I'll bloody report you. Tell The Red Cross how you really treat us."

John and I gasped. Tubby had made a serious threat.

A Japanese guard nodded to his offsider, and together they dragged Tubby across the dusty earth and threw him into a bamboo cage north of the barracks.

John and I exchanged glances. This wasn't good.

The cage was neither wide enough to lie down, nor tall enough to stand. Being open to the elements made it a death-trap on hot days. The gaps between the lashed bamboo were easily accessible to rifles, bayonets, and soldiers' cruel hands, but not large enough for even the skinniest man to escape.

I limped to the railing and bent over to get a better look, but Captain John called me inside. "We have postcards to write. Not as good as letters, but they have more chance of being delivered." His voice was remarkably calm and his face gave nothing away. "Right, choose one of the Jap's 'obligatory messages'." He opened the door of a storage cupboard where a POW, no longer alive, had scrawled the entire list of compulsory phrases—all lies about fair treatment, decent food, and the like. Rumour had it that a twist of human-hair dipped in blood had painted the rust-coloured words.

Where would the POW have gotten blood?

As if in answer, Tubby called out in pain.

Desperate to block out the sound, I started babbling, "It's gonna be tricky to personalise my message when I've gotta use these." I flicked my hand towards the phrase list. "They're blatant frickin lies. And we're only left with twenty-five free words. What sort of message will that be?"

John's mind was elsewhere and I absent-mindedly chewed the pencil.

"Don't do that," he said.

"What?"

"Don't put a pencil in your mouth. The bitter taste hasn't come from stirring gin and flamin' tonic. It's the flavour of festering filth."

I took the pencil out and spat on my shirt sleeve, hoping to rid myself of germs. Any number of diseases circulated the camp and a bout of dysentery was the last thing needed by a man with a wounded leg. I didn't like my chances of getting to the shitting trench in a hurry. There was no way I'd make that hundred-yard dash in time.

I copied the first from the list. "*We have plenty of recreation.*" I stabbed a hole in the postcard. "What's the word you Aussies have meaning *far from the bloody truth*."

"Bullshit." John smiled and took out a cigarette stub doing its third round of service. He often 'smoked' without lighting up. Said he found the action comforting. He did the rolling motion, too, rubbing his thumb and forefinger around an imaginary smoke, often during a pause in his stories. When he did light up, he'd have a few puffs, pinch the end and save it for Ron. It was weeks before I realised *Ron* wasn't a person. It was the Aussie shortening for late*r on*.

He leaned over to check my writing. "If our other words were actually 'free' we could add something colourful." He picked up my postcard and read his made-up message in a theatrical voice. "*We have plenty of recreation...* laughing at soldiers hobbling to the dunny after chewing a pencil, trying not to end up with shit in their pants." John '*read*' it again, counting the extra words. "Bloody heck, it's yours and my lucky day. Under the twenty-bloody-five. Done and dusted."

"Would a mother enjoy a letter about shit?"

"Of course not. I'm having a lend of you, Kid. Anyways, they'd never let it through."

A sharp scream jabbed me right in the guts, and John swallowed what was left of his laughter. He struck a match, setting fire to the entire cigarette.

When the screaming stopped, I forced myself to continue the conversation.

"Could we write something in code?"

"Encryption only works if both the sender and receiver know the cypher." John's eyes darted from the floor to outside, but he kept talking. "A bloke I met in Palestine bought two copies of the same book before he enlisted. He left one with his wife. He taught her how to understand a code with three numbers in a series. For instance, if he wrote 132, 21, 4, she'd know to turn to page 132 of her book, find line twenty-one and read the fourth word."

"Wouldn't the Japs be suspicious seeing lines of numbers?"

"This was back when we all thought we'd win the war; it wasn't a plan to send coded messages after capture. Though it might have been useful." John leaned back and closed his eyes, taking a long drag. "This bloke planned to write 'intimate' messages to his sweetheart, but he lost his copy of the bloody book after the first letter and had to end all the others with: *Same 'loving' intentions as last time.*"

I half laughed, but a terrifying warble from the bamboo prison strangled my vocal chords.

"Go on, write," John said. "You must have thought of something."

"I have, what about this? Except I'll write it in Dutch." I counted the words before I read. "Moeder, Vader and Pieter, I miss you and look forward to coming home. *We have plenty of recreation*, but when I get back, I'll take you out for *oliebollen*."

I blew a chef's kiss into the air. "It's the sweetest dessert of deep-fried pastry with sultanas and sugar—"

Tubby's cry made us both jump to our feet.

"Can we help him?" I asked.

"No. The guards react worse with an audience. If we don't feed the frenzy, they'll get bored."

The thought of a friend, at evil's mercy, chilled my blood. By the time we'd finished our postcards, the cries were barely audible. Yet, they scratched the inside of my head like a gramophone needle I couldn't stop.

"What was that?" A hard-hitting gurgle made my skin crawl.

"The Japs never ratified the Geneva convention. That's the sound of complete disregard," John said.

"I don't understand."

He hung his head. "We better go outside. I think it was poor Tubby's last gasp."

The other POWs stayed inside the hut while we edged around the end of the building and found Tubby crumpled, lifeless in his cage. I dry-heaved at the garrotte wire strung so tightly around his neck it had cut through his throat. A sour tang flooded my stomach and rose to my mouth. Had there been food in my belly, I would have thrown up.

John sidled close to the guards and bowed respectfully. "*Kare o umete mo idesu ka.*"

They each nodded yes.

My belly tightened, and I shot angry glances at both John and the Japanese. "What did you say?"

John lowered his shoulders and stared at his empty hands "I asked them if I could bury the body."

He fetched the small gardening shovel from under a tree and began digging in the corner of the compound, beside the growing row of heart-rending bamboo crosses.

When John became weary, I wrested the shovel from his hands and dug another section of the grave. By the time we swapped again, a line of POWs was waiting to take their turn.

One by one, men dug into the earth and the rest of us watched in sacred silence.

Two of Tubby's friends etched his real name and serial number into a hand-crafted cross, while Cullen slowly and reverently washed the blood from Tubby's corpse.

Not a word was uttered until the grave was deep enough to blanket Tubby under a rich protective layer of earth. We threw symbolic handfuls of dirt to let our mate know he wasn't alone.

When John spoke out, we stood, heads down, in private prayer and the quietude crumbled under the enormity of his words.

"Death, please carry this man gently on his new journey.

Mother Nature, we thank you for cradling his current form until it joins the earth once more.

God and spirits above, look after us all. Forgive us for what we have done and for what we've lacked the courage to do. Please give us strength to forgive ourselves."

John saluted towards the raw, new cross, then clicked his boots before turning to address the Japanese. I bit into the inside of my cheek with my teeth, hoping the Captain wasn't about to end up resting in a grave of his own.

"*Jibun o yurushite,*" he said.

The guards bowed their heads.

"What did you say to them?" I whispered.

"Forgive yourself."

"Why? Why?" My skin crawled with disgust. "They don't deserve forgiveness."

"When this war is over, those soldiers will carry remorse for their terrible deeds. Unless they forgive themselves, the self-hate will grow and their families will suffer for their guilt. I do not wish this passed on to the next generation."

Chapter Twenty-Seven
Melbourne 1925

The wedding arrangements fell into place. It was set for six o'clock on a Friday afternoon, but Sam, William and Mrs Cora arrived before five because Mrs Cora insisted the groom be early.

After the news of his mother's passing, Cecelia developed a fiercely protective love that wrapped Sam's grief in sweet-smelling softness. A month after the death, they sat out in the bush where Sam felt he could breathe. Cecelia wore a peculiar expression, the one women have when rescuing a wounded bird. Sam's wings and heart were broken, and she wanted to mend him.

"I'm sorry I didn't get to meet your mother." She twirled a strand of Sam's hair. "I would have waited for her to arrive and had a large family affair, but I think we should get married as soon as we can."

"I want to give you all the things you deserve," he said.

"Don't worry, you will. You'll be looking after me for the rest of our lives."

Sam was taken aback. He still planned to buy her the fancy ring, and work hard to save money, but he was secretly glad about an intimate ceremony. The fewer people keeping up the pretence of him being Catholic, the better.

The day came and standing at a Catholic altar, made Sam feel more Jewish and more fraudulent with each stretched-out minute.

After five church bells chimed, time slowed and so did Sam's heart. The next hour dragged on forever with Jesus, his virgin mother and all the painted saints, watching and judging.

What if Cecelia had found out? His butterflies grew razor-sharp wings, setting his gut in battle with the gnawing doubts in his head. There was no uncertainty about his own feelings, but he feared his dear Cecelia had come to her senses.

Waiting awkwardly in front of the priest, Sam adjusted his bowtie and smoothed his unruly hair. He forced a smile at Mrs Cora and William, who waited calmly under the stained-glass window of Jesus. No point worrying them.

The church bells rang again, six solemn clangs. Cecelia's boss, Mr Spencer, dressed as always in a Bohemian riot of stripes and coloured velvet, hurried to a seat in the centre of an empty pew. Surely, if Cecelia had woken that morning realising she'd mistaken pity for love, her employer wouldn't be here as a witness.

The priest paced the aisle, scanned the grounds outside, and pushed back the sleeve of his vestments to check the time.

Still no sign of Mr and Mrs Lakeman or their daughter.

Mrs Cora adjusted her peacock feather hat and sidled up to Mr Spencer. Snippets of their whispers echoed around the holy vaulted ceiling.

"Cecelia works at my bookshop…"

"The one in Bourke Street with an unusual name… What's it called?"

"The Hill of Content," Mr Spencer said.

"Is that the name of a book?" Mrs Cora asked.

"No, the Fitzroy garden elm trees whispered the name."

Sam watched Mrs Cora as she arched an incredulous eyebrow. Another story to tell her bridge ladies. Sam feared it was likely to be part of an epic tale, where her poor young lodger was jilted at the altar.

He hunched his shoulders and fought the ache in his chest as he mentally rehearsed a speech of regret. He counted to five-hundred, then gave himself another hundred seconds to accept she wasn't coming.

The heavy church doors groaned and Mrs Lakeman entered alone, dabbing her eyes with a lace handkerchief.

Sam's heart slowed to an almost dizzying stop.

He needed to compose himself. To accept with good grace whatever excuse Mrs Lakeman gave.

Sam reached a hand toward her, but instead of taking it, she nodded to the priest and took her place in the front pew. The priest passed the nod to the organist and as if by magic, or God's will, the cathedral filled with music.

William tapped Sam's shoulder and whispered, "She's here."

An angel—all gossamer and light, lace covered arm hooked through her father's, stood silhouetted in the light. Mr. Lakeman, sombre and proud, slowly stepped down the aisle, delivering his daughter to Sam.

She smiled at Sam with what he imagined was the perfect blend of innocence and desire. Her bravery astonished him. Her confidence made his entire body tingle with shame at his cowardice

He experienced more than the miracle of God in this place of worship. There was an extraordinarily powerful force—an intoxicating weave of love and like and lust.

For Sam, the ceremony was a blur.

Outside the church, Mrs Cora threw handfuls of petals, which Cecilia picked off Sam's clothing and out of his hair. She pressed her mouth close to his ear. "Our marriage document lists your name as Solonsch. Solonsch? I must have been too nervous to notice when we had the meeting with the priest."

"It's my legal name but I don't use it anymore."

"Why didn't you tell me?"

Sam raked his hair with his fingernails, then smoothed it, like a bird preening its feathers. "It's my father's name and I've given up everything he gave me."

He was relieved when she smiled and he drew her as close as

propriety allowed.

Would he have to tell her everything? No. Sam would never ruin a fairy-tale by revealing the sordid truth.

They'd kissed inside the Church, but she melted into his arms and they kissed again. He wanted to skip the wedding reception and head for the hotel. As if Cecelia were reading his mind, she closed her eyes slowly, her eyelashes tickling his cheek. "I wish we were alone."

The taxi pulled up outside The Victoria Hotel in Little Collins Street, and the doorman took their suitcases.

For the second time in their whirlwind love affair, Sam scooped Cecelia into his arms and carried her. This time over the threshold of their hotel suite.

She blushed and tilted her head right back, exposing the smooth skin of her neck. "The last time you picked me up like this, you were taking me to safety. Now, I feel a frisson of danger."

Sam flexed his arm beneath her clutching fingers. "Too flamin' right," he said. "We might not leave this room alive."

The next morning Sam woke to find Cecelia half-naked, unwrapping wedding gifts at the foot of the bed.

"Why are you frowning?" he asked.

"This." She passed Sam a book. "It's from Mr Spencer. It's most peculiar."

"Well, he owns a bookshop and knows you love to read." Sam stopped speaking and raised his eyebrows when he read the title. "Ideal Marriage: Its Physiology and Techniques?"

"It's not for sale. It's a proof—an advance copy. The book won't be published until next year. Mr Spencer's note says it will become valuable, but only if we keep it in pristine condition."

"Why are you looking so puzzled?"

Cecelia climbed onto his lap so they could look together. She blushed as she read the introduction, "*There is too much joy untasted which could enhance life's worth. ... I am certain that many men and women, even if they dare not say so, will breathe their thanks in the privacy of their nuptial chamber.*" She turned to the front page. "The author is a medical doctor, so it must be true."

Sam's chest grew warm, the heat spreading as Cecelia read snippets, stopping to giggle, but returning to read more. "*So, above all, I would impress on all married men: every considerable...*" She paused and fanned her face with the book, then handed it to Sam. "You might have to read the rest.

"*I would impress on all married men: every considerable erotic stimulation of their wives that does not terminate in orgasm, on the woman's part, represents an injury, and repeated injuries of this kind lead to permanent—or very obstinate—damage to both body and soul.*" Sam flicked back to the contents page. "*Chapter IX. Sexual Union and Communion Part One.* Do you think we should try this union thing again now? This time we can follow the manual."

Cecelia reached across Sam, brushing against him as she moved the brocade curtains enough to share a glimpse of the outside world. "It is overcast. We might as well stay indoors. But I do believe we did perfectly well without help."

Her smile sent shivers straight to the body parts Sam noticed were explained in Chapter three.

As they left the hotel, the doormen sniggered and whispered to each other.

Sam ignored them.

His world was only large enough for two.

"I've got a honeymoon hangover," he said to Cecelia as he hailed a cab. "I'm charged up and exhausted all at once."

He had cheered inside when Mrs Cora selected a large room at the back of her house. The furthest away from William and Mrs Cora without being in the garden. Cecelia's rapturous bleats and moans were for his ears only, and he needed to hear them again. The only real cure for a hangover was more of the same.

Chapter Twenty-Eight
Melbourne 1926

"Cecelia not coming down for breakfast?" Mrs Cora slid her chair closer to Sam and pressed her pink painted lips together, the way she did when she shared new gossip.

"She begged for a few minutes extra lie-in," Sam said. "I'll take something up before I leave for work."

Mrs Cora rested an elbow on the table, slowly cupping her chin. "Did she ask for toast like the last few days? No butter? No jam?"

"Yes." Creases appeared between Sam's eyes. "How d'you know?"

"I know it was three or four months ago, but you must recall the words of your wedding ceremony?" She clasped her hands in imitation of the priest. "Are you prepared to accept children lovingly from God and to bring them up according to the law of Christ and his Church?"

Sam gulped a mouthful of tea but struggled to swallow. He did remember the ceremony. But surely Mrs Cora wasn't suggesting Cecelia was with child. Not so soon. Sam and Cecelia wanted children... eventually. But right now, their bubble of happiness was the perfect size for two.

He shook his head. "She got too much sun yesterday; I suspect.

The way she splashed and skipped through the waves like a dolphin, I wouldn't be surprised if she has a touch of sunstroke."

"Perhaps you're right," Mrs Cora said, clearing her throat. "Ever since Fay arrived, Cecelia's been the perfect hostess. She's probably over-tired."

Cecelia had been most welcoming to Fay, and to Millie and Jane whenever they came into the city. She'd shown off the best and worst parts of Melbourne with equal enthusiasm; painting everything in such a positive light like she was auditioning for the job of ambassador for the State of Victoria.

But Sam's brain wouldn't let go of Mrs Cora's insinuation. Over the past two weeks, Cecelia had stopped bouncing out of bed in the morning and been less inclined to bounce around on top of the bed.

He wrapped two pieces of toast in a linen napkin, folding it carefully and tucking in the corners to keep them safe, then pushed in his chair. "I'd best check she's okay."

Upstairs, Sam cracked open their bedroom door and stood back, watching Cecelia cradle the washbowl from the nightstand. Her crossed legs were half covered by her cast-off nightgown, and a wet washcloth was draped over her bare neck and breasts. Sam's eyes blinked like a camera shutter as he took a photograph with his mind's eye. A beautiful picture.

"How are you feeling?" He took tentative steps, expecting her to lift her face with the smile that made everything okay. But her shoulders heaved as she retched into the bowl. Sam lowered himself to the floor behind her, lifting her hair and wiping the washcloth over her shoulders and the nape of her neck. He needed to be helpful, despite struggling to keep himself together.

Mrs Cora was right. His gut and heart both knew, and they demanded his head agree. Was he ready for this? Cecelia would make the most loving mother, of that he was sure, but what practice or experience did he have of a loving father-child relationship? Where would a man learn this? Were there books about fatherhood?

He pushed aside his doubts and pulled Cecelia backwards into his arms, then he offered the napkin wrapped parcel like a gift. "Toast, madam? Perhaps this will settle your stomach."

She locked her eyes on his as if searching for the truth. "Oh, Sam, I'm not entirely sure, but I think we're going to have a baby. I hope you're happy."

He ran his hand gently over her flat belly, tears dampening his eyes. "How clever we are."

"She's asleep." Sam looked at the floor instead of Mrs Cora, and grabbed his crib box, ready for work. "Cecelia and I will be late for dinner tonight. I'm already behind on today's delivery runs, and now I have to stop in the city to visit *The Hill of Content* and let Mr Spencer know Cecelia will arrive on a later bus."

"Do you mind dropping me in town?" Mrs Cora grabbed her hat, gloves and handbag without waiting for Sam to say *yay* or *nay*.

When he held open the van's passenger door, she beamed like she'd won a £1000. "It's none of my business, but it is a baby, isn't it?" Her smug smile grew wider.

"It seems so. I must work harder now if we're to have a place of our own."

"Of course." She bit her lip. "But there's no hurry. The house is large enough for us all to have privacy. And the stairs won't be a problem until the little tacker is crawling." She held a gloved hand to her chest and sighed with delight. "A baby will bring life back to this old place."

Although the morning run into Melbourne was smooth, Sam concentrated on the road, trying to think of anything but the baby. He'd always believed he was capable of anything, but being a good parent seemed beyond his reach. Today, especially, he felt like a lost child.

"Cough up. What's worrying you?" Mrs Cora's eyes bored into the side of his head.

He pictured his black-hearted father wearing an awful half-smile, dangling his wife's favourite possession. A precious vase. A gift from Bubbe.

Sam took one hand off the steering wheel to touch his cheek, imagining the bruises under his mother's eye after her refusal to pick up the broken pieces.

He was the son of this brute. Mother had claimed he took after his father. It appeared to be true; Sam reflected on his own gambling —wagering his freedom for extra cash.

The overwhelming problem he now faced was the thought of the bad seed taking root and unfurling. What if Sam's actions rivalled Solomon's?

"My father wasn't a wonderful role model. That can mess up a kid's life."

Mrs Cora poked out her tongue. "A clever man learns from others' mistakes. Besides, it takes many people to influence a child."

Sam slowed down and parked by the curb. He blew his nose and took a few deep breaths. "My *Bubbe*. My beautiful, precious grandmother believed in me even when she shouldn't have." Sam smiled at Mrs Cora. "You have many of her qualities."

Mrs Cora dabbed her eyes. "I'll be okay to walk from here. The haberdashery shop is just around the corner."

She squeezed Sam's hand. "I'm going to buy softer-than-soft baby wool. Through the winter you'll get sick of my clickety-clacking as I knit booties and bonnets for your bundle of joy."

"You'll be like a grandmother to the little one," Sam said. "I don't know what Cecelia's mother will want to be called, but..." Sam bit his lip. "Mrs Cora? Perhaps the baby could call you *Bubbe*?"

Instead of answering, Mrs Cora smiled through tears as she clambered out of the car.

Chapter Twenty-Nine
Melbourne 1926

Sam stood hands on hips, staring in disbelief as Cecelia loaded yet another suitcase in the back of the lorry. "We're only going to Adelaide for the weekend. Filling up the back with luggage leaves less room for the merchandise."

Cecelia supported her growing belly as she bottom-shuffled across the bench seat of the lorry close to Sam. "Sorry for squashing you," she said to Sam's sister, Fay. "I'm trying to make more room. I've wondered what happens on these trips, and this might be my last chance to go."

Sam threw Fay a look—Cecelia can't find out these trips are illegal. He needed Fay to distract his wife while the 'business' took place.

Fay ignored his reminder and drew cushions from a soft carry bag she'd brought inside the cab. "Here you go." She tucked one behind Cecelia's back. "The other's for you to sit on."

Cecelia laughed and leaned over Sam while Fay tried to shove a cushion beneath her bottom. "We're jammed in like two sardines and a cranky puffer fish."

Sam climbed out and lit a cigarette. "What else have you got in that bloomin' bag, Fay? It's as round as Cecelia's belly. The pair of you have brought enough stuff for a year."

"Who knows what we might need on the road." Fay nudged Cecelia and the pair chuckled like schoolgirls on a trip to the country fair.

Sam loved how well they got on. His other sisters didn't visit often. They used the distance from Melbourne to the outer suburbs as an excuse, but he knew it was because he'd asked everyone in the family not to say anything about being Jewish. He'd never intended to keep secrets from Cecelia, but when you don't tell the truth straight away the mole hill turns into a mountain.

At the border crossing, Sam waved at his policeman chum. There was a second, unfamiliar, officer who didn't wave. He discounted the sickly feeling in his gut—this run would go smoothly.

"We'll have to buy extra beers for the new fella," he said, exchanging a look with Fay who knew the ins and outs of the trip, the contraband in the back and the bribery at the border.

"Why are you buying beers for the police?" Cecelia asked.

"It's hot out there. I'm doing our police force a kind turn." Sam twisted his wedding ring nervously.

"I'm not a fool," Cecelia said. "I saw you and Fay looking at each other. Tell me what's going on."

Sam explained the 'drink up don't look deal' to Cecelia as light-heartedly as he could, then added, "It's a ridiculous archaic rule. The crayfish can swim from one port to the other, but we can't drive them. They're changing it because it isn't dangerous. Except to the crayfish." He forced a laugh.

"So, you've been breaking the law?" Cecelia looked from Sam to Fay, then back at Sam. "You told your sister but not your wife? I hope you've made thousands of pounds?"

"It's not that lucrative." Sam bit his lip then stared at the road ahead.

"If it hadn't been for Mrs Cora having a house full of farmers and me insisting on accompanying you at the last minute, you would never have told me." Cecelia's soft voice hardened.

Sam stroked her knee. "Come on, as I said, it's an outdated law."

"No penalty then?" Cecelia turned to face him, her eyebrows merging in anger, but her eyes afloat with fear. "I thought as much. It's one thing to be invited by His Majesty to stay at an establishment with broken-glass topped walls, it's another to implicate your pregnant wife."

The atmosphere in the car cooled significantly.

"I've come up with an idea," Fay said after a few minutes of stony silence. She unfolded the map of Australia which Sam kept in the glove box and pointed out the border between South Australia and Victoria. She tapped her fingernail on two spots. "There's a wheat property straddling the boundary. I saw gates as we drove past. What if, on the way back, we enter the farm in South Australia and cut across the corner, exiting in Victoria?" Fay traced the route with her finger. "We would miss the border patrols altogether."

"But there's no road." Sam looked at Cecelia and shook his head.

"There'll be decent farming tracks through the crops. It's worth shifting a few fallen logs."

Cecelia nudged Sam with her elbow and clasped her expectant belly. "A baby needs two parents, Sam."

Sam looked at his pregnant wife and felt the warmth of her love. He needed her too. "You're right. I promise we'll get through the border okay, and this will be my last trip."

Cecelia shrugged. "If the border police ask questions, don't dare include me in your lie. I will not get on my back and groan while you tell them I'm giving birth."

"I'm sorry for pushing my luck," Sam said, his eyes pleading forgiveness. "We will hide the crayfish under the false floor and I'll buy lots of extra beer as bribes."

He drove the next two hundred miles with one hand on the steering wheel and the other arm protectively around his resting wife. He would not put Cecelia at risk. The regular trips to Adelaide gave him a taste of danger and adventure, but he wouldn't risk his marriage. He'd tell Jacob this was his last.

"Pleased to meet you, Cecelia and Fay." Mr Feldt kissed both ladies on the cheek then pulled out two chairs at the restaurant table. "I hope the food is good. Recommending a local eating establishment puts me in rather a bind. I'll feel responsible if the food isn't up to its usual standard."

"You aren't cooking it are you?" Sam laughed.

"I'm no cook. But I did cook a meal for my wife a few days before we got married."

Sam thought about himself and Mrs Cora preparing dinner for Cecelia. "Did you impress her?"

"Oh no, no, no. I wasn't trying to impress her. I wanted her to be disappointed from the start, not wait until she saw me naked on our honeymoon."

Cecelia giggled and blushed, Fay pantomimed a yawn. "A comedy duo in the making. Come, Cecelia. We'll escape to the ladies' room before they start Charlie Chaplain and Fatty Arbuckle impersonations."

As soon as the women were out of sight, Jacob slapped his hand over his mouth. "I hope I wasn't inappropriate. What a delight your wife is. She laughed at my joke."

"She has a keen sense of humour." Sam puffed out his chest with pride.

"A good looker, too. Unfortunately, my wife and daughters don't find me funny. They have a similar manner to Fay. I'm sure they're amused underneath their masks of boredom, but I must say, they've maintained a solid disguise for years." Jacob guffawed loud enough for diners at a nearby table to *tsk* and *tut*.

Sam smiled. He liked this about Jacob. A man poking fun at himself, was not something he'd grown up with. He didn't want to end their arrangement, but he had to. There just hadn't been the right moment. He opened his mouth, but Jacob interrupted.

"Hey." Jacob checked to make sure the women were out of earshot. "I didn't know you were married. I'd planned to offer you my older daughter's hand. She's not as sweet as your Cecelia, but I thought it would give us something else in common. Both being miserable."

Sam spluttered on his mouthful of beer and seized a napkin to wipe his mouth. But Jacob looked solemn.

"I'm sorry I didn't tell you about Cecelia."

"I'm pulling your leg. Can't you tell? My wife's a good old gal and my daughters are my pride and joy."

Sam studied Jacob's face. He could tell he meant it with all his heart. Soon he'd have his own child to love.

Jacob was still laughing at his own joke when Cecelia returned. "What's so funny?"

"Nothing really," Sam said.

"*Bupkis*. A bit of banter, that's all," Jacob added. "Sharing our Jewish humour."

A tic quivered under Cecelia's eye. Sam had seen that same twitch when she found out his real name. When she touched the gold cross hidden under her blouse, he twisted his wedding ring, trying to hide inside his head. What if she was questioning the sanctity of their marriage? Could such a shock send her into labour?

He looked at Fay for backing, but she was feigning complete captivation in a loose thread on the hem of her sleeve. He willed her not to pull it any further. There was enough unravelling going on.

"You're Jewish?" Cecelia asked Jacob.

"We're ready to order." Fay almost tackled the passing waiter.

"You and Sam have so much in common," Cecelia continued, ignoring the waiter poised with note pad.

"Yes," Jacob said. "He's almost a son to me."

"I'll have steak, medium rare," Sam croaked through the driest of throats.

"You'll miss Sam, then." Cecelia scanned the menu.

Jacob looked puzzled and picked up his menu, too.

Fay and Jacob made small talk throughout the meal.

The silence between Sam and Cecelia was uncomfortably loud.

Jacob accompanied them back to the hotel then left them in the foyer. Within seconds of waving goodbye, Cecelia dropped all semblance of politeness. Sam unbuttoned his too-tight collar.

"You're Jewish," she said. There was no uncertainty in her voice. "First you told me your name was Douglas when it's actually Solonsch and now it seems you've had an episode of religious amnesia?"

Sam started to speak, but Cecelia held up her hand. "You made a bare-faced promise to honour me, right under God's roof. You aren't even Catholic, are you?"

"I believe in one God. The same God for all. And my God doesn't read signs outside holy buildings to find out what brand people have assigned their religion. Does it matter what team you follow as long as you abide by the rules?"

Cecelia's lip quivered and her cheeks flushed with anger. "But they're not the same rules. You aren't even Christian."

"Neither was Jesus," Sam said, trying to hide his concern. "He was a Jew."

He needed to make this right, but Cecelia's face suggested he was digging a deeper hole for himself. He had never seen her like this. Could he fix it?

Behind Cecelia, Fay was signalling him with her index finger across her throat in a beheading action. A shudder ran from Sam's head to his toes. What an awful way to die.

Chapter Thirty
POW Camp, Batavia, 1942

When John spoke of Sam and his wife, his gaze carried an intensity that prickled the back of my neck.

Suddenly, *Koembang,* a violent wind, howled like a lost soul, disturbing the palm fronds—sweeping them across the POW compound roof like brooms clearing a stage for the next part of John's story. I hoped Cecelia wouldn't leave him.

He nodded in a *now-you-know* manner then sat on the bed, his jaw moving as if he was chewing on the words that had been so hard to speak.

The wind whipped again reminding me of ghosts.

Eventually, he turned to me, the weight in his eyes made him seem a different man. "Sam's name change from Solonsch to Douglas didn't shock you?"

I gave him an easy smile. "I've known for a while."

John cleared his throat and tore a page from the Japanese book he'd rescued from the scrap pile. After using his fingernail to crease the folded edge, he ripped himself a cigarette-paper sized square. "I haven't always been honest. I hope it's not too late to start."

I loathed myself for wanting more of something which gave John such pain, but I asked anyway, "Will the stories continue?"

I needed them to keep going. I only endured the other twenty-three hours in this shithole because of the one hour a day where I got to escape with Sam.

"I don't know, Kid."

Before John rolled his mix of tobacco and leaves, he studied the Japanese writing then shrugged. "For all I know, this book could hold all the answers to every question in the universe, but they're nothing but lines and squiggles."

Why now? I wondered. John could have pretended forever. "What made you tell me you're Sam?"

"Because I want you to understand how much I trust you. I need you to trust me in return."

What did this mean? Was there something larger, more important than the stories to come? I sat up to prove my readiness. "Tell me what to do and I promise to do it."

"I need you to distance yourself. Complain to the others about being stuck with the idiot who thinks he knows everything. Ask the commandant if they can move you away from me. Kick up a real stink."

My eyes prickled. "But then I'll never hear the stories."

"They won't transfer you. But I need you to do this. You must set yourself up to survive. Make it clear you're the victim, not an accomplice."

There was a shift in the way John spoke. A minor shift that many might not have noticed, but I had grown so accustomed to the shades of meaning in his voice that I could pick the slightest change.

I shuddered and sweated in the tropical night, but my bones ached cold. Maybe these stories went beyond entertainment? A darker purpose I couldn't grasp? Whatever it was, it was coming my way as swiftly as the *koembang* wind.

"What are you planning, Captain?"

"It's about stuff I've already done. Now go to sleep."

Prior to a second inspection by the Red Cross, the Japanese seemed keen to show the world they were following the Geneva Convention, they even asked men to speak on the radio and transmit messages of well-being across the air-waves. As long as the 'volunteers' attested to the fair treatment of prisoners, the individuals were given luxuries, and the Japs agreed on more flour and rice for the rest of us. They also passed on what was left of the Red Cross parcels they'd hoarded. Real cigarettes, chocolate, aspirin and tins of food—this all seemed heaven-sent.

Since Tubby's death, where many of us had shown ourselves capable of digging a hole, all men who didn't have one foot and a toe in their own graves were directed to work in the new camp garden, growing vegetables from Red Cross donated seeds.

Outside, working alongside other men, with guards watching, provided the perfect opportunity for staged discord.

John was tying beanstalks to bamboo stakes when I made my move. I let go of my stabilising-chair to wrestle twine from his hands.

"You're doing it all wrong," I yelled, then turned to the guards. "He's doing it wrong. There should be three stakes forming a teepee. A single stake will topple the second someone farts."

For a millisecond John raised an impressed eyebrow. "Piss off! Isn't it enough I'm forced to listen at night while you whine like a kid, now you're bothering me all day?"

I grabbed John's collar and whispered through gritted teeth. "Hit me. Push me."

Knowing the push was coming allowed me to stage the fall without further injuring my leg—but I yelled blue murder as I examined the old wound. "Did you see that? Bastard fucking knocked me down. Move me into another hut!"

The Japs denied us camp food for three days but didn't separate us. John dug up the can of corned beef he'd buried for an emergency.

A few nights later when he started on Sam's next episode, he did so in a voice so weightless, it almost floated away. To cover our exchange, I complained when Hiro made his rounds. "Get this bastard away from me, I need sleep."

Focusing on John's voice was difficult with the sound of rain outside and guilt whispering inside my head. I couldn't put John at risk for my entertainment. "Don't tell me more. You're endangering yourself."

John wrapped his arms across his chest and leaned against his bedside window sill. "Thanks for your consideration. But I need to continue. The stories might be a distraction for you, but they're something entirely different to me."

He reached under the mattress for his two prized Capstan packets. One was full of homemade rollies, the other held a genuine Capstan fag. John swore he'd never smoke it. The homemade fags were awful, but by half sticking his nose in the original packet and inhaling the pure tobacco smell he could trick himself into believing he was smoking the real deal.

"I'm sure you've heard of people having their entire lives flash before their eyes," he said. "You know, in the moment of death."

I leaned closer to John. It was too dark to see him clearly, but I was compelled to make sure he was okay. He was breathing easily. "You're not dying now."

"No. I'm getting in early. None of this movie reel played at the flamin' speed of light for me. What's the point? I want to meander through my past and think about everything I've done. Good or bad. See if I've bloody missed anything. You know?"

"Is it working?"

"Well, my tally shows a fair whack of misdeeds, but I've done worse things without realising. I've spent most of my life seeing how events affected me, when I should have been concerned about others."

In response to a flash of torchlight and footsteps, we hit the pillow and closed our eyes. Hiro stopped near my bed and I listened to him listening. He marched through the hut continuing his nightly patrol and left us alone.

"You still awake, Kid?" John whispered.

"Yes."

"Did you understand?"

"Not exactly."

"I'm viewing my life as an outsider. I realise now, much too late, that marrying in a Catholic church wasn't insignificant to the bride. I ignored the plaster angels staring down from the ceiling in warning. Back then it was all about *Sam*, and about him getting everything *he* wanted."

Chapter Thirty-One
Melbourne 1926

Cecelia decided moving in with her parents would be more convenient. They'd be able to help with the baby. Sam was working long, honest hours, trying to save for a house of their own.

Sam didn't want to share his Cecelia more than he had to. He dreaded moving out and losing their luxurious, private room and Mrs Cora's easy, thoughtful company.

It would be okay. They'd only live with the in-laws for a few months.

Sam revved the motor, driving faster. The sun was setting on another long day and he was eager to get back to Cecelia, who'd be outside, sitting on the low stone wall near the driveway, waiting for him to wrap his arms around her.

On a primal level, Cecelia's need for Sam made him feel more of a man.

When he turned off the highway, he chuckled at the joke Sparra told over smoko and wondered whether to share it with Cecelia.

"To achieve marital harmony," Sparra had said, all cocky, "you need a woman who can cook and clean... a woman who's an animal in the bedroom." Sam had smiled smugly when Sparra delivered the punchline. "But you better make sure these women never meet."

Sam was a lucky man.

With only three weeks until the baby was due, he was still learning about his wife. How generous and forgiving she was. Finding out about Sam's dishonesty was a mere rut in their journey. "Clean slate," she'd said. "You've admitted your mistakes, we'll start afresh."

Throughout the day, Sam's thoughts had returned to his late start that morning. How passionately she loved him, warts and all.

"Take the day off and spend it with me." Cecelia had licked her lips and sighed in a way that made Sam catch his breath.

Even if Sam had been told a pregnant woman could be sexy, he wouldn't have believed it until now.

She'd slipped her nightgown to the floor, and clasped her arms around Sam's neck, her ripe belly pressing into him. Sam was aroused. He might once have laughed, but there was nothing comical about a woman so confident with her changing body. Especially one breathing hotly onto his neck.

"I wish I could, but there's so much work to do. I will take a couple of days off when you have the baby."

His voice had said no, but his hands roamed across her bottom, more rounded now. More yielding to his touch.

Cecelia lowered her eyelids. "So, you'd leave me here imagining the taste of your kisses and the warmth of your skin beneath my fingers? Leave me wishing we could spend every moment joined as one."

Sam's skin tingled with anticipated pleasure. "I could stay for one more cup of tea."

Her laughter rang like a victory bell.

It had been almost an hour before Sam forced himself out of bed.

Cecelia had stood naked as he dressed, setting her arms out like a balance scale, weighing her choices. "I don't know what I want more. I'm so ready to see the little one's face and count his or her tiny fingers and chubby little toes." Her full breasts moved with her arms when she tipped the scale in the opposite direction. "But I want more time alone with you."

"It's too late for choice," Sam said, kissing her quickly. "I really must go."

Now, as he drove, he imagined his naked wife and her balance scale act. He'd raced through the deliveries to get home.

But, instead of Cecelia waiting on the wall, it was Mrs Cora who raced to greet him, tapping on the car window before he had the chance to climb out. "Cecelia's having the baby. She's at her parents' house. One of the boarders, Mr Don Hogan, was about to leave for his farm when it all started, but he kindly helped me get her into his car."

Sam switched off the engine. Although the car's vibrations stopped, his body still shuddered. He gripped the steering wheel and took a deep breath, then started the car again. "I'll go now," he said, reaching for the gear stick to put the lorry in reverse.

Mrs Cora tapped on the window and shook her head. "No hurry. She was in the early stages and these things take time. You might as well have a bath and a hot meal before you spend hours wearing a track in your mother-in-law's carpet."

Sam wished he'd brought another packet of cigarettes and a warm coat. Mrs Lakeman didn't allow smoking inside the house. Spring evening air had a nippy bite and he shivered more than ever when he imagined the winter, and being made to smoke outside.

Although he'd promised not to, maybe he could make a few trips to Adelaide and top up the coffers. Then they could buy their own house and he could smoke where he liked.

Sam went inside and warmed his hands next to the fire. "It's taking a long time," he said.

Mr Lakeman looked up from his newspaper. "When Cecelia was born, the labour went on for days."

"If I knock at the door, would they let me in for a few minutes?"

He stared as if Sam had gone mad. "It's not a man's place. And you're lucky it isn't. God sends the most awful pains to women. Eternal retribution for Eve's misdeed."

"Then God's not very fair, is he?" Sam scuffed his boot a little harder on the rug. Better wearing away more pile than kicking his wife's father.

He sat on the armchair in the corner and made a point of not starting further conversation.

Sam dozed on and off, jumping at every crackling log, hoping for news. Before dawn, Mrs Lakeman appeared at the top of the stairs. Sam tried to read her face, but all he came up with was that she'd turned the colour of old porridge.

She held a trembling finger to her lips as she walked towards Sam, then she paused to look back towards Cecelia's room. When she started down again, he saw the fear in her eyes.

He covered his face with his hands; he didn't want bad news. Although he barely remembered it, his youngest brother had died at birth and his mother had never been the same.

Mrs Lakeman lurched against the bottom newel post and dragged herself to the kitchen. Sam reluctantly walked behind her and took the kettle from her trembling hands.

He couldn't bring himself to ask about the baby. If Sam didn't hear the actual words, he could pretend Mrs Lakeman was merely exhausted.

As she reached for the teapot, the kettle shrilled, but it wasn't loud enough to drown out the powerful infant cry.

Mrs Lakeman was just tired. Sam was tired, too. Too tired to hold back tears of relief.

He put his arms around his mother-in-law and helped her into a chair. "Is it a girl? Can I go up?"

"You have a son, Samuel. The physician and midwife are with Cecelia. She's not well."

"Tired, I imagine."

"Her blood pressure is extremely high."

"Is that normal after a birth?" Sam drew sharp breaths, willing her to say *yes*.

"No, Samuel, it isn't. We need to pray."

Sam's mouth was too dry to respond, and time slowed. He followed Mrs Lakeman to the foot of the stairs and watched her trudge up to the room.

He stood until his legs faltered, then he carried his armchair into the hallway, facing the front door. He collapsed into the seat.

The doctor's hat and jacket hung from the dark timber coat stand. Sam stared at the doctor's things so long, he could still see them when he closed his eyes. He found hope in their presence. The doctor would only stay if he believed he could save Cecelia.

Eyes on the doctor's effects.

Eyes on his wedding ring.

Reflected in the mirrored panel of the coat stand, the midwife descended the stairs, a large metal bowl in her arms.

"Can I go up?" Sam pleaded.

The midwife shook her head in a tight-lipped 'no' and kept walking. The slosh, slosh, slosh of liquid breaking the deathly silence.

Mrs Lakeman followed, eyes searching the wooden treads. "Blood," she said to herself, then stumbled down to the next step. Sam looked at Mr Lakeman, expecting him to dash to his wife's aid, but he stared at the newspaper. Never turning a page.

"Let me help you," Sam said. Not that he had anything to give.

"I'm going to church." She grabbed her Sunday best hat and gloves, steadying herself on Sam's shoulder. "My prayers will be heard more clearly when I'm closer to God."

The door clicked behind Mrs Lakeman and Sam resumed his watch.

Eyes on the doctor's effects.

Eyes on his wedding ring.

The midwife's feet thudded on each timber tread. Up the stairs. Down again. This trip she was carrying a wad of blankets, but instead of heading to the copper out on the back veranda, she lowered the bundle into Sam's arms. He almost dropped it when it whimpered.

"Your son." She peeled the blanket away from his face. "He's a good little sleeper. Have you chosen a name?"

Sam and Cecelia hadn't got that far. Cecelia had read suggestions from her list and although he'd watched her perfect lips, and joined in with her excitement, he couldn't recall the details. He said, 'Cecil,' before his brain processed whether it was an approved name.

Mr Lakeman sprang to life. "Not Cecil. Cecelia would never choose that."

His venom coated words were a shock, and unless he backed off Sam feared he'd take a swipe. Cecelia might be her father's little girl, but she was the love of Sam's life.

"It's not you," Mr Lakeman said, apologetically "The name. There was an awful Cecil in her class at school."

His voice startled the baby and tiny hands reached out as if grabbing for comfort. Sam pulled his son closer.

"Awful fellow, kissed her without permission, then the others taunted. Cecil and Cecelia."

Sam kissed his baby's forehead, feeling numb and guilty. "Sorry, lad. I don't know your name. We'll wait for your mum to tell us."

"What about Cyril?" The midwife's voice was shaky. "It means masterful."

Sam gazed at the tiny soft cheeks and tried to open his heart, but his love stuck in his throat. It would neither come out nor settle down. "Cyril sounds like a good name. Yes." He recalled another name from the list. "James. Cyril James Douglas."

When the midwife reached for baby Cyril, a shiver of loss ran through Sam's body.

She patted Sam's shoulder. "I can't promise, but I'll ask the doctor if you can see your wife."

Sam shifted his weight from one leg to the other, rocking a baby no longer in his arms. He had a son. But he would trade the infant for the mother in a heartbeat.

"Come up," the midwife called. "A few minutes only."

The doctor—a tall man in a black suit, bearded with a crooked nose, met Sam on the landing. Blood spattered his white shirt. Cecelia's blood. His expression made Sam think of the Grim Reaper.

"In many ways your wife is lucky. The pregnancy complication I believe her to have often kills the mother quickly. I've tested her urine and done bloodletting to remove excess fluid until her kidneys resume functioning."

Sam clenched his fist to his heart, nodding rapidly at every word. "How long until she's fully recovered?"

The doctor grasped Sam's upper arm with a jolting intensity. "I haven't explained myself well. There are miracles, but most mothers with this condition last only weeks or months."

Sam faltered outside Cecelia's room. What had the doctor said? Months for her to get better?

"Go inside while I take some fresh air." The doctor opened the door and gestured for the midwife to join him. "There's nothing to do but wait. We'll leave you alone."

The room had the rusty smell of blood, making Sam retch. He inched towards the bed, standing back for a moment, frightened by the doctor's words. He knelt at Cecelia's bedside. Her delicate features were distorted. Her bloated cheeks pressed her eyes closed. Everything abnormal; the laboured breath, the swollen cracked lips, her body slumped on the mattress.

He kissed each puffy finger, noting the scratch where the wedding band had been removed.

"Cecelia, can you hear me?"

Did her eyelashes flutter, did her fingers flicker against his hand?

"We've saved money for a house, but I'll spend it on doctors." He buried his head in the pillow next to hers. "I'll organise my sisters to help with the baby. Mrs Cora, too. She will be beside herself with joy when she meets Cyril."

No response.

"Our little boy is a beauty. I hope you don't mind the name."

Her fingers pressed into his palm. He was sure of it.

"The name isn't important; we can change it."

He tilted his head backwards and pressed the tip of his nose to stop the dripping tears. "I love you, Cecelia. I'll whistle your favourite bloomin' tune for hours just to watch you dance around the living room."

He rested his cheek on hers and closed his eyes. "Please come back to me."

Chapter Thirty-Two
Melbourne 1928

Cecelia's cry awoke him. Sam reached across the bed to pat her back and calm the stuttered breathing she had during a bad dream. "It's okay, love. I'm here."

His hand skimmed her empty pillow. She must have gone downstairs for water. He turned onto his back, arms above his head, smiling, eyes closed at the honeymoon warning she'd given him about her dreams. Sam had promised to protect her, and for nights on end he'd happily encircle her in protective arms, entangling his legs with hers.

He drifted off to sleep then heard her cry again. "What's wrong?"

No answer.

He jolted awake.

His heart drummed. Two years of waiting for a miracle, but Cecelia was never coming home.

He pulled on his clothes before daylight. Today and tomorrow Fay had Cyril. Two days with Aunty Fay, two with Cecelia's Great Aunt Mary, a day with Mrs Cora, then the weekend with Sam. But this was a temporary and unsatisfactory arrangement. Sam needed to work longer and longer hours to help Fay and Mary support themselves because they were losing income

Since Mr Lakeman's death months after the birth, Mrs Lakeman couldn't cope with the child. She claimed he cried too much. Was too demanding. Must have taken after his father. Cecelia had been no trouble, an angel of a child.

Sam drove through graveyard quiet streets and turned slowly down the long paved driveway of the Catholic convalescent home. At this hour, he wouldn't be allowed inside, but one of the kindlier nursing nuns would wheel Cecelia into the grounds.

After tapping on the nursing-station window, Sam settled on the bench and watched the gardener dead-heading roses. He shuddered when the old man removed all flowers in a state of decline. Sam knew it was to encourage fresh new blooms, but he suffered the thorns of infinite loss.

"Good morning, my love." Sam kissed Cecelia's cheek, then nodded thanks to the nun. He wheeled the reclining chair under her much-loved trees. Even though the first stroke had affected half her face and body, she'd been able to speak when they brought her here. She'd kept up her good spirits for longer than Sam thought possible.

She'd admired her favourite trees. Just like those in the Fitzroy gardens, that Mr Spencer from the bookshop claimed whispered the name of his store.

"They're the perfect tree shape, like a child's drawing, except golden instead of green." Cecelia's voice was a hazy whisper, but Sam worked hard to understand. Her crooked-smile was still beautiful as she watched the elm leaves wave in the breeze. "This will have to be our Hill of Content for a while." She'd drooled and squeezed Sam's hand with what little strength she had. They'd both laughed. And then they'd wept.

For the past two years she could no longer speak or move; at times she could barely breathe, but her eyes were alive and she could hear. Sam read to her as often as he could, stolen moments as he raced from one job to the next.

Early on, he'd brought Cecelia poetry books, but the Catholic nuns, with bland faces and harsh voices, had ordered him to take them away. God, they declared, hated unholy writing.

"Miracles are rare." A nun had clasped her hands too firmly for kindness when she'd seen the poetry book. "It makes sense that the devout are first in line. The only book allowed on these grounds is the Holy Bible." Her thin lips moved, and her voice was female, but a trick distorted everything. For Sam, she became Solomon.

Cecelia's tragedy shook Sam so much he hedged his bets and converted to Catholicism. Praying in both the church and synagogue—hoping to improve the odds.

Since then, the nuns nodded approvingly at Sam's gold-embossed leather-bound Holy Bible. He bowed his head back at them, wearing a smile that took him back to boyhood. Instead of Robin Hood between the pages, he was smuggling a copy of Wordsworth's poems.

"Are you ready for another? Do you remember where we were?"

The pressure against his hand was barely there, but the lightest squeeze showed she understood. Cecelia no longer looked like his healthy young bride, but Sam found her beautiful. He kissed her lips. "Our baby's coming to see you today."

Sam turned away, covering his face with a handkerchief.

He would have to tell her soon that Cyril was going into a foster home. Fay was bringing him to say goodbye.

He pushed Cecelia across the grounds, fretfully filling in time with a short poem.

"Look! They're here." Sam waved as Fay and Cyril walked past the imposing wrought iron fence. Fay pushed a pram so large it would've been a mighty effort to lift on and off the back of the bus while restraining little Cyril—the escape artist. Fay kept one hand on the empty pram. The other was losing the battle as Cyril asserted his independence. He was determined to use his own legs as transport and the large twig in his hands rattled and clattered along the railings, proclaiming his arrival.

Fay wrestled it from his hands and he zoomed ahead, arms becoming plane wings, a loud throaty engine desecrating the peace.

Sam *shhhed*, a finger at his lips. The hospital staff frowned on visits by even the quietest of children. They'd granted special permission for a child this young to visit, but the nuns weren't expecting a boy like Cyril.

"Our little boy is coming up the driveway." Sam stroked Cecelia's cheek. "He has your smile."

Fay almost caught Cyril, but the little lad ducked beneath her arms and ran to join the gardener in the rose bed.

"He's crouching his pudgy legs, imitating the old man to a tee." Sam described Cyril's actions for Cecelia. "Now he's stroking his chubby chin with little fingers—inspecting the flowers. He looks ready to give horticultural advice."

When Cyril grabbed the open-jawed secateurs and roared, running at Fay, aiming the sharp serrated teeth at Fay's leg, Sam scrambled to his feet, and within seconds, he had Cyril tucked under his arm and had given the pruning shears back to their rightful owner. "Sorry, mate. Kid's got more energy than the sun."

The gardener didn't smile as he gathered his tools and headed towards the main building.

Sam knew he'd complain, he quickly moved the boy to his hip. "Come on, give your Mummy a kiss. You haven't seen her for a long time."

Cecelia's dull eyes found a tiny sparkle as Sam held Cyril over her chair. "Look how much he's grown."

Very carefully, Sam sat little Cyril, eyes wide as saucers, on the wheelchair next to his mother. For a moment the child was stunned. Then, his screams travelled for miles. He kicked and scratched her, calling out hysterically. "Not Mummy."

Sam snatched the boy and slapped his thigh. "Stop. Your mother loves you. You love her, too."

Fay rescued Cyril, and Sam fought for every breath. The red welts against the baby skin wounded Sam's heart.

Nuns marched down the path, and Fay quickly waved goodbye as she plonked the crying child into the pram. She called to Sam over her shoulder. "I'll catch the bus and meet you at Mrs Lakeman's. You stay with Cecelia. The foster home meeting is at one."

The nuns hesitated seeing Sam weeping in broad daylight, and returned to the hospital with barely a tut.

Tears ran down Cecelia's cheek, over the scratch mark and down to her lip. He wiped it away, coughing several times to move the painful lump from his throat.

"I'll read you a poem." The words caught in Sam's throat. These weren't the words he needed to say, but he couldn't tell her how unbearably hard looking after their son had become. She had it much worse and he couldn't inflict further disappointment.

"*My Heart Leaps Up*," he read.

> *My heart leaps up when I behold*
> *A rainbow in the sky:*
> *So was it when my life began;*
> *So is it now I am a man;*
> *So be it when I shall grow old,*
> *Or let me die!*
> *The Child is father of the Man;*
> *And I could wish my days to be*
> *Bound each to each by natural piety."*

He rested his head and wept against Cecelia's breast. "I'm sorry for getting angry at our boy. What chance does he have, but to do wrong? *The child is father of the man.* My father made me what I am, now I'm making Cyril what he is. I'm so sorry, Cecelia. Your mother wants Cyril raised by a good Catholic family. Fay and I were against it, but now, I see she is right. *The child is father of the man.* Our son needs a better father."

Cecelia caressed his hand with the lightest movement, a small tap signalling him to look at her. He closed the book and rested his elbow to peer into her eyes.

Sam had always been so proud of his ability to read faces. Now, he wished for oblivion. The message in Cecelia's eyes was clearer than the words on the page. She needed God to take her soon.

CHAPTER THIRTY-THREE
POW CAMP, BATAVIA, 1942

Once he'd finished telling his story, John curled up on the bed. "I'm in too much pain." He ignored me and the world, remaining shut off until the next afternoon.

I'd watched John cope with physical pain, but this raw emotional pain of the soul seemed more than he could process.

Although I wanted to help, I had to leave him alone. The gossip group shared the latest magazine smuggled from Bicycle Camp. The subdued sighs suggested they were not poring over curvy women like they'd done last month with the much-prized *Femmes D'aujourd'hui* magazine. Despite being a publication catering to women's interests, every image of the female form had prompted '*cor blimeys*' and '*have a gander at them*'.

And it wasn't only the pictures which proved entertaining. Cullen, after reading an article on beautiful homes, had flounced between the beds, waving his hands flamboyantly while pretending to redecorate the hut. My father would have winced at those hand gestures. Cullen acted so like my brother. But Pieter would have laughed and jumped up to show Cullen how to do it with flowers and style.

I edged closer to see what they were looking at, but they kept this new magazine well-hidden. Eventually Silent-G passed it to me, rolled and tucked in a sock with an accompanying top-secret wink. Silent-G mildly disappointed me by not attempting a clandestine handshake.

The inmates of Bicycle Camp had produced, at great risk, a hand-written, hand-drawn journal. It included pages of meaningful poetry, drawings of bleak landscapes, anecdotes on what POWs missed most, and touching tributes to mates no longer around to read them.

Even if John had been his usual self, this magazine wasn't the mood-lifter I'd hoped.

For the benefit of the men, John and I had ramped up our displays of mock contempt, making it impossible to do anything but ignore him. Although I'd never hugged John, if any man deserved comfort, he did.

John had a special brand of brilliance. One that had gotten me through many a rough day. The exceptional spirit with which he faced the guards, took the beatings, and negotiated extra food for his fellow prisoners was seeping out, as if the memories of his dying wife had punctured a hole and the man lying on that bed was a shell.

One sad memory did what months of torture camp failed to do. Broken him.

For the first time in a good while, I felt my own survival threatened. Seeing John in that deflated state, I realised my biggest fear wasn't losing my life in this God-forsaken place, but losing my will to live.

When I'd asked John to find me a walking chair, he'd adapted one by cutting holes in the back for handles. I'd thanked him. Said he was clever. Then he'd quoted a saying, he reckoned came from the Ancient Greeks. *Necessity is the mother of invention.*

It was my turn to help John.

If necessity is the mother of invention, what is the father's role? I decided a man's forte was stealing an idea and adapting it to fit the current need. My current need was distracting John. We needed a project.

"We could make our own camp magazine?" I asked the fellas.

"You're touched in the head, Young Dutchy." Silent-G said. "There's punishment for those who record stuff in the camps."

"We'll make sure not to write anything derogatory about the Japs." I glanced at John who had rolled to face us, so I pulled back my shoulders. "I'll take the blame."

Cullen curled his mouth and held up the Bicycle Camp mag. "I don't know. I'm not saying it isn't okay, but it isn't a barrel of flamin' laughs."

"That's why we'll do ours entirely different. You've given me an idea and come up with the perfect name. *A Barrel of Flamin' Laughs*."

"What could our lot produce?" Silent-G sneered at the men in their beds.

"We've got a variety of talent. Double-Double, the Dutch Dentist, is quite the cartoonist." I smiled at Cullen. "And you could have a page with hints on furnishing prisoner of war huts."

Cullen leapt to his feet and pirouetted before repeating his old spiel. "My guide to budget style using found objects to imbue a true POW ambiance."

John sat up and rolled a cigarette. "Any more of that, Cullen, and you can call it The *Camp* Magazine."

Cullen laughed and camped it up again.

"What about you, Silent-G?" I asked. "Any hidden talents?"

"I could share me recipes. Adapted from Gran's originals." Silent-G mimed spreading something across his palm. "Maggot and tomato pâté on thinly sliced cornmeal and sawdust bread."

"See," I said. "We're laughing already. Who else's in?"

"You're taking over the place, Young Dutchy." Cullen smirked. "You might be in need of a name change. Major General Dutchy has a good ring, eh?"

I didn't intend to take charge, but it felt good to be seen as more than The Kid. John half-smiled and gave me a two-finger-salute before turning his fingers upward in a *fuck-you*. The wink was almost imperceptible, but my chest swelled to twice its size.

A new red-haired fellow, Bluey, rubbed his chin "My penmanship's not up to scratch, but I can throw together a bawdy limerick or two."

"I can write a neater copy." I said, blowing my knuckles and shaking my hand. "I can still feel the sting of the wooden ruler when my lettering wasn't perfect. Those Lutheran nuns had a good strike rate."

"What about him?" Cullen pointed at John. "I know you're not on speaking terms, but he tells fair-to-middlin' jokes."

I shrugged, then called across the hut. "Know any jokes, John?"

"I'm looking at one," he said.

"Fine. I'll find someone else."

"I'm more of an anecdote man." John got to his feet. "Humour in the raw. Like after my army medical and the doc said I'd almost failed. 'What's wrong with me?' I'd asked. 'I'm fit as an ox.' But the doctor insisted I was colour blind. 'I'm what?' I remember staggering backwards and shaking my head. The diagnosis came completely out of the red."

I shoved my chair through the central courtyard, making snake tracks in the dirt as I headed to the garden. Other POWs were hollowing shallow trenches ready for planting, and although they looked up when John complained loudly about my being an annoying twat—the men and the glassy-eyed guards seemed disinterested.

Despite our fake gripes, John and I enjoyed the enforced work in the vegetable patches. Morning and afternoon, when the sun had less sting, the Japs made the daily call for the semi-able-bodied to get outside and work.

The guards ignored John when he yelled, "I'm getting away from The Kid." Then crossed the yard to work in the tomato patch.

Instead, they yelled at me, "*Asoko*. Over there." One guard aimed his rifle at my chest, then laughed and indicated John. I needed no further signal. I dropped my head obediently, and pushed my chair after him.

"It's been a while since they've questioned you," I whispered, shuddering at the word *questioned*, because there was no word powerful enough to describe what those bastards considered an enquiry. "I think the Japs have given up on finding out about your activities in the jungle. None of the guards seem to care whether or not we talk to each other, and the men certainly don't. Can't we go back to our old ways?"

"We're playing the long game," he said, bending to pull a weed.

"Hang on. I've made something for you." I untied a stem of bamboo I'd strapped to the chair.

John turned it over, inspecting my modification—a broken dinner fork I'd bound to one end of the stick. "Thanks. But what is it?"

"Probably won't work, but I've splayed the fork's tines, to help you pull weeds without bending over. Save your sore back."

He turned and stared at the barbed wire for a moment. Then he nodded and dug carefully around a weed, flicking it into the air to land on what he called *the drying bed*. "Works a flamin' treat," he hummed under his breath without looking at me. "You doing alright producing your magazine?"

John knew the answer, I'd seen him watching, seen him coming back to life, but I went along with his charade. "Except for sourcing paper, it's coming along fine."

"Good. I'll look forward to reading it. If I'm allowed."

"Of course. Some of your jokes have been illustrated by DeeDee. He's even drawn you 'pishing' blood."

For two weeks, John ceased his Sam tales, and I hadn't pushed it because the last episode had taken such a toll. But he seemed almost his old self and I selfishly wanted them back.

"Will there be any more stories?"

John stopped weeding. "I can't revisit Cecelia's death, or saying goodbye to young Cyril." John sighed deep enough for me to feel it in my gut. "I believed the lad was better off with a proper family. For a few years after she died I could barely wipe my own nose, let alone look out for a helpless child. I've given that phase as little thought as possible. Too much pain, too many dodgy deals, unnecessary brushes with the law, and unsuspecting women who didn't deserve my detachment and disdain. I'm not retelling any of that. No point visiting Hell before I have to."

Chapter Thirty-Four
Melbourne 1936

It took Cecelia another two years before God was kind enough to take her. For the next six years Sam stayed with Mrs Cora and dreaded passing her in the hallway—her disappointment a damning judgement of his actions. Eventually she moved him into an old servant's room. He came inside only when he thought she'd gone out.

So, he was totally shocked, when one morning they came face to face and she didn't step aside. Instead, she pressed her hands against the hallway walls to block him. Her determined look didn't hide the core of sadness.

"You're welcome back in this house once you've sorted yourself out, but for now, you must leave. For years I've given you leeway, thinking kindness was the best way to help, but it hasn't worked. I cannot, I will not, condone drinking or drunks in this house."

Tears spilled down Mrs Cora's cheeks and as she wrung her hands, he felt them squeezing his heart.

He was already brimming with self-loathing, but Mrs Cora's disillusionment shook the remaining solid ground beneath his feet. This was as bad as Bubbe giving up.

"Under normal circumstances, I wouldn't involve a third party in an intervention," she said, "but I'm at a loss so I contacted Fay. You two have always been close." Mrs Cora collected her handbag, hat and gloves, sniffing back tears. "I wish you all the best, but I'd rather not be here when you leave."

When Fay arrived, she almost knocked the door off its hinges. There was a no-sympathy-from-me expression when she grabbed Sam's arm. "Sit here. We are going to talk."

Her stare could cut steel, and Sam was taken back to his mother's scoldings. "The Melbourne constabulary have your mugshot on every wall. Petty stuff. Silly, stupid deals. You're not daft but you're acting like a child. I can't believe you've taken impulsive risks I'd expect from an idiot."

Sam put his head in his hands. She didn't understand, he didn't care what happened to him now. He wanted Fay to go away.

"I've given up bailing you out," she said, "but I'm not giving up on you."

She held him tightly in her arms and he felt safe. He knew he was in for another whipping of cruel truths. But at that moment, the close contact with someone who cared for him made him realise he did want help.

She reached into her bag for a letter. "I've written to that fellow in Adelaide, Mr Jacob Feldt. He's been generous enough to respond with an offer. We've decided to invest our money in a project for you. A fresh start."

"But I can't leave Melbourne." He thought about Cyril, about Cecelia's grave. "You have no idea how I—"

"Do not start with me." Fay waved the letter at him. "You've been allowed more than enough self-pity for a life-time. I won't get into a tit-for-tat about grief, but you're not the only person to have loved and lost."

Sam hadn't given much thought to Tom, the man Fay had lost to war. He thought she'd just got on with her life, but she looked at him and for the first time he saw the lines of sadness etched around her eyes. She'd never loved again. This was a glimpse of how deep her grief actually ran.

"I'm sorry."

"I don't need your sorrow, I've enough of my own. I'm not dismissing yours either, but I am ordering you to climb out of the bloody hole."

"But what about Cyril—"

"Don't you dare! You've paid that boy fewer visits than me. How many in the past year?"

Sam hung his head. He hadn't seen the boy for two years. Fay and Cecelia's Aunt Mary were the only ones visiting Cyril. The Catholic church restricted family visiting to four days a year. Better for the boy in the long run, they'd claimed.

Knowing what Sam was like, they were right.

"There'll be regular business trips between Adelaide and Melbourne. You can visit your son then." Fay stood and brushed down her coat, dismissing any further objections. "Go have a bath. I'll help you pack."

Despite the cool temperature, he ran a cold-water bath and held his head underneath to straighten his thoughts. Cecelia's death wasn't his fault, but others had pulled themselves together, and he needed to do the same.

Despite being the most overcast Adelaide day Sam had seen, streams of light cut through the darkness. God poked his fingers through the clouds and prodded him roughly. This was a message: Not everyone gets a second chance, so pull up your bloody bootstraps.

Jacob Feldt brought Sam and Fay to the fruit shop they now owned. Sam would take a wage and the profits would be split three ways until he could buy them out. Although the entire frontage was badly in need of renovation, Sam's jaw ached from smiling.

The patch of mismatched green paint covering the previous owner's name was shiny enough to look wet. The latest layer of lettering read: *SAM'S FINE FRUITERERS*.

He tripped over his words as he read it out. "*Fam's Fine Fruiterer.*"

Fay and Jacob laughed and Sam played along like the Sam of

old, pretending to adopt a speech impediment. "*Fam* is my new name."

One of Mrs Cora's favourite sayings was—*laughter is the best medicine*—the cure was working.

During the journey from Melbourne, Fay filled Sam in on details of the new business venture. Jacob had thought Sam should use another name in case his misdemeanours came back to haunt him. Sam agreed. He was ready to strike the last few years from his life.

"I thought of Bubbe when I suggested using the name Sam Kohn." Fay said. She pointed to the much smaller writing below the main signage: *proprietor Sam Cohen*. "It's obvious our crackly phone connection played a part in choosing your business name."

"I made a spelling mistake?" Jacob covered his mouth. "We could paint over the name, but I've already filled out the registration papers."

"No matter, I like Cohen just fine."

Jacob slapped Sam's back as he'd done many times before.

The darkness hadn't consumed Sam entirely. The more miles he'd left behind him, the freer he felt. As the car had swallowed the road toward Adelaide, the weight of his worries seemed unable to keep up.

There was a subtle shift, like wakening from a never-ending nightmare. He wasn't yet the live wire, the *bren* of old, but a touch of the larrikin had reawakened and this new city was a blank page to fill with new words.

Chapter Thirty-Five
Adelaide 1936

Sam's fruit shop was sandwiched between a row of commercial buildings with private premises above. Behind the customer sales area, the narrowest and steepest stairs Sam had ever seen separated a small kitchen and bathroom.

He took a deep breath. He might not get to choose his feelings, but he could control his actions. A voice in his head offered him the choice. Drag your miserable body up the stairs like a loser, or show your appreciation to Fay and Jacob.

Sam seized the chance to change direction and leapt the steps, two at a time. He leaned over the railing and saluted as he yelled, "Land ahoy."

"Looks as if you've found your sleeping quarters," Mr Feldt said, stacking old pallets.

Fay whistled the old Henry tune from the bottom of the stairs.

"Trouble ahead?" Sam asked. He skipped halfway down, feigning a playfulness that began to feel real. He adjusted his make-believe spy-glass. "Pirates on the high seas?"

"More down-to-earth problems, brother. How will you carry a bed up such narrow stairs? Chop it into smaller pieces and nail it back together?"

"That's a problem for another day. Check this out." Sam used his shirtsleeve to clean a circle in the grubby window, but letting in the sun wasn't an improvement. The light spotlighted dust, dead cockroaches, layered cobwebs, and long out of fashion wallpaper that was lifting and curling. He smiled at a section almost slithering out the door. "Even the paper's trying to escape."

The place was a complete shambles. Totally neglected. But the kind of mess he could fix. Energy coursed through him and Sam wanted to start right away.

"You'll have to tear this down." Fay tugged on a dog-eared corner of the escaping wallpaper.

"Don't rip it down. I might be able to restore one wall." He smiled. The repeated pattern of grapevines and trellises reminded him of glorious afternoons in Mrs Cora's garden.

He would prove himself to Mrs Cora. He'd scrub and scrape and bring both the room and his life back into order. If his back hurt and his knuckles bled in the process, so much the better. Sam had long stopped feeling anything. A bit of pain would remind him of what living is.

As if Fay had read his mind, she turned to Jacob, who was shaking his head at the work ahead. "If you don't mind, Sam and I will skip lunch today, and get a head start on the cleaning before I catch tomorrow's coach back to Melbourne."

"Tell you what, after I pick up the Mrs and my daughters I can drive back via Unley Road. I'll grab a box of cleaning materials from home and drop them in."

When Jacob hollered a coo-eee up the stairs, the angle of the sun shone obliquely through the grimy windows. Two hours had passed like minutes.

"I'm leaving the cleaning stuff down here." Jacob said.

"Hang on." Sam hurried down, brushing the filth from his fingers before shaking Jacob's hand. "Thank you… thank you for everything."

"No trouble at all. In no time you'll be making us money. Give me a secret stash to bet on the ponies." He held a finger to his lips. "Shhh. I haven't told Mrs Feldt about the arrangement."

"Haven't told me what?" A stern-faced woman with a siren of a voice blocked the doorway. "Another business deal of yours, eh, Jacob?" She put her hands firmly to her hips. "Naturally you've thought this one out and it's not a useless gamble."

"Yes, my dear. I'd like you to meet young Samuel—"

"What are we going to do next—" Fay stopped halfway down the stairs. "Sorry. I didn't realise."

"No problem. Mrs Feldt, meet Fay and Samuel Solonsch. Good Jewish people," Jacob said.

"Move, mother." The taller of two women in their twenties levered Mrs Feldt out of the way. "Hello." She raised her eyebrow. "I'm Bessie and this is my sister Lily. Do you mind if we have a look now we're inside?" Without waiting for as much as a nod, she squeezed past Fay on the stairs and headed up top.

Fay and Sam exchanged shocked looks. They would never have dared speak to their mother like this, yet the admonishing look from mother to daughter was easy. Bessie's pushiness was without malice.

"Don't come up these stairs, Lily," Bessie shouted down. "Not if you're still afraid of ghosts. Of any place I've ever visited, I vote this as most likely to be haunted." She leaned dangerously over the balustrade, prompting Sam to hold out his arms.

Bessie laughed. "You silly man. The arm bones break easily. You'd be better off throwing yourself on the ground to break my fall. Not that I would fall. I'm no fool."

Sam flexed his outstretched arms. "You've mistaken me for a chivalrous man. I was merely warming up my muscles for the heavy cleaning ahead."

"Touché," Bessie said, squeezing past Sam.

Sam hid his smile. This statuesque woman was feistier than Cecelia or even Fay. He'd met many women as weak as himself, but being surrounded by people who didn't need saving was refreshing. Because he wasn't a man to save anyone.

"Father. Mother. We'd better get to lunch and leave this charming couple to turn this wreck into a home."

She curtsied and smiled from the door. "Good luck. You'll need it."

After handing Fay's luggage to the coach driver, Sam studied the regular-formed bricks making up the bus station's outer wall. Adelaide was a neat and tidy town. Although he was determined to fit in like the red bricks, during the past two weeks, Fay's wonky-shaped humour had enriched the place.

"Safe trip." His voice faltered as she boarded.

"Come here." Fay stepped down and almost squeezed the breath out of him with her bear hug. "No excuses now. Write and let me know when you're coming to Melbourne."

"When you see Cyril, can you give him this?" Sam folded Fay's hand over a coin. "It's not the one Bubbe gave me, but it was minted the same year —1836. It might be better if Cyril thinks it's from you." Sam coughed weakly, pretending a tickle in his throat was causing the shakiness. "We can't tell Cyril any Jewish fables or his Catholic family would have a conniption, but if you don't mind, I'd like him to know it's a family tradition. I want Cyril to know he has family who love him and believe in him."

Sam's eyes glistened. He wasn't sure what affected him most, leaving his son with a foster family, the memory of Bubbe and her unconditional love, or his favourite sister waving goodbye.

Within a month, the shop was ready for business. Sam had spent days cleaning and bringing in stock that wouldn't spoil quickly. In the evenings, he'd carefully penned flyers for the opening.

SAM'S FINE FRUITERERS
Grand Opening Monday 5th of August 1936

Opening hours 9-5
Deliveries 8- 9 am and 5-7pm.

He and Fay wandered the neighbourhood before she left, chatting with everyone they passed. Those walking dogs, pruning roses, and gossiping over fences were all handed flyers.

Two days left for the final touches.

He was whitewashing the flagstones outside the shop door when Jacob pulled up in his black Ford.

"The Cavalry have arrived!" Jacob trumpeted through his hands then opened the car door to let out his troops. Bessie and Lily laughed as they marched towards the door armed with brooms. Both wore mop caps and aprons— Lily's over a dress, Bessie's over what looked like men's trousers.

She stamped her feet and saluted. "Assistance requested? Awaiting instructions, Sir?"

Sam's cheeks reddened, and he pointed out the board he'd made to hold the daily delivery orders. "Pretty much all done, but I've clipped my last minute to-do-list up there."

"No wonder you and Dad get on so well. He is a list-aholic, too." She pulled the paper from the clip and studied it. "I'm impressed. You've been doing things on the list and not just writing them down. I've known people with that affliction—procrastination. Very dangerous."

Sam leaned against the shop counter, regarding this woman curiously. "I know a great joke about procrastination."

"Well?" Bessie raised her eyebrow.

"I'd rather tell it later."

Bessie and Lily ignored him and got on with cleaning windows he already thought sparkled.

Jacob was right, his daughters didn't laugh at weak jokes. Jacob had said Sam was lucky having Cecelia, who'd giggled at every silly thing Sam said or did. His scalp prickled when he wondered if she'd still be laughing now, after all these years. Probably not. Sam had so wanted to be the man she loved that he'd become him for a time. Losing Cecelia was heartbreaking, but if she'd lived, he would have lost her, eventually. She wouldn't have divorced him, but she would have stopped loving him.

The Feldt women threw themselves into the work. Lily tackled the windows, her slender arms moving ballerina-like in elegant circles, while standing on tip-toe to reach the higher panes of glass. But Bessie impressed him most. His mouth hung open when she hoisted a fruit display table with her hip and pushed a cleaning rag under one side with her foot, and dragged it effortlessly in the corner to sweep underneath. He remembered Jacob suggesting Sam marry one of his daughters. He wasn't looking for a wife, but neither of these women would be fool enough to take him.

"What are you looking at?" Bessie stared right back at Sam.

"I'm sorry, I should have lifted it for you. It's heavy, I know—I've lifted it myself."

"If you're expecting me to congratulate you on your physical prowess, you're wasting your time. You could be working." Bessie resumed sweeping the floor.

Sam wasn't sure if he liked this woman, but he certainly admired her. "Not for one second did I expect a compliment. I was trying to be decent, but I'm out of practice."

Jacob looked up from striking another item off the list. "Learn from an older man's mistakes, Sam, never argue with Bessie. She's cast in the same mould as her mother. Lily is more like her namesake, as fragile and pretty as a flower. Bessie and the Missus are fine looking women, but they're indefatigable and indestructible. Pick your battles."

This challenged Sam's notions about the softer sex. He wouldn't consider *indestructible* a feminine trait, but he found it unusually comforting. Bessie was more attractive because of it, and even more so because she had no interest in him. He could admire her traits without getting emotional. He pushed his rapidly thinning hair from his eyes to risk another glance. Suddenly, Sam wished he wasn't balding.

After the final sprucing. Bessie and Lily retired to the bathroom to freshen up for the family lunch.

"I'm not taking no for an answer this time," Jacob said. "You're coming with us. I'll go fetch the Missus and we can go together. There's room for three in the back seat."

"Wait, Dad." Lily held up the hem of her skirt, eyes wide with horror at a rip in the side. "I must go home and change."

Lily's ever-present smile disappeared, and Sam worried she might cry. He was at a loss when faced with sadness and wondered if he should apologise. Before he could say anything, Bessie pushed Lily through the door.

"Cheer up. It's not life or death. Dad can take you home to get Mum, and Sam and I will walk to the restaurant."

Jacob looked Bessie up and down with narrowing eyes. "Don't you need to change, too? Into a dress?"

Bessie's high-waisted trousers, with two rows of buttons from the waist down her hips, and looked for design only, had Sam wondering how she'd got them on. They had none of the baggy-ness of men's pants. These appeared glued onto her torso but flared from the thigh.

She twirled, displaying an equally close-clad bottom. "This is my favourite outfit."

Jacob's shoulders slumped in defeat. He flicked his fingers in a pathetic wave and left.

With the Lily and Jacob gone, Sam pulled out one of two dining chairs and poured Bessie a glass of water. "Thank you for your help today. Excuse me while I change my shirt. I'll be back in a moment." He raced upstairs, wanting to give his shoes a quick polish. You can tell a man by his shoes.

"Have you done anything with the room up there?" she called.

Bessie's voice was coming from near the top of the stairs, so he leaned over the railing and there she was, perched a few steps below him, sipping her drink. "Not much. My sister Fay helped me clean, and we put up curtains to hinder birds flying through the opening."

"You know what?" Bessie said. "I'm not as smart as I look. I didn't click at the family resemblance. I thought Fay was your wife."

"No. My wife died nearly five years ago."

"Oh." Bessie stared at Sam for a while, as if looking inside his head. She finished her drink and returned to the kitchen without a word.

Sam dressed quickly and came down to find her. "I shouldn't have blurted that out."

"I'm the one who's sorry," she said, her eyes travelling over his shirt. "You look very nice. Though not as nice as when we first met."

The back of Sam's neck tingled with unease. Was Bessie flirting? She was expecting a response, but the only thing he thought to say was. "Should I change?"

She shook her head 'no' and continued flipping through a shop-fitting catalogue. He waited for her to look up so he could see her face. No hint of a smile. No pink tinges to her cheeks. No nervousness. She wasn't flirting. She was being Bessie. Straightforward as women come. Sam was intrigued by her earlier comment. "What was I wearing?"

"It wasn't the clothes; it was my grass-is-greener syndrome." Bessie laughed. "You know, I never go to a restaurant without looking at someone else's plate and wish I'd ordered that."

Sam's temple pulsed. He felt as if he'd been seen. Truly exposed for his moments of envy and of wanting more than his lot. Even today he'd been jealous of the easy relationship Jacob enjoyed with his children. "Perhaps being human means we all want what we don't have."

"I'm not talking about food." She stared, waiting for Sam to nod his understanding. "The thing is, I've convinced myself the men I could have loved either died in the Great War, or married their sweethearts. The left-overs are either morons or those who prefer men."

Sam took Jacob's advice and agreed. "You are probably right."

"Other women's choices look the dishiest." She sighed and stood. "Let's get to the restaurant early."

Sam smiled. "Good idea, that way we can study the menu and watch other diners. Inspect their meals as they're brought out. If you spot something you like, I'll go and ask the name."

Bessie slapped her thigh. "Are we talking about the husbands? Or the meals?"

Chapter Thirty-Six
Adelaide 1936

On the afternoon of the shop's grand opening, the entire Feldt family turned up.

Mrs Feldt punctuated her thorough inspection with not so discreet throat clearings that Sam couldn't quite decipher. He settled on their being disapproval of her husband's impetuous business investment.

Lily smiled and fluttered her eyelashes at the customers, both male and female. They'd be disappointed when they returned because eye-lash fluttering wasn't part of Sam's sales technique. Though, he'd consider practising it in a mirror, if it brought in more clients.

Mr Feldt touched everything, nodding in the way he did when reading the race guide at the track. Sam would have placed a hefty bet on Jacob's being satisfied with his stake.

Bessie, on the other hand, folded her arms and squinted. Sam waited for her to find fault.

"Why don't you put the bananas next to the plums instead of the pears? Yellow and purple are a better contrast. Both fruits will stand out."

Sam couldn't imagine customers in these difficult financial times buying fruit based on colour. Only the rich purchased on a whim, and the rich weren't visiting fruit shops. He met Bessie halfway. "The bananas have to stay furthest from the windows to slow their ripening, but I'm happy to swap oranges with plums. You can help if you like?"

Bessie jutted her jaw in what Sam interpreted as a jaunty celebration of a win. Her passion for winning reminded him of Jacob.

"Whose idea to hang ribbons and balloons out front?" Jacob asked. "Great idea. Seems to have worked; your shelves are half empty."

"Mine." Sam copied Bessie's jaw movement. A win for Sam. "I wanted those new flashing neon signs, but the cheaper frippery has done the trick."

Bessie humphed. "No wonder men are attracted by lipstick. All show, no substance. Rather than the decorations, I think the blackboard you've put outside, advertising the price of your tomatoes drew the crowds. Where did you get out-of-season tomatoes at almost half price?"

Jacob gave Sam a warning glance, then shot a side-eyed look at his wife.

From conversation with Jacob, Sam knew that while Katie Feldt suspected merchandise had often 'fallen off the back of a truck' the details of these dodgy deals were kept between the men.

Sam leaned back on the counter and took out a cigarette. "I didn't buy them cheaply at all. I sold them at an intentional loss."

All heads turned towards Sam. Had he gone mad? Mrs Feldt fanned her face and Lily steadied her mother using a firm elbow grip.

Bessie put her hands on her head and leaned back to shake her wavy hair. Her smile was broader than Sam had seen. She was a pin-up girl with guts and backbone. After a second flamboyant toss of her hair, she rested her chin on her fist. "Do tell. I can't wait to hear your reasoning."

"I considered advertising in *The Advertiser* or *The Sunday Mail*, but they wanted a pretty penny—much more than the loss on the tomatoes. I needed customers inside the store. Once they came in for the bargain, I switched on my full charm, told them a joke or two and sent them away with a memorable experience. I need new customers."

"So, it worked?" Bessie asked.

Sam responded by pointing to the Orders Board. Fifteen of the sixteen bulldog clips held sheets of paper. "Deliveries for the morning."

Once Sam finished serving the last of the customers, he turned the sign to CLOSED. Jacob offered him a beer, and the ladies had made a pot of tea and arranged pieces of fruit on a plate.

As the Feldts collected their coats, ready to leave, Sam handed out brown paper bags. "Take whatever vegetables you want," he said. "It's been a grand day for a grand opening."

"Not me." Bessie refused the bag. "Another reason never to marry. I have no inclination for cooking."

Sam waved goodbye then surveyed his shop, from the shiny new sign outside, to depleted produce displays within.

His hand was on the light switch when he noticed every slot on the Order Board was filled. His name scrawled on a new note.

S,

I'm not easily impressed, but you've done a dandy job.

B

There were two sure ways to set life on the up-and-up, success and friends. Sam took the smallest paint brush from the cupboard under the sink and labelled the top clip on the board. *Classified*.

As he wrote Bessie's initial on a fresh piece of paper, he struggled to recall any famous platonic relationships in the novels he'd read or the movies he'd watched. Sam enjoyed her company. He and Bessie would break new ground.

Mila Douglas

B.
Your friendship means a lot.
If we were together on a sinking ship with only one life-buoy... I'd really miss you.
S
P.S. That was a joke!

Chapter Thirty-Seven
POW Camp, Batavia, 1942

Captain John sauntered out of the hut like a man on a Sunday stroll, facing Hiro, the most charitable of the Japanese guards shoulder to shoulder, his last five cigarettes resting on his open palm. Hiro didn't take his eyes off the cigarettes, but once the negotiations were sealed with a grunt, he disappeared into the guards' quarters, reappearing with a wad of plain paper.

I shrugged and smiled. Nothing surprised me anymore. No point in asking what deal he'd struck, because I'd get the same answer, 'No questions, no trouble.'

John made the exchange and smiled his way back to the group watching from the veranda.

I looked at the others, waiting for snarky comments about John dealing with the Japs, but they were all joy. Cullen even air punched like a spectator celebrating a goal at a football match—minus the cheering.

Armed with the paper we desperately needed; we set to work in earnest. The Camp Magazine would soon be up and running, easily copied from the collection of notes scribbled on the back of baked bean labels and scraps of paper.

We talked amongst us ourselves, agreeing we needed someone to keep watch while our production line was running. The guards were so used to John poking his nose in, calling out, asking them questions in poor Japanese, there'd be nothing unusual in him continuing, albeit for a different purpose. He offered before we asked.

So, on the afternoon when John hurried up the steps, whistling, my gut-sense warned that John wasn't monkeying around. I immediately thought of Sam and his sister whistling whenever there was trouble.

I hissed, "Hide the magazine."

The men, concealed the pages like a well-oiled machine, before John made it through the door.

I kept one sheet of paper, pretending to write a letter home, and glanced towards the door. John moved too quickly for a wounded man and his haunted look set off alarms.

He shook his head and whispered. "It's not the magazine. I heard *Kempeitai* guards talking. 'No information from Captain Douglas, time to 'ask' the friend.' They're on their way."

My white paper, blank, except for a salutation, suddenly swam with black spots. I grew dizzy with fear.

Two unfamiliar Japs nudged John out of the doorway and made a bee-line for me.

Without a word, they dragged me into the yard and threw me face down on the ground.

By early dusk I could barely lift my bruised face from the dirt, yet still they beat me. Through my swollen eyes, I glimpsed flashes of my father. Scowling and disappointed. He'd expected his brave soldier son to put up a better fight.

But I wasn't brave.

John would have lifted his head and faced his aggressors, Instead, I stared at the drops of rain falling, watched tiny rivulets wash my dislodged teeth where I'd spat them onto the ground. Then I stared at the blood stained *Jika-tabi*, the Japanese jungle boots. I'd long found them fascinating in a horror-comic way.

John had shared an English saying once. You can tell a man by his shoes. I'd taken it literally and compared the boots of men in camp.

This time, I got to see the Japanese boots up close. Really close. No laces on the *Jika-Tabi*—rubber soled and canvas topped with split-toes like cloven hooves. The big toe separated from the rest.

Between kicks, I pictured the boots of allied soldiers—hoping to keep myself sane. The Australian boots were tan leather, six pairs of eyelets, lacing right up. The British, also tan, had nine eyelet pairs and two buckles. Another kick, another tooth, and the rain fell harder.

Us Dutch soldiers wore black boots, seven pairs of eyelets. But the US paratroopers won the race for most laces. Dark brown, tying well above the ankle. Twelve bloody pairs of eyelets.

But now, no amount of rain would wash the image of *Jika-tabi* from my mind. I did not doubt, they were the footwear of villains.

The next kick connected with my cheek bone and I turned my head, offering them the other cheek, keeping one open eye on the boot. The foreignness chilled my veins.

The Dutch also had sayings about shoes, *Met lood in de schoenen;* it translated to leaden shoes and meant doing something you dread.

That saying described me.

The Japs asked me over and over what John talked about during the night. I said I hadn't listened. That I didn't understand enough English. But between the beatings they kept asking.

I couldn't hold out much longer. I'd have to tell.

The weather came to my rescue with thunder shaking the ground, crashing and zizzing a warning siren that came too late. The lightning had already struck.

It struck again.

My mother taught me to count the seconds, *één, twee, d*—the cymbal crash beat me to *drie*. This storm was so close the vibrations churned my innards and blocked out everything but a voice whispering inside my head. *I am done. I am done.*

The cloven-hoofed boots moved to safety, leaving me to hope the end was lightning fast.

I could hardly make out the words over the thunder, but in a brief respite, John called out again, "You deaf yet?"

"No, but it's the end of the road for me."

As he hobbled to my side, a flash of lightning lit his face; Capt. John was smiling.

It was difficult making words around swollen lips. "How the hell do you find that funny?"

"I've come to the end of that road more than once, yet here I am, still around to annoy you." John's emaciated arms propped me to a sitting position, and he wedged his knees behind my back, cradling my shoulders.

"They'll see us together. Leave me."

"Forget the enemy. We're in a peep-show and Mother Nature is showing her wonders one flash at a time."

"I watched a peep show film once." I ran my tongue in the gaps between teeth, tasting blood. "I watched a woman undressing, but ran out of coins before she was nude."

A light sword slashed the sky, turning night into day, then rounds of thunder rolled. I kept my eyes open. "Barbed wire. Not worth seeing."

"You wasted yer coin looking at the fence." John's laughter rolled like the thunder. "You were probably staring at the woman's shoes instead of the parts you paid for."

Although my jaw burned and blood still dripped, I laughed a little. Sam might well have peeked inside my head and glimpsed my fixation with shoes.

When the sky exploded again, John lifted my head. "Look beyond the boundary," he yelled.

Pink and purple bougainvillea entangled in a wild embrace. Vivid green banana leaves, large enough to use as bedsheets, waving hello. There was beauty out there.

"And?" John asked when the lightning moved on to terrorise the mountains. "What did you see, when you really looked?"

"Exquisite things, out of my reach. Knowing I'll never see them again up close doesn't make dying easier."

"You're not dead yet." He slapped my bruised back a touch too hard.

"I didn't tell the Japanese what they wanted to hear. But when the storm hit, I was close. They're determined to know what you've been talking about."

"Then tell them."

"I can't. I can't live with making things worse for you."

"I wasn't hiding our friendship to protect me. It was to protect you. If they know about us, you may as well tell."

"That would make me a traitor, I'd be forever despised."

"I don't know about that." John lifted me slowly to my feet. "God blanketed Egypt with plagues, yet billions still love him."

"I can't believe in God," I whispered.

John nodded, close to tears. "Come on, Kid, I'll get you inside."

Safe on my bed, John cleaned my face and put three displaced teeth in my hand. "This could be the miracle we're looking for. Find the bugger that fits the gap in the front. Press and hold. I've heard teeth are like trees. They grow back if they're re-planted quick enough."

"I thought that was going to be one of your jokes."

John had a sadness that made me weep. "Well, I won't disappoint you, Kid." He forced a wink. "What's black and bad for your teeth?"

"I know the answer." I said. "A kicking Japanese boot."

Chapter Thirty-Eight
Adelaide 1936

Sam was serving when Bessie flitted into the shop like a whirligig. She kissed his cheek and pinned a note on the board. "See you tonight."

She'd disappeared before Sam could calculate the cost of the three and a half pounds of peaches he'd bagged. Or ask Bessie what she meant.

"Hang on," he said to the elderly fellow, then ducked his head out the door, almost losing sight of her as she strode across Unley Road. No woman on Earth walked faster than Bessie Feldt, at least not in heels as high as those.

The customer passed Sam in the doorway. "Here's your money and here's some advice from an old bloke. Chase after her. Women like that, and I didn't do it nearly enough."

Sam smiled politely, but shook his head. Bessie wasn't his girlfriend, there'd be no point chasing her.

He put the money in the till and picked up a black cap, no doubt belonging to the man who'd left in a hurry. The man would come back for it. Then he unclipped Bessie's note and sat on the shop counter to read.

S
My good friends, Edith and Clara demand to meet my mysterious male friend. In case you don't know— I'm referring to you. Pick me up at 7:00pm, and we'll collect E and C. Wear clothes suitable for an evening outside.
B

Mysterious male? Sam wondered what Bessie had told her friends. They'd exchanged notes for months, and although he'd escorted her to the movies, spent evenings at the Feldt house and were comfortable with each other, she'd never introduced him around. Perhaps they just needed a lift?

As he tucked her note into his pocket, he had an idea. The patent-leather hat left by the customer, was like those worn by chauffeurs in the ritzy parts of Melbourne. He tried it on. If Bessie wanted a chauffeur, he would look the part.

When Bessie answered the door, she threw her head back and laughed. "What on earth?" She stepped back to inspect his all-black outfit. A flash of recognition crossed her face. "Should I call you Sam, or is that too familiar an address for a servant?"

"Call me whatever you prefer, Ma'am." Sam kept a stiff upper lip and waved her towards the car, opening the car door.

"This is going to be a hoot."

He bowed like he imagined he should, then used his lower vantage point to watch Bessie hitch her skirt as she climbed in.

"Driver! I hope you weren't checking my legs? One finds it incredibly hard to source reliable help."

"Sorry, Ma'am," he said with a wink. "Of course not. I was merely examining the tyres. Your safety comes first."

Bessie directed Sam to the well-lit corner where she'd asked her friends to wait. "I hope they don't dress in matching outfits. Women should drop that habit when they finish school. Other than that, they're totally different, but you're going to love them."

Bessie was right, the women wore similar outfits. Sam employed his trick to remember names, Clara with the clear eyes and Edith with the evening shoes—their main point of difference.

"This way, ladies," Bessie said. "We have, Sam… err…. Driver Solonsch at your service."

He opened the door with a flourish and Edith blushed.

Clara scooted across the back seat. "If you'd given fair notice of a dress-up evening, I'd have worn a French maid's costume."

Sam wasn't sure, given the poor lighting, but Clara appeared to wink in his direction.

"This was an improvisation on Sam's part," Bessie rolled her head and eyes in one dramatic move. "Our chauffeur should come with a warning label pinned to his chest."

"Oooh," Clara said, "what would it say?"

"Funny in small doses. Whatever you do, don't feed the bear." Bessie flung her hands in the air. "He doesn't understand the most essential component of humour. Restraint. He'd spend an hour trying to squeeze orange juice out of a rock if he thought he'd get a laugh."

"Bessie, you can be so cruel," Edith threw Sam a sympathetic smile. "If it means having an escort, I think the least we could do is laugh, even if he isn't funny."

"Ladies," Sam said. "I am not deaf. And I am not slow at telling jokes. It's just that Bessie is a fast listener."

"See what I mean?" Bessie let out an obvious sigh. "The punch lines are soooo feeble."

Sam glimpsed Bessie through the rear-view mirror. She smiled at him.

While waiting for table service in the open-air eatery, Bessie borrowed Sam's silverware to drum on the table in time with the two-piece band. It wasn't a racket. Not at all. She played a sophisticated combination of drum strokes with her right hand and followed with her left, rolling through the beats like an expert. The guests applauded Bessie along with the band.

Sam raised his eyebrows and clapped too. "Hidden talent?"

"You didn't know?" Clara asked. "I'm surprised Bessie didn't tell you about her medals. Principal drummer in the orchestra."

A female drummer? Medals? Sam had much to learn about this woman.

"I can still do a trick or two if the situation warrants it," Bessie said, "but I'm no longer part of the band. I've moved on."

Clara idly twirled a strand of hair around her finger. "Bessie has new dreams. She changes them with the times."

"We all should." Bessie said. "I'd like a real chauffeur, but I guess that's off the list. I'd also like a collection of diamonds. Imagine wriggling your fingers and being able to light up Victoria Square in a gas strike." She laughed, and Sam basked in the warmth. Bessie didn't need diamonds. Her laughter did a first-rate job of lighting up the place.

"I haven't changed *my* dreams," Edith said. "I still want a husband. Still want children. I want a family to love. I'm almost thirty, but wanting a happy home shouldn't be an impossible dream."

The group fell silent and Sam looked hopefully to the band. Poor Edith. People rarely spoke with such honesty. If telling a joke could lift the mood, he would have told ten standing on his head.

The waiter distributed their meals and Bessie grinned at Sam as she pointed to each plate.

His eyes followed her finger. "Yep," he mouthed. "We're both wishing we'd ordered what the others chose."

"Well, although no one is interested in what I wish for, I'm going to tell you, anyway." Clara waved her fork in the air like a magic wand. "I'd like a man. Except, I'd like one of the ancient variety. Amiable of nature, rich as all-get-go, and preferably one foot in the grave. If necessary, I would lie back and think of Mother England, but I'd only have children if there was a fleet of nannies paid to hold clean, smiling faces to their Mama for a kiss."

"Even that's not for me." Bessie laughed.

"What?" Clara asked. "The laying back with your eyes closed?"

Edith glanced quickly at Sam, then covered her ears and blushed.

"You don't want children, Bessie?" Sam asked, trying to save Edith.

"Golly-gosh, no. Diamonds are much easier to look after. You can't give babies a quick wipe and lock them in a safe."

Edith appeared forlorn when she gently tapped Sam's arm. "What about you? Do you want children?"

"I had… I have…a son. After my wife died, a loving foster family took him in." Sam looked at Bessie, who looked away. She knew about Cecelia, but he'd never told her about Cyril. He wondered if Jacob had said something.

"Couldn't you get the lad back if you remarried?" Edith blinked back tears.

Sam looked at Bessie. Was she pairing him up with her lonely, despairing friend? She was drumming her long red fingernails on the tablecloth. He'd never considered a drum beat capable of conveying emotion, but her entree performance was positively joyful, and this erratic tapping was no sweet dessert.

He turned to Edith, "I don't know if the boy would accept me as a father now. He's nearly ten. I should have fought to keep him, but I was too selfish."

"Balderdash!" Bessie's voice carried the distance of two tables. "Selfishness is taking a boy out of a caring home environment. The family no doubt loves him, and it would be cruel to move him now. Your son should stay exactly where he is."

Chapter Thirty-Nine
Adelaide 1937

After finishing dessert, Jacob tapped a finger against his nose. "Wonder if we should restart the interstate run? There're some good fruit deals to be had in Melbourne, and things we could take to trade. What do you reckon, Sam?"

"When would we start?" Sam agreed too quickly. The men had rehearsed the conversation ready for his regular dinner with the Feldts and decided it couldn't look like a done deal or Bessie and Mrs Feldt would veto it.

"Who'd look after the shop?" Sam backtracked to sound less eager. They'd already decided if neither woman offered help, they'd run the shops for half days with Jacob working at both.

"As long as it's not a hair-brained scheme, we'd be better off hiring a part-time assistant," Mrs Feldt suggested. "Teach him the Tobacconist and Fruit trades and he can work shifts at both, covering for Sam during interstate runs."

Jacob winked at Mrs Feldt and kissed her cheek. "A fine head on fine shoulders."

Mrs Feldt gifted him one of her rare smiles. "In the short term, I suppose I could look after the Tobacconist shop, freeing you to make deliveries. Will that give Sam enough time to get to Melbourne and back for Monday?"

"Perfect, darling Katie. Thank you."

Jacob winked at Sam. While he didn't know exactly what deals Jacob had in mind, he recognised his enthusiastic glow. Nothing like slightly risky, lucrative transactions to get the blood pumping.

It was Sam who suggested the idea, offering to pay off his shop debt sooner, but his sudden interest was prompted by the cryptic request ending Fay's last letter. *P.S. You need to visit Melbourne. Soon!*

"And while you're away …" Bessie tapped Sam's empty bowl "I'll fine-tune your business practices." She drummed her fingers up his arm. "You're great with customers, they adore the way you remember their orders and the name of their blasted dogs, but there are short-cuts that could save you time."

Sam imagined the pile of notes he'd find when he returned.

Jacob produced his gold cigarette case and jerked his head towards the door. "Join me?"

Outside, he spoke quietly. "The usual crayfish run, then check out car deals while you're there. Get our old mate Sparra to see if there's anything going at the wharf."

"There's always something going at the wharf." Sam forced an easy laugh to hide his eagerness and concern about the trip.

Why did Fay want him to come so soon?

Sam delivered crayfish late Thursday and visited Sparra first up next morning.

"Mate. I'm glad you're back. There are two German ships in and I can't do proper business using sign language."

By lunch Sam had bagged Sparra and himself a bargain. Sam's new vehicle had the slightest of dents, which he was sure the motor garage near his shop could panel beat out. As per Jacob's new plan, he'd make a killing then buy another.

Sam beamed when Sparra lined up a mate to buy his old lorry, and laughed when Sparra said, "Smooth as flamin' clockwork.

Happy as pigs in shit. Join me and the blokes for beers?" Sparra asked.

"Not today, but definitely next time. I've business to sort."

An hour later Sam was driving his new car through Melbourne. Worryingly, he had no idea what this family business was. Fay had simply instructed Sam to meet at Mrs Cora's on Friday afternoon at two. No further details.

He parked on the road away from the house, then crept slowly around the back, drawn to the idea of retracing old memories rather than face what was waiting inside. He cocked his head hoping to inhale the familiar floral scent, but the garden didn't have the same atmosphere. The jasmine trellis was bare except for the canes and a handful of stubborn leaves reluctant to let go.

When he spotted Fay and Mrs Cora waiting under the grapevine, he stood back and took a deep breath, watching Fay bite her bottom lip and Mrs Cora pick at skin around her fingernail. Was this the place he'd spent so many glorious afternoons? His memory had tricked him. He'd stared at the bedroom wallpaper in Adelaide so often, he'd grown to believe the perfect, plump bunches of grapes were a window into Mrs Cora's yard. Sometimes he saw Cecelia, pink-skinned, vibrant and happy.

The bleakness of the grapevine, and the expressions on the usually smiling women's faces unsettled him. He raced towards them; arms open and ready for hugs. Mrs Cora saw him first and steadied herself against the table as she stood.

"You look wonderful, Sam," she said.

She was being kind; Sam knew he looked worse for wear. "You haven't changed a bit," he replied. A smile accompanying his lie. Mrs Cora was older and fragile, was this the news?

"Fay keeps me informed." She wiped a tear trickling over her chin. "I am sorry about pushing you—"

"You did the right thing. I would have wallowed forever, or drunk myself to death." He wrapped his arms around her shoulders. "I've missed you."

He took Fay's hands. "I don't need to be a mind reader to see trouble. What is it?"

"It's young Cyril."

A whoosh of vertigo made the garden spin. "If anything's happened to the boy—"

"No. Cyril is the picture of health." Fay squeezed Sam's hands tight enough to stop them shaking. "But… he's been in trouble. Fighting. Refusing to obey teachers. Vandalising church property. Quite a list for a ten-year-old."

Sam sat stunned, eyeing one woman then the other. He'd expected bad news, maybe Mrs. Cora's illness or Fay's financial difficulties, but not this. He should have been fuming at the boy's mischief and misdeeds, but despite knowing Cyril was partly to blame, Sam shouldered the responsibility. He was the guilty party. Cyril was his son. Solomon's grandson, too. He'd blamed his own father for passing on the bad seed, now Cyril would blame him. There are two influences at work in making a fine citizen. Good genetics and a loving family. Sam had passed down the bad seed and allowed his son to be brought up by strangers.

"Mrs Cora and I applied to have Cyril released into our care, but the Catholic well-being committee refused." Fay held her head in her hands. "The boy needs a tight rein, they said. They disqualified Mrs Cora because she isn't a blood relative and doesn't have a husband to use a firm hand. I was rejected for not being able to furnish them with a letter of recommendation from a Catholic priest."

"I'll take him back with me," Sam said. "He can help in the shop before and after school. There'll be no time for trouble."

"I pre-empted that. You also need to prove you're taking him to a good Catholic home. Religion is more important than blood." Fay stirred a heaped teaspoon of sugar in her tea and Sam watched it dissolve—the eddies and tea leaves and murkiness echoing the mess he was in.

"What *can* we do?" he asked.

Fay shifted in her seat. "Cecelia's aunt Mary has been visiting Cyril regularly. She is in excellent standing with the church. Her nephew in Bendigo has children around the same age, and she's arranged for him to take Cyril for a year. If it doesn't work out, they will move our boy into an orphanage until he's fourteen. After that he may live with Mary."

Sam checked his watch. "Which school does Cyril attend?"

"St Mary's Boy's School," Mrs Cora said. "West Melbourne, on Howard Street."

He picked up his keys. "Who's coming? If I'm quick, we'll catch him before the home-time bell."

Sam started the engine before Fay and Mrs Cora closed the passenger door. Both women braced themselves against the roof and windows as he took corners sharply, and passed other vehicles at a faster than sensible speed. Mrs Cora risked herself further, by letting go to make the sign of the cross.

He parked near the double-fronted, black-stone building, the large gothic crosses on the peak of each gable making him shudder. He fixed his eyes on the arched entry and waited as uniformed boys poured into the street.

"There." Fay pointed to one of many and jumped into the middle of the road. waving frantically. "Cyril! Cyril! Over here."

Sam watched a boy turn and wave. He barely recognised his own son. Perhaps he should get out? Dazed and dumbfounded, he wound down the window and studied his son from the safety of the car. Cyril's hands were firmly in his pockets as he spoke to Fay, but he glared at Sam from the corner of his eye.

Sam looked for his own features in the lad. With his baggy grey school-shorts reaching just above the knee and his shirt blousing out, two sizes too big, there was nothing about the physique he could compare. Other than the colouring, Cyril didn't resemble Sam. He tried picturing Cecelia, but details of her face had leached away.

"How long does it usually take you to walk home?" Fay asked.

"Dunno. Half an hour, an hour? Depends whether I stop to skim stones over the creek or play a game of marbles."

Sam bit his knuckle to stop himself from jumping in with a story about himself and his brothers. He wanted to tell him about the Prussian steels and about his great grandmother.

"You remember Mrs Cora, of course," Fay said, then she lowered her voice. "Your father is here, too."

Cyril kicked a pebble at the car wheels. "You're not supposed to visit me at school." Then he pointed at Sam without making eye-contact. "And you're not allowed at all. I chucked away the stinkin' coin you sent me. Aunt Mary took me to visit Grandma and she said the police locked you in gaol."

The words punched Sam in the gut. If Mrs Lakeman actually knew about brushes with the law, he'd never see the boy again. "Your gran must have me mixed up with someone else. I live in Adelaide now. I own a fruit shop. When you're a bit older, I'm hoping you'll come work for me."

Cyril's eyes were hard and unblinking. "Did you run over my mum with your car? Is that why she died?"

Guilt gripped Sam by the throat, his plans to whisk the lad away suddenly seemed silly and ill-thought-out. Cyril was growing into a man who hated his father as much as Sam despised Solomon.

"No. No. No," Mrs Cora said. "I was there when it all happened. Your mother was riding a bicycle and…" Mrs Cora held her hand below the knee, "a snappy dog, about so high, bit her leg." She pulled her shoulders back, her voice clear and strong. "Your dad was the hero of the day. He saved her and carried her into the hospital."

Cyril frowned, then looked from Mrs Cora, to Fay and to Sam. He shook his head. "I better get home." He picked up the school bag he'd dropped on the ground. "Bye, Mrs Cora, bye, Aunty Fay."

"Bye," Sam said.

But his son didn't look back.

Sam was eager to escape Melbourne, and accept responsibility for his parenting failure. What would a mature upstanding man do? Move on, take a wife, and make a new family.

The next day he drove from sunrise to sunset, stopping twice to top-up the petrol using an enamel jug to decant from a metal drum into the car. He pushed Cyril from his mind, but he kept coming back. Sam was more dysfunctional as a father than Solomon. At least

Solomon provided his children with food and shelter, Sam had struggled to provide anything beyond a defective gene.

Not far out of Adelaide, while Sam was distracted — thinking about Bessie and how lost he'd be without her company, a kangaroo jumped in front of the car.

Although Sam had hit 'roos before, and learned to accept it as an unpleasant consequence of motorised vehicles, when he hit this particular animal, he felt the life drain from its body along with the blood. Holding his handkerchief to the wound, he knelt beside it, but the creature died in his hands.

He wept as he dragged the corpse under a tree, then checked its pouch, praying there wasn't a joey. Sam couldn't bear the thought of creating another poor orphan.

The badly bent front wheel took the brunt of his feelings. He bashed the rim back into shape and managed to change the damaged tyre, but had to drive slowly. A small price, travelling in a car which limped home, when the kangaroo would never move from its roadside grave.

Loftes' motor repair garage was less than a block from the fruit shop, Sam parked outside and rang the bell. The proprietor, Loftes, or Lofty-Can (self-nicknamed because he reckoned he could do everything) answered.

"I know it's late, but could you take a look at my wheels? I'll pay extra, and I'll send over a basket of vegetables when I open shop."

Lofty-Can carried a lantern down the stairs, illuminating the shiny red paint, stopping at the damaged wheel. "What you done here?"

"Hit a poor 'roo." Sam touched the dried blood on his sleeve.

"This isn't your lorry, whose bloomin' car is it?"

"Damaged goods from the Melbourne wharf. The Aussie car dealers won't take anything less than perfect. Insurance payouts are more lucrative than fixing and selling."

"Why aren't the smashed-up cars sent back on the ship?" Lofty-Can asked.

"The freight company are instructed not to return cars to Germany. Takes up room for return cargo. The blokes sell them off, pretending they were totally destroyed, probably declaring half the cash and pocketing the rest."

"You'd better insure this car yourself. She's a fancy girl for these parts." Lofty-Can opened the large garage door. "Bring her in, I might as well start tonight. She'll be good as new by lunch time."

Sam crossed the road, inspecting his shop from the outside in. Someone had done an excellent job keeping it clean and organised. Bessie? He looked under the clip marked *Classified*, expecting a pile of notes, but there was only one.

S

Welcome back.

I've employed a new shop assistant who's working out very well. His name's Herbert, you'll meet him on Monday.

Although your paper calculations are impressive, I've thought up a new method to save you time. Also, for Herbert's in case his mathematics aren't accurate. In the till drawer you'll find my handy price-calculating-table. Cost per pounds/ounces recorded across the top, weights down the left. The pre-calculated cost of items by weight can be found in the juncture of these lines.

I also have a money saving suggestion for you. Rent out your upstairs room to Herbert, and you can move into our house. There's plenty of room, it's free, and we can see how well we get along when we spend more time together.

B

P.S. Lily and I want to visit Victor Harbor on Monday. Herbert will look after the shop.
Please pick us up at ten.

The trellis wallpaper had lost its power to transport him to a better place. When Sam closed his eyes, instead of grape-vines and flowers he saw Cyril scowling, felt the kangaroo dying in his arms, and thought about Bessie's note. It now seemed she wanted more from their relationship than he'd realised.

He climbed out of bed and checked out Bessie's fancy price calculator. He also found an abandoned book, which hadn't been under the till when he'd left. He perused it at the kitchen table while drinking a milky cup of tea. It was written in German by Austrian author, Rainer Rilke. He couldn't recall any Austrian customers, but he flicked through the pages of prose and poetry, until one line jumped out at him: *Love consists of this, that two solitudes protect and touch and greet each other*. Sam leaned back in his chair, his eyes closed, saying the line as written in German, then translating it into English.

What an apt description of the love he felt for Bessie. None of this overpowering sentiment, instead, this was a promise to be there, to hold, to protect. Sam copied this verse and another in his neatest handwriting, then slipped it inside his wallet.

He couldn't fix the kangaroo, but perhaps if he and Bessie married, there'd be a chance to offer Cyril a family. Maybe father and son could mend their relationship?

But, to propose, he'd need a diamond. That would need money.

When Sam collected his car from Lance Loftes, he couldn't even see where the dents had been. The wheel rim was good as new, two brand new tyres were blacker than crows, and the wrecked tyres had been thrown in the boot for a trip to the rubbish tip. Lofty-Can had lived up to his name.

Sam spent the rest of the day moving a pile of packaging from outside the shop and packing it tightly into the boot with the tyres. He decided the rubbish run could wait until Tuesday.

In the dying light of the afternoon, Sam drove his car up and down the deserted city streets, looking for insurance brokers. He settled on The Queensland Insurance Company, mainly because it wasn't too far from the Feldts at Halifax Street. If he arrived at 9:00am, he could insure his new car quickly and collect Bessie at ten.

To save time, he wrote all necessary details: name, address, and occupation along with particulars of the motor vehicle.

Year of manufacture: 1935.
Make: Opel. (Same as the Vauxhall except made by the sister company.)
Colour: Burgundy red.
Condition: Near perfect.
Value: ?

Sam didn't wish to presume a value of the car before an assessor decided, but he ran through all plausible arguments for pushing up the agreed price. He'd want a good amount if he were ever to make a claim.

Although he arrived at Halifax Street ten minutes late, Bessie was so busy chatting to Lily and Clara she didn't notice. This was another thing special about Bessie; she never made a big deal over unimportant things.

The trip south from Adelaide to Victor Harbor took almost two hours, but the women commented about the luxury of his new car, Bessie particularly taken by the colour which matched her dress.

"Okay," Sam asked. "What do you ladies want to look at first?"

"The horse-drawn tram," Bessie said. "There's a picture of me and Lily travelling across the causeway to Granite Island. We were little girls then. I'd like another in the same pose."

The sight-seeing photographer followed them around the island after cottoning on that Sam was out to impress the women. Being a Monday, business was quiet so after taking photographs of Bessie and Lily, he took a picture of Sam holding the horse's reins and pretending to drive the cart.

While Clara and Lily bought drinks from the vendor, Sam pulled Bessie aside. "I read your 'classified' communiqué."

"And?" she asked.

"I hope I've interpreted it correctly." He reached into his pocket, fiddling with his wallet until he found the love quotes. "I would very much like to get to know you better."

"And?" Bessie's teasing smile a contrast to her hands-on-the-hip stance.

"Will you marry me?"

"You must ask my father first," she tossed her head around and laughed.

"I already asked." Sam tilted his head and winked.

"Okay, I'll play. What did he say?"

"He said he's already married."

Lily and Clara returned with a tray of drinks, but Sam was on a roll. He whipped the whole tray off them and displayed the folded notes with letter 'B's facing towards Bessie, before lowering himself onto one knee.

The other women stepped back, Clara holding a hand over her mouth.

"Will you marry me, Bessie?" he extended the tray, and she picked up the carefully copied declarations of love.

"*Love consists of this, that two solitudes protect and touch and greet each other.*" She studied Sam from different angles.

He hoped she agreed.

"And this one?" Her voice was almost a whisper. "*Once the realisation is accepted that even between the closest people infinite distances exist, a marvellous living side-by-side can grow up for them if they succeed in loving the expanse between them, which gives them the possibility of always seeing each other as a whole.*" Bessie blinked back unexpected tears. "You understand what I want in a marriage. My answer is, yes."

Chapter Forty
POW Camp, Batavia, 1942

Storm followed tropical storm, drawing dense clouds in their wake until they reached a tipping point and rain fell as if sky buckets were up-ended. John watched from the verandah; the air so saturated his cigarette wouldn't light. He 'smoked' it anyway.

"I hope our gardens aren't bloomin' ruined," he said to no-one in particular. "Poor leaves will have to breathe underwater. Not a bad skill for the wet season."

While he wandered up and down the verandah, I nursed my injuries on the bed, his constant stream of commentary negating any need to look for myself.

"Water's above the brick border... Almost up to the termite caps... Blimey, Sergeant, step number four's going under—"

"Can you bloody well stop?" Cullen shouted over the noisy bullets of rain. "You sound like a submarine captain preparing to submerge."

"Clear the bloomin' bridge." John laughed. "Dive, dive, dive."

When I arrived in Batavia, I wondered why so many buildings were raised above the ground. Now, I understood. As water seeped through the floorboards, the prisoners scurried into action, like lines of ants they lifted bags of rice and precious possessions onto their shoulders. Silent-G grabbed his bible. Cullen snatched family photos, tucking them safely under his hat.

John interrupted his clearing up to check on me. "Anything you want moved to higher ground?"

I shook my head. "No, I'm fine."

What would I save? This sodden place held nothing of importance.

A muddy river rose halfway up the legs of the bed. The mattresses would go under next.

Captain John took command. "Those who are able—pile beds on top of each other. Move the bottom mattresses up. Belongings on top."

For a while, the rain settled, and we all stared at the water level, waiting for it to go up or down. The men were in parade-ground zone, listening for a call of 'at ease'.

My mind wandered. I dipped my toe into the water, but instead of a stinking prison hut, I waded through Amsterdam's wetlands in autumn when farmers caused shallow flooding. In my head, a calendar of seasons turned until bulbs beneath the surface sprouted. I blinked, and row upon row of purple and yellow tulips emerged. If I ever got home, I'd collect armfuls of flowers and decorate the house with Pieter. I'd face my father, and tell him how wonderfully brave his other son was.

Then, without warning, the river drained. The floodwaters tickled my feet goodbye, subsiding as quickly as they arrived, leaving layers of rich black dirt in its wake.

"Scrape it into a pile," John called out. "This is pure silt. We are gonna grow ourselves some bloody bewdyful veggies. They'll be big enough to win every flamin' ribbon in the Royal Adelaide Agricultural Show."

The men scooped fertile mud with their fingers and our collective hopes rose with the growing pile. Our hut was back to war-time normal.

I returned to biting the belt leather, gently pressing my wobbly front tooth back into place. The leaden feeling returned, *Met lood in de schoenen*. Was it worth the effort to save the tooth? The Japs were intent on finding out about John, but they'd beaten him so many fruitless times they'd given up on him. How many others had they questioned? Would my tooth be knocked out again before it took root?

"They'll come back for me soon," I whispered.

John, with his mud-stained face and hands, parked next to me on the bed. "I've been thinking about it. We're not gonna wait for the Japs to take you. As soon as you can walk, you'll go out there, and ask for the *Kempeitai*."

Hair prickled the back of my neck. "I'd rather not."

"I've a plan. We're not fighting fire with fire, we're gonna fight as if we're armed with them bloomin' Russian rocket launchers, we've been hearing about. The hardest part of this, for you, will be facing the men inside the camp. You'll have to keep up the pretence of hating me. Some will believe you're dobbing me in."

"What will I say when I ask for the guards?"

"Tell them you've remembered snippets of my stories. Tell them in Dutch, tell them in English, try sign language. Stretch it out, take your bloomin' time. Make it clear you don't know which, if any, of the tales are significant. Little by little plant the seed of an idea that I've confided in a code you don't understand. Suck them in, Kid. For now, we're buying time. I reckon they'll be real nice to you. You need it. That leg of yours is not looking so good."

I shook my head. "I'm not doing this for my leg."

"I know. You're doing it because I asked. And doing it despite the danger. At some point during the questioning, I want you to hold back information until they agree to move you to a camp where no one knows you."

Chapter Forty-One
Adelaide 1937

Sam chucked the insurance company's letter on the shop counter, and went outside to cool his hot-headedness. Rearranging the fruit on the pavement display failed to distract him. Pent-up annoyance coursed through his body, exiting through clumsy fingers, juggling oranges out of his hands, into the street.

Jacob drove up the road and parked out front, lifting his palms in the air when yet another poor orange escaped.

"What's up?" He offered Sam a ready-rolled cigarette from his engraved gold case. "Whatever it is, one of these will fix it."

"Is that the line you hand out at the tobacco shop?" Sam took one anyway. "Next, you'll be chucking in bottles of snake-oil for ailments tobacco won't fix."

Jacob pretended to write 'snake-oil' on his palm with his finger. "Good one. Suggestion noted. Now, what's worrying you?"

Sam waggled the lit end of his cigarette to indicate the insurance papers inside. "After setting a price on the car, which they valued themselves. They took the year's premium in cash. Now, the stinkin' thieves have decided they need proof of purchase, which I do not have, and the premium is non-refundable."

Jacob rested his cigarette on the gutter and grabbed his car keys. "Go inside and find a pen and paper. I'll be right back."

Sam watched Jacob search the glove-box of his car, then went inside to do as he was told.

"Sales documents for my car, we'll just copy these." Jacob waved a rectangular leather wallet.

"But it came from Germany. From a flamin' ship. There was no motor vehicle dealer."

"All the better. You speak *Kraut*, but can you write it?"

"Fairly well." Sam see-sawed his hand. "I attended school in Prussia for a while and the lessons were in German."

"We're on. Copy the format of this document, but in German. Put the ship's name and the seller where my document names the dealership and the salesman."

"I have no idea of the bloke's name. He wouldn't have given me his real name if I'd asked. It was hardly above board."

"What name would you give if you were pretending to be German?" Jacob blew smoke rings.

Sam peered through as if spying through peep-holes, then smiled. "Hermann. Hermann Schmidt. The most German name I've ever bloomin' heard."

"Right. You do up the first draft, then I'll rewrite it." Jacob grabbed an apple. "Something to eat while I'm waiting."

Sam nodded his approval. "Good thinking. Then the document's not in my handwriting."

A month later, the day after Sam's official engagement to Bessie, the insurance problem grew hotter, in fact it burst into flames.

He turned up at The Feldt's front door, wheezing from the two-mile run.

Bessie stepped back at the expression on his face. "You look as if you've seen a...?" She steadied herself against the wall. "Should I start writing my story for a women's magazine? *The World's Shortest Engagement?*"

"What? No." Sam pulled her into his arms. "I have no second thoughts on that count."

"Then what's wrong?"

"The police knocked on my door this morning. My car. Someone reported it burning a few blocks from home. The police are asking questions and they're pointing the finger at me."

She dragged him into the living room. "Dad. Mum. Sam needs help."

The morning of the hearing, Jacob and Sam stood outside the old blue-stone courthouse building waiting for Bessie.

"Crooks all of them," Sam said. "The insurance company accusing me of setting fire to my own vehicle so they don't have to make the payout." He kicked the wall. "Now we have to throw extra money at lawyers."

"Don't go in with that frame of mind, son. Hiring a professional was the only way to go."

"I know what to say. I'm bloody innocent."

"We're between a rock and a hard place," Jacob said. "We don't want the coppers looking into our other business dealings."

"If only we hadn't tried to sell the car," Sam said.

"Who'd have thought the anti-German sentiment would have carried over to manufactured goods?" This time it was Jacob's turn to kick the wall.

"Bloody insurance companies are always ripping off customers. No Robin Hood deeds there. They take from the poor and pocket the riches. Time they paid up," Sam said.

Jacob tapped his nose. "Keep calm and keep everyone happy, Bessie's coming."

Bessie straightened Sam's collar before brushing the shoulders of his pin-striped jacket. "Just be yourself. I've never met a single person who doesn't like you."

Jacob and Bessie walked up the courtroom stairs at the opposite end of the judge's bench, and Sam stayed below, waiting with his lawyer.

The sound of chatter from the gallery reverberated around the timber-panelled court room. Sam was relieved when court was called into session. He'd expected a jury—instead, a tired old man in a wig, who looked like he'd rather be home by the fire than listening to case after case of minor significance.

When the judge called Sam's case number, all parties approached the bench then waited as the Judge read the charges and the witness statements.

"What is the significance of a jug being found at the scene?" the Judge asked.

Sam could answer this question, but knew when to speak and when to keep schtum. He believed if the other side jumped in argumentatively, they would lose.

The prosecutor for the insurance company held up his copy of the witness statements. "You'll see before you that the garage proprietor reported discussing insurance on the car in question and a shop assistant identified the jug as one belonging to Samuel Solonsch. The police at the scene believe combustible liquid was poured from this very jug before the car was set alight. It was left behind."

The judge raised his eyebrows at the defence lawyer, but Sam seized his chance. "I agree with the police, your honour. The jug was mine, and I came to the same conclusion."

"Why was it at the crime scene?" The judge asked.

Sam took a deep breath to answer, but the prosecuting lawyer interrupted.

"We contend Samuel Solonsch used it to set fire to his own car. The value of which was inflated."

The judge waved his hand dismissively. "Mr Solonsch, how do you answer to this allegation?"

"I kept the jug in the car along with a drum of fuel for long trips. As to the inflated value of the vehicle, the assessor from Queensland Insurance Company inspected the vehicle before assigning a value."

After shuffling papers, the judge produced the assessor's valuation and the purchase documents. "This seems to be true. Do you have other points to make?" This time he stared at the prosecutor.

"The purchase documents have not come from an authorised sales-yard. They aren't from Adelaide and not even from an Australian company. We can't trace the source, but our assertion is that Mr Solonsch forged the documents."

"This is your handwriting, is it not, Mr Solonsch?" The judge pushed a signed statement across the bench to Sam. "And this?" He placed the sales certificate beside it.

Sam pointed to his statement. "Yes, Your Honour. I wrote this account."

Sam's lawyer tapped his finger on the sales certificate. "This is not my client's hand writing."

The judge flicked through the papers on his desk. "I can't find an alibi statement."

"Your Honour," Sam's lawyer said, "there were many witnesses who can attest to Samuel Solonsch attending his own engagement party."

"Step closer," the judge ordered. "I need to see your face under the light. If this is true, why did you buy the car interstate?"

"I was visiting my son. His mother died some years ago, and he's been in foster care ever since. He barely recognises me, refuses to acknowledges me as his father." Sam placed his hand to his chest. It wasn't an act. "I thought a flashy motor would impress the lad. It didn't and it's not giving me much joy at the moment."

"You seem disturbed about the boy, but I think there's something else on your mind," the judge said. "Is there anything you wish to disclose? Remember. This is a court if law."

"Yes. I believe the court should spend more time investigating insurance fraud. Not by the clients, but by the vendors. Just last month I read in the newspaper where a farmer's tractor exploded and the insurance company ruled it suicide so they wouldn't have to pay his widow the life insurance policy."

By the judge's eye-roll, Sam knew he had taken his liberty a step too far. He shouldn't have gone on the offensive. It would have been better for him to agree with everything that came out of the judge's mouth.

Sam turned and looked up at Bessie seated in the gallery, then slicked back his hair before making a crestfallen nod. The judge made notes in a large black book. If found guilty, then it might be Sam writing about the world's shortest engagement. Bessie would break it off in a heart-beat.

He flinched when the judge struck his gavel. "I cannot form a definite opinion on the events before me. We will never know who lit the fire. For this reason, I order Queensland Insurance Company to pay Mr Solonsch all money owing, along with court costs."

'Thank you, Your Honour." Sam portrayed himself as a subdued and grateful man, but the inner Samuel was leaping and shouting, 'Take that, you flamin' mugs!'

Bessie waited outside the courthouse. "Dad's gone back to work, but you and I have business to discuss."

"I'll buy you whichever diamond ring you like," he said. "You're a good sort, Bessie Feldt. A man like me is lucky to have a woman like you beside him."

"Listen for a minute before we get to the size of the rock. I'm not going to ask you directly whether you had involvement in the fire. In fact, I'll never ask a question unless I'm prepared to hear the answer. For this reason, I need you to promise. When I do ask something, you must always be honest."

Chapter Forty-Two
Adelaide, 1938

Once Bessie was escorted into the womb of the hospital, from which men not wearing white coats and stethoscopes were barred, Sam made his way around the maze of disinfectant reeking corridors to *The Fathers' Waiting Room*. The room was thick with cigarette smoke and anxiety, and he managed a feeble smile at other expectant men. He told himself to be thankful for this gift—a second chance at fatherhood, but under his breath he repeated his mantra for Bessie. *Indestructible.* Jacob had told him she was indestructible, and right now this was something he needed to believe. *Indestructible.*

Sam riffled through the bag Bessie had thrust into his arms and looked for the note. She was right—as always. Excessive idleness gave him too much time to think and he needed to stop thinking.

S

Copy my sample announcement and invitation (paper-clipped at the top of the pile). Write one for each of your siblings and one for your darling friend Mrs Cora. Leave a suitable space for writing in the baby's sex, birth weight, name, and date of arrival. Address the envelopes, too. Once our baby is born, fill in the missing details (using the same pen!).

I know you think your family won't travel this far for the naming ceremony, but let me remind you, I was right about the wedding.
As always,
B

Sam replayed the last two panicked hours.

His, not hers.

"Surely, it's time for the hospital?" Sam had tried to reel in his emotions but his voice was all rising terror.

"I'm fine, Sam. It's early labour and I'm not leaving until I get everything I need."

What else could she need? She'd packed a birthing-bag weeks ago. As far as Sam was concerned, the hospital was the safest place to be.

His mother-in-law had argued, but he'd dug in his heels without giving reasons. He couldn't tell her he felt responsible for putting this baby inside Bessie, and that he was praying not to kill another wonderful woman.

Bessie reached around to massage her back and Sam tried to help, but she groaned and waddled in the opposite direction.

"Come on. The car's this way."

"Sam. I'm in pain, but it hasn't addled my mind or interrupted my natural compass." She held her hand up in a stop, and her cursing eyes implied words a lady never says out loud.

He breathed deeply and pressed his lips tightly as she dropped a bag atop the piano and lifted the lid to play a tune.

A few bars into the song she moaned, squeezing her eyes shut, but then she smiled and stroked her belly.

"Don't forget those. She pointed to the message clip she'd proudly hammered into the polished timber architrave. "Those new notes are important."

Sam offered a silent prayer to his heart, hoping they'd continue their unique form of communication until they were frail and too blind to see.

"While I'm doing the hard yards of bringing a baby in the world, there'll be plenty of waiting time out in the fathers' room. I've left you a few jobs to keep you out of mischief."

Other than Fay and Mrs Cora, Sam had seen little of his family since leaving Melbourne. Jane had married and was busy with children. Millie? Well, Millie had always kept to herself. William, now living in New South Wales, was a step further from Adelaide. Too far a detour for Sam to make on a quick business trip. Besides, after Cecelia's death William had tired of Sam's erratic behaviour and a rift developed.

Yet, a year earlier, William had travelled to Adelaide for the wedding. All Sam's siblings were there, except Joe. He'd stayed in England with his wife, living close to Solomon. Joe and Sam didn't share the same relationship with that man.

Previously this made Sam livid, but waiting for his and Bessie's baby to be born, Sam became hopeful that a man, bad seed or not, could form healthy relationships with his children.

"Mr Solonsch?"

Sam braced himself as he walked towards the physician. He looked into the doctor's eyes, gauging the temperature of the news, readying himself before any words were spoken. Tepid. There was nothing out of the ordinary. Sam's heart rejoiced. He added *ordinary* to *indestructible* on his short list of favourite words.

"Is Bessie okay?"

"Your wife can tell you herself. Follow me."

Sam walked in a daze, and although the doctor offered little information, the few comments he made were comforting. "Healthy. Without incident. Boy."

The doctor marched into the maternity ward where patients' names sat in holders beside each door. The doctor checked his notes, then entered the room labelled '*Mrs Samuel Solonsch.*'

Sam peeked past the doctor's shoulder, nervous about what he would see. His hyper-tensed muscles relaxed at the beautiful sight of Bessie sitting up in bed. She was peaceful, smiling, and looking far healthier than Sam felt.

"Come see our boy," she said. "I don't know who he looks like. But he is exquisitely beautiful."

Sam peeled the blanket half-covering a tiny face. "He is precious." He touched the silky soft cheek, then touched Bessie's. "He isn't as beautiful as you." Tears welled up behind his blinking eyelids and he held a hand against his throat to calm the burn.

"Oh, Sam." Bessie took his hand. "I'm sorry if this has brought back painful memories. It must remind you... you know... your wife." Bessie's whisper was barely more than a breath.

He watched her lips through the damp haze of emotions, not wanting to miss a word.

"How awful it must've been," she said.

"Nothing about the two days compare," he said. "Today has been perfect. The most perfect example of magnificence in the ordinary and the indestructible."

"I must be tired." Bessie's bright laughter echoed off the walls, lightening the dreary hospital grey. "I have no idea what you're talking about."

She leaned back and unbuttoned her night dress. "Hand me the baby. I'm thinking Louis John suits his little face." She held the baby to her breast. "We're both learning how it works, but I'm sure we'll get the hang of it."

Staring open-mouthed with wonder, Sam watched his son search for the nipple and Bessie help him fasten on.

"What are you gawking at, Sam? Did you think my chest was here to fill up the darts in my dresses, or to give you something to look at?"

Sam's laughter was a mixture of genuine amusement and absolute pride. At least parenthood came to one of them naturally.

The following day, Mrs Feldt burst into the hospital room moving faster than Sam had ever seen her. She stopped just short of Bessie and the baby, as if deciding which human she most wanted to smother with kisses.

Jacob followed behind as if entering a temple, flowers for Bessie in one hand, and what were probably the most expensive cigars from his tobacco shop in the other.

"Congratulations." He slapped Sam's back. "You're a father. More importantly, I'm a grandfather, a *Zayde*."

Sam took the cigar, imitating Jacob, who although possessing every smokers' accoutrement known to man, still preferred the old school method of clenching the end of the cigar with his sharp front teeth, rotating it to slice a neat groove, then chomping off the tip.

Jacob flipped the hinge of his lighter then took a few puffs. Pungent, aromatic smoke filled the room.

"Please! Not in such an enclosed space," Mrs Feldt said. "If you want to smoke, you'll have to go into the hallway."

"Quite right, but we don't want to leave. We'll save them for later." Jacob stubbed his cigar in the large metal ashtray under the window, checking it was extinguished before putting it in his jacket pocket.

Sam followed suit.

Jacob was the best example of a father Sam had ever met. He loved his children more than gambling, he knew how to laugh with them, make them feel safe, and he taught them to be strong and proud.

"Come to Zayde," Jacob said to the baby, then crooned sweet words in Yiddish. "My little one, I've so many tricks to teach you. That is the job of every Zayde; to help his grandchildren get into mischief."

Everything was going to be all right. Jacob was a good husband and father. Sam would use him as a role model.

Chapter Forty-Three
POW Camp, Batavia, 1942

Staggering down the hut stairs was like walking to the gallows, the pain in my leg insignificant when compared to the broken-glass guilt. These were the steps of a traitor and despite John believing this our best chance of survival, my remorse was immeasurable. Yet I had no choice.

Hiro's face, usually disinterested, lit up with interest. He stubbed his cigarette on the ground. No one wasted tobacco like that. Were my intentions that transparent?

I inhaled, vainly hoping the jasmine vine strangling the guards' shelter would offer a calming fragrance. But I smelled nothing.

"I'd like to talk to the *Kempeitai* officers. I have something to tell."

From the veranda, the reproachful eyes of my fellow POWs sent daggers. Hiro nodded, his eyes comprehending.

He jerked his chin towards the hut. "Wait barracks." His addition of poorly spoken English was unnecessary. We both understood the gravity, if not the details.

Back in the hut, no one spoke to me and the prisoners became protective of John. Of course they did. Everyone loved his jokes, his easiness, his apparent immortality. Even those who'd mistrusted his dealings with the Japs, admired him. I couldn't hear what they whispered, but felt their thorny accusations pierce me with blame.

Later that afternoon Japanese soldiers escorted me through the barbed wire wrapped gates and shackled me in the back of the Isuzu military vehicle.

This was the first time since the Japs imprisoned me that I'd seen the town of Batavia. My platoon had arrived in the Dutch-East Indies before the Germans occupied Holland. We'd stayed to protect the colony, but the enemy in Java ended up being Japanese.

I knew this town well. Schools, hospitals, business offices, once well cared for and full of life, now requisitioned by the Japanese, reeked of neglect. For a culture obsessed with position and control, the Japanese ignored the creeping decay. Neatly trimmed lawns of old, were now weed infested and overgrown. *Ontong*, the flying foxes, ate nuts and fruit then flew over the city like bomber planes splattering pellets of seed-filled manure.

The Japanese restrained the POWs, but the jungle was reclaiming the island.

The guards accompanied me into a government building where a Dutch woman acting as Japanese-English translator greeted me softly, as if I'd arrived for afternoon tea. The atmosphere seemed unusually calm, but her tightly pulled hair, protruding ears, and nervously twitching nose suggested a mouse warning of a trap.

A Japanese officer wearing a look of contempt leaned against the wall. He flicked a riding crop against the window sill, refusing to meet my gaze.

When he faced the window, the interpreter moved her hand from the top of her head upward to the top of mine, signalling our difference in height. She glanced at the officer, then pointed quickly to the chair. "Sit down, I will record everything."

The officer shot a clip of rapid-fire Japanese syllables, and she raised her eyebrows in my direction. "The interrogators helped you remember? What exactly?"

"For the record, I dislike the man called Captain John Douglas, and I do not wish to get on the wrong side of the Japanese army. It is the greatest army in the world."

After an exchange in Japanese she said, "The commander says that's enough. You will get no leniency for stating the obvious."

I stared at a hook on the wall wondering what picture had offended the Japanese enough to remove it. Staring at tarnished brass was easier than looking at the commander, the translator whose eyes darted around the room, or the guards stationed at the door.

I cleared my throat. "I thought little of it at the time, but John told lots of stories. I had no choice but to listen, I was stuck in the bed beside him. You can check with the superior officers of our camp. You can ask anyone. I begged time and time again to be moved."

When the translator explained this in Japanese, the officer in the corner struck the desk with the leather crop. The translator jumped more than I did.

"Get to the point. What sort of stories?" the translator asked.

"Tales about a boy and a man. I thought nothing at the time. They didn't make sense. They were in English."

The hook on the wall blurred as I squinted to take in the whole room. The commander slumped against the window, bending the riding crop and twisting its neck over and over.

The commander was either going to ask me to leave or order a punishment for wasting his time. Maybe I'd over-followed John's instruction to drip-feed information. Had I done it too fucking slowly?

I risked standing as if I'd finished, like John and I rehearsed, then I bowed and said thank you. *"Arigatou gozaimasu.".*

The Japanese commander yawned.

"I have taken enough of your time. I was foolish to think Captain John's tales contained hidden messages."

There was a toing and froing in Japanese, then the commander sat upright.

"What messages?" the translator snapped, echoing his tone along with the words.

"There were inconsistencies in Captain John's stories, which made me think there was a reason for telling them." I tapped my head, then placed my hand on my heart. "There's no point repeating the ramblings of a mad man when they're probably not important."

"Start now."

The translator's eyes widened.

The Japanese officer had spoken English.

Chapter Forty-Four
Adelaide July 1939

Baby Louis John was the star of the Feldt household, an entertaining creature with plenty of admirers and no competition. When he took his first steps, alien beings looking on might have assumed from Sam's reaction that this child was the first human to walk upright.

While Sam played with his son, Jacob spent the morning preparing for the two-up school down by the River Torrens. Louis John toddled over to the desk and reached up for the chalk and betting board used at the races.

"He's gonna be a gambler like his Zayde." Jacob said with pride. "Come on kid, put a mark where you reckon I should make a bet on the horses. Pick me a winner." He held the squirming lad over the chalkboard waiting for him to draw.

"Dad," Bessie said. "If you're looking for inspiration from a fourteen-month-old child you have major problems."

"I'm not denying it. But I can feel it in my waters. This kid's my lucky charm."

Sam watched his son juggle the piece of chalk in his chubby hand, and laughed when, instead of drawing, he pushed it between two fingers and giggled, angling his head exactly like Zayde then smoking the stick of chalk like a cigarette.

Even Mrs Feldt snorted, although she tried to hide her mirth. "Don't teach the boy all your bad habits. Tell him, Sam. You're the father."

Sam covered his mouth to hide laughter. He didn't mind at all. Yes, Jacob had some shady behaviours, but Sam wasn't one to cast any stones. All he saw was a man with an enormous heart. Sam determined that Solomon's biggest sin was not showing love.

"Are you going with Dad?" Bessie asked Sam. Her unblinking eyes made it clear she expected 'No' for an answer.

"Not today. Sorry Jacob, I'm going to spend time with this little fella. Not because I'm jealous of him imitating you instead of me, which I am, but because I'm taking my lad to the beach."

Jacob winked with a lopsided smile. "Got you. The women have plans and you're keeping the kid out of their hair." He jumped when Katie Feldt tapped his shoulder.

"Do not stay out too late, Jacob." She gave him a clumsy hug. "I don't know why you need to run a two-up school. Surely someone else can do it today. We've got all the kids coming for dinner tonight. We won't wait for you."

Louis John grasped Jacob's leg, so he retrieved a wooden paddle and pennies from his pocket. "Watch this, little fella. The coins have to spin twice, or it's a dud throw." The baby watched the money twist and land. "Heads," yelled Jacob.

Louis John's babble may or may not have sounded like 'heads', but everyone clapped.

"Come on, love." Jacob kissed Katie's cheek. "Give my lucky pennies a kiss?"

"Watch out," Sam said. "Lucky she's not Catholic, instead of giving the coins her blessing she might give 'em the last rites."

Jacob twirled his wife in an affectionate dance. "I love you, Katie."

"Don't try distracting me. I'm telling you straight. We *will* eat without you."

. . .

Sam's assigned job in preparation for the *Shabbat* meal was carrying the small square table from the veranda into the formal dining room then pushing both tables together into one. One end of the long table was set up for the head of the family—Mr Jacob Feldt. The other end had a high chair for the real king, little Louis John.

While Mrs Feldt cooked up a kosher storm, Bessie and Lily laid the table using rose patterned china, silver cutlery, and crystal from the carved sideboard.

Sam failed to distract Louis John who managed to reach up and grab utensils faster than the sisters could arrange them.

"Come on, what have you got this time?"

Sam pried the tiny fingers to rescue a serviette ring engraved with Jacob's initials. "I can see why you took this. Look at it. A little silver wheel."

Sam rolled it across the rug to bright-eyed squeals. "Your turn," Sam said, then watched his clever son copy. He swallowed hard and pushed aside a memory of Cyril imitating the gardener with secateurs. Another, less painful memory jumped in its place. Himself in Bubbe's kitchen stealing the pastry balls. He'd been so dead afraid of proving her faith in him wrong, but it seemed life was okay after all. He hadn't turned out as bad as he'd feared.

"See this serviette ring," Sam chuckled. "We're going to call it a rare Prussian Wheel." He was still laughing when there was a knock on the door.

"That'll be Dad. Probably lost his door keys. Can you get it, Sam?"

Sam swung Louis John into the air. "You ready to show Zayde what you've taken off the table? He'll probably tickle you half to death—"

He opened the door.

Two policemen stood outside.

Hats in their hands.

Heads bowed.

"Mrs Katie Feldt?"

Sam pulled his son closer with trembling arms. "Come through."

The policeman's serious nod was weighted with bad news.

At the sight of policemen, Mrs Feldt dropped the tray of braided Challah bread. Sam helped her to a chair, and she took the serviette ring from the baby's hand, tracing her husband's initials.

"That's all we know," a policeman said. "Your husband was found dead on the edge of the embankment near Glanville West. It looks like a heart attack."

Chapter Forty-Five
Adelaide, November 1939

Following Jacob's death, there was a mood shift in the Feldt house. Bessie had lost her father and Sam had lost the father he'd chosen, but there is no hierarchy in grief.

Mrs Feldt barely left her bedroom, and Lily's visits became less frequent. Bessie stopped playing the piano, stopped drumming her fingers on the table, and stopped running her hands over Sam's skin.

A crushing emptiness replaced Sam's easy banter, and when he caught his own reflection, but saw Solomon's scowl, he struggled to breathe.

The recent declaration of another war added to the sense of an upside-down world. The gap between Sam and Bessie mirrored the hole Jacob had left behind. Sam's usual bag of triviality and jest was no fit for what ailed them. The rift grew.

Much of their communication was through notes, because facing each other felt way too hard.

B
I'm off to Melbourne in a couple of days. We're running out of stock. The war's already thrown transport into chaos.
I can take Louis John with me so he's off your hands.

Love always,
S

Her reply was brief.

S
The boy stays here, with me and Mum. Be quick, but drive carefully.
B

Bessie no longer adorned her notes with pet words and declarations of affection. Her love was locked in grief, and Sam couldn't find the key.

On his way home from the Melbourne run, Sam drove past a pair of tall, besuited men standing beside the highway in the middle of nowhere. He slowed to a stop and wound down his window, angling his head to gawk up and see their faces. "You fellas lost?"

"Walking to Adelaide," The darker-haired fella drawled like a cowboy from an American movie Sam had seen.

"Walking? Australia might be an island, but it's pretty bloody big. You know you've six-hundred miles to cover?"

The cowboy's eyes bulged and he turned to his partner. "That's like Utah to Wyoming. It'll take us weeks."

"Long legs might get you there quickly, but I reckon it's quicker to drive." Sam reached across to open the passenger door. "I'm Sam."

"Thank you," said the cowboy. Up close, he looked about twenty. "I'm Bob. This is Hank."

"Barb? Short for Barbara?"

"B.O.B. Bob. Short for Robert."

"Pleased to meet you Cowboy Bob, and you, too, Hank the Yank. Throw your cases in the boot and hop in."

"The boot?"

"Ah… the trunk. The compartment at the back."

They shinnied clumsily across the seat.

"Relax if you can." Sam choked on a chuckle. "Might be hard with your heads touching the roof."

Folding their legs, they slid down the seat.

"Good. That'll keep the kink out of your necks. You fellas are a long way from home."

"We came to Australia to play in basketball tournaments. But with the war across Europe, they called most of the team home. Hank and I are the 'lucky' ones. The church elders begged us to stay."

Sam rolled a cigarette with one hand while keeping the steering wheel straight with his knee. "Going to play basketball in Adelaide?"

"No. The Mormon pastor enlisted in the Australian Army necessitating a replacement. They picked us because part of the pastor's role is delivering food to the poor." Bob shrugged his shoulders with what looked like defeat. "Hank was the only man on the team who can drive."

Sam lost the thread of the conversation, but it was an interesting distraction. "So why didn't you go back, Bob?"

"We work in missionary companionships. Hank and I come as a pair." Again, the shrug. "Hank delivers food and I deliver the sermons."

Unlike Bob's booming voice, Hank's was timid and whiny. "Bob thinks he's drawn the short straw, but my driving experience has been on the other side of the world and the opposite side of the road."

"I'd rather drive than preach. What on earth will I say?"

Both men sighed like an ill-wind.

"Mormon? I haven't seen a church with that signage and I know the city of Adelaide like the back of my hand." Sam lifted a hand off the steering wheel, pretending to inspect the back. "What's that spot?"

The hoped-for laugh didn't come, but Sam wasn't offended, he remembered arriving in Australia with William, and how much they'd appreciated Mrs Cora's welcome. It was Sam's turn to do the same.

Hank took an envelope from his breast pocket. "Here. Wright Street, Adelaide. Church of Jesus Christ of Latter-Day Saints."

"Church of Jesus…what?"

"Mormon for short."

"Good. The other name's a mouthful." Sam pulled over and parked under a tree to light a cigarette.

"Come on, Hank. Time for driving practice. Not many cars out here in the bush, so you've time to learn which side of the road you're on." Sam turned to Bob. "Once Hank's got the hang of it, we can work out what you might say to your flamin flock."

After a dozen miles and many bends driven on the correct side of the road, Sam was confident enough in Hank to concentrate on Bob. "Right-o. There's a notebook and pen in the glove box. No use coming up with ideas then forgetting them."

Bob rested the pad on his knee, pen at the ready.

"Right-O, Cowboy, I reckon you're starting out with three advantages. You're American, that'll get the parishioners' attention. They'll be thankful for your height, too. Everyone'll see you, right from the back. And your voice. Loud and bloomin' clear."

Bob's smile was tentative. "Should I read passages from the Bible?"

"Not until you've hooked 'em. The readings are better woven into a relevant conversation."

There was no nod of comprehension.

"I better explain myself. If you heard what people across the country are whispering over the neighbour's fence. What would it be?"

"The war. Losing men and women. Everyone's talking about it."

"Make that your first heading."

Sam watched Bob write WAR in shaky capital letters. "Now. If we can work out some questions, we can think of some answers."

"How will war change our lives?" Hank suggested, his eyes fixed on the road. "I'm worried about that."

"What about you, Hank? What do you think people are worried about?"

Hank's knuckles were white as he gripped the steering wheel. "How am I going to feed my family?"

"It's a fine thing, that you'll be delivering food to the needy." Sam sighed.

Bob scribbled food and money in his notebook, then looked at Sam. "And you? What keeps you awake at night?"

Sam stared at the scorched-earth nothingness ahead. The dying light backlit the clouds with a colour to rival the earth. A congregation of altocumulus gazed upwards towards cathedral like beams of cirrostratus, wispy tails of golden twilight. It was a heavenly moment.

Sam thought about his bad seed, about Bessie, his sons, and whether he'd ever be the man they needed. But he wasn't about to share this today.

"Too many worries to list, but I reckon you've got a couple of bewdies. We'll build on those. If your parishioners connect with what you're saying, they'll feel less helpless. If you manage that, you'll have done a bonzer job."

"Wake up, Sam." Bessie prodded him with one finger as if he were infectious. "There are two sleeping giants in the dining room. Do they belong to you?"

"Sorry, love, you weren't in the bed or I'd have told you."

"Mother had another of her bad days. She can't sleep alone. I curled up next to her."

Since Jacob's death, Bessie and Katie Feldt clung to each other. Sam recalled his mire of grief in the years after Cecelia died. What if he lost Bessie to the darkness? What if his second chance family were split by tragedy? What if Louis John grew up to look at Sam like he'd looked at Solomon?

For Louis John's sake, he hoped they'd clamber their way out soon.

"I know it's not wise to invite hitch-hikers home, but these men are barely in long pants, and a long way from home. I had no idea where to leave them in the middle of the night."

He yearned for one of Bessie's usual snappy retorts. Feisty. Definite. Clear. Instead, she traipsed silently into the kitchen and Sam edged towards the dining room—a place he'd avoided because it held lingering echoes of bad news.

He hadn't wanted to scare Mrs Feldt with two strange men in her living room, so he'd directed the Mormons somewhere out of sight, throwing in blankets and pillows.

Sam braced himself at the door. When he walked in Bob and Hank jumped to their feet.

"Thank you again, Sam. We'll pack up and be off." Even Bob's softest voice bounced off the walls.

The Yanks had opened the curtains and dust motes danced in the sunlight. Bessie wheeled in a tea-trolley with cups and a pot of tea, and balanced a tray on her hip holding an enormous pile of buttered toast.

"Food," she said, with a touch of her old self. "I'll fetch Mum and we'll eat breakfast."

Her self-possession took Sam aback. Bessie was the most capable woman he'd ever met, even now, she'd never reveal frailty to strangers. He smiled at her and she smiled weakly in return. Her flash of sunniness warmed his chest.

Mrs Feldt also forced herself out of bed. To greet the visitors, she'd dressed in her going out clothes. She took her usual place, with baby Louis John on her knee. She ran her hand over Jacob's empty chair and pushed it right in. No one would sit there.

"Hank and Bob," Sam said. "Mormon missionaries from America. Meet my wife, Bessie, and my mother-in-law, Mrs Feldt."

Sam suppressed a chuckle when Mrs Feldt tipped her head a long way back then lifted one hand high over her head. "Did you men walk into this room without ducking?"

"No," Bob said with a laugh.

They exchanged looks then Hank stood to show how his tilted head still touched the door surround.

Mrs Feldt smiled. "What on earth do they feed children in America? Fertiliser?" She tickled Louis John's foot and pointed to the men. "We could cook you some of these magic meals."

After breakfast, the Mormons taught Louis John how to play basketball with a scrunched-up piece of newspaper. Bessie stayed in the dining room to watch when Sam cleared the dishes and Mrs Feldt went with him.

"Hank's offered to give Bessie driving lessons. We've got Jacob's car and she can run you all around when I'm in Melbourne."

"You're not going to teach her yourself?"

"No way. Jacob gave me advice: never try telling a woman what to do."

At the mention of Jacob, Mrs Feldt's lip quivered and Sam patted her arm.

"I'm going to help Bob prepare a speech," he said. "Would you mind keeping Louis John for a couple of hours."

"Try taking him off me." She put her hands on her hips, but there was twinkle in her eye. "The boy is the most precious thing I have left."

Piano music drifted through the house, luring Sam and Mrs Feldt to investigate. Bessie sat at the piano while Hank danced with Louis, and Bob's booming voice carried a decent tune.

Sam wasn't fool enough to think all was healed, but these strangers had opened a pathway, a moment's escape from grief. He took this as a positive sign.

Two weeks later, Elder Bob walked into the temple a bundle of nerves. Sam, not being a member of the church, watched through the open door, pacing edgily from one foot to the other as he waited.

The congregation whispered uneasily and shuffled in their seats. Their previous Bishop had been older and the Latter-Day Saints had sent a novice to replace him. But the unsettled atmosphere disappeared when Elder Bob spoke.

His deep and assured voice bounced off the walls.

No one moved.

Hank stood beside Sam and they listened together. "Bob's in the zone. I've seen him do it on the basketball court."

Sam recognised threads of the ideas they'd discussed, but Bob's speech was more than that. Much more. Bob spoke directly to Sam as if he had a window into his personal fears.

He told of the belief that all men and women have the right to worship God in whatever manner they believe. He covered the concept of a pre-mortal life where souls dwell with God, the father of all. And Sam heard how He helps everyone develop different talents—to prepare them for their unique role on earth.

None of this 'bad-seed' business. No original sin.

Sam was the way he was because God needed his peculiar traits. Not so different from Bubbe and her legend of the Nistarim.

When Bob spoke of how those who showed genuine kindness to others, would be reunited with their loved ones, Sam pictured those he'd lost.

His mother, Bubbe, Cecelia, and Jacob.

If there was a means to spending the afterlife with his entire family, Sam would work harder on being kind.

Perhaps the Mormon church was what Sam needed? But he couldn't join. He'd changed religions before and God hadn't rewarded him.

He stopped looking at Bob and watched the congregation. Sam wasn't alone in this uplifted state. Elder Bob had drawn everyone in. By the time the sermon ended, the Temple vibrated with a connectedness Sam felt in his soul.

The parishioners hummed with goodwill as they passed Sam and Hank at the door.

"Man! He made every basket, owned the court," Hank said, his eyes wide with pride.

Sam patted Hank's shoulder. "I've no idea what you mean, but Bob did a great job and he did it with a voice like God—only louder."

Chapter Forty-Six
Adelaide, 1940

Sam flipped the sign from OPEN to CLOSED and shoved a hastily hand-painted OUT OF STOCK sign on the shopfront window's ledge. Sam's usual meticulousness was gone, the lettering as rough as the old packing crate lid: Queensland Bananas. No deliveries of those in months.

He'd had to let his assistant go. Not enough work for one, let alone two. There was barely anything on the shop shelves and purse strings had tightened along with supply.

There wasn't much to do, but he fiddled around, delaying the trip home. Bessie, Louis John, and Mrs Feldt were like a three-legged stool who'd found balance on uneven ground. Sam was the fourth leg, and his presence created a distinct wobble.

The empty room above the shop became Bob and Hank's home. Good men. Despite their religious beliefs, they helped Mrs Feldt and Bessie with the tobacconist stall. Nicotine and alcohol sales had barely dropped. These 'necessities' calmed war frazzled nerves in a way an apple couldn't.

Bob and Hank often thanked Sam for his kindness, but he knew his kindness needed to be more widespread. He'd up his game if it meant a ticket to the after-life and basking alongside his loved ones, like Bob had described in his sermon. Sam shuddered at the thought of spending eternity knocking on some bolted bloomin' heaven door, watching Cyril and Louis John through a window while he stood outside with bloody Solomon.

After he'd swept the shop again, he made a pot of tea and collected Fay's letter from the counter. The postman usually pushed it through the slot in the door, but this letter was so fat, the mailman had brought it inside. Sam hoped it would be juicy. His sister wrote good gossipy letters.

He carefully rolled a cigarette, then after hefting the envelope, rolled another. A two cuppa, two ciggie job he reckoned.

Dear Brother (my favourite, but never tell or I'll deny.)

Sam leaned back in his chair, smiling as he inhaled the smoke. She would have written the same to William and Joe.

Sibling news first, from least interesting to most. Millie and I have been inundated with alteration jobs since the war started. Men wanting uniforms with a better cut, hoping they'll attract more girls.

Jane's children are delightful and she's doing well.

Joe has written another apology. He's delayed his plan to move to Australia, yet again, this time until after the war. He and his family are fine.

William, you ask? I've taken in his uniform, made him look smarter than ever—do you catch my drift? Yep! Our William's joined up! Had to lie about his age (again!). Isn't it ironic that Will put it up in the first war, now put it down because he's over forty?

Now for second juiciest news. Remember that farmer fella, Don Hogan, who used to stay at Mrs Cora's, especially for the 'Melbourne Agricultural Show'? Well, he's proposed. When she told me, she was all sighs and giggles, like a besotted schoolgirl. He's a widower, and he's handed the farm to his sons. Got enough money for Mrs Cora to stop taking in boarders. I'll send you a photograph when I get one.

I hope you haven't skipped ahead my impatient brother? I bet you're wondering about the biggest news of all.

Well, I've met up with our young Cyril. He's much happier living with his great Aunt Mary. She is a lovely woman and adores him. Remember he told us he'd chucked that coin away? He showed it to me. Shined it up and everything. He was disappointed in life when we saw him, that's all.

I've been meeting him for afternoon tea and he can't hear enough about you. His aunt Mary told him you were a hero for saving Cecelia the day you met. He's been nagging me for stories about your younger days. Loved hearing about you running off to join the navy. When I told him how torn apart you were having to leave him when his mother died—he smiled and cried at the same time. Yesterday, he said to me, "My dad was a real-life hero, wasn't he? Not just one out of books."

Then he told me how much Mary worried about the war. Apparently, he tried comforting her. "Don't worry. We're going to win this one. My Dad and uncle William will win it for us."

Love you always (as long as I'm your favourite sister)

Fay xxx

Sam's cigarette had burned out, leaving a ghost of ash on the cracked saucer. He read the letter twice, ignoring his stone-cold tea.

He wiped at his tears until his eyes were red, but couldn't keep them under control.

Chapter Forty-Seven
Melbourne, May 1940

The sea of cars on Collins Street whooshed past, and Sam gripped his hat with both hands. Only ten more steps and he'd be across the road, inside the army recruitment office. From what he could tell, given his limited view in the momentary breaks of traffic, the place was empty. He'd expected a line of men queueing down the footpath, offering themselves up for duty. To fight in the Mediterranean and the Middle East, connecting with the Commonwealth forces.

The news broadcasts incessantly called for heroes. *Sign up. Do your bit.* Hero was a hollow word until Cyril said it. Then it reverberated in Sam's chest. Their relationship wasn't completely broken.

He hesitated at a gap barely wide enough for him to cross even if he dashed. He wasn't that much of a hero.

It was increasingly difficult to keep the fruit business going. There were already shortages of stock and soon there'd be rations. What then? How many men signed up for matter-of-fact reasons? The army wage was guaranteed, a regular income. A hero's way of feeding their family.

What a bastard he was leaving a note instead of a hug. In the

Great War, he'd sent postcards to his loved ones, finding this the easiest of goodbyes. How little he'd changed over the years.

His original plan in coming to Melbourne had been to visit young Cyril in person. To really mend things. But Sam would sooner wrestle a bloomin' crocodile than look into pleading eyes, or risk being haunted by unpleasant farewells.

Bessie would understand. He'd written it better than he could have said in person. He wasn't abandoning her, but making something of himself, doing something useful. Maybe she'd love him again when he sent a photograph of himself in uniform. He'd post one to everyone, if he ever managed to cross the flamin' road.

Fifty yards to his left, a grey-haired woman with a limp battled the traffic by pushing her trolley of rags ahead of her like a shield. At the same time, a truck turned the corner, blocking all vehicles from his right.

Moses had parted the sea.

Inside the recruitment office, the clerk was anything but biblical. "Saw you across the street, mate. Was counting seconds on the clock, wondering whether you might run the other way. Glad you didn't. The war might feel distant over in Europe, but mark my bloomin' words, the bastards are coming for us. All of us. Men. Women. Kids."

Sam put his hat on the table and sat opposite, listening as the clerk talked him through the form.

"By the look of you, you've waited for the age limit change. The number of blokes I had to turn away last year was a disgrace. Thirty-five was a ridiculous cut-off. In my opinion, we could've gone past forty, but I don't make the rules." He looked around checking that the door to the back room was shut. "But I've been known to bend them."

Sam followed his motto of saying little in situations where talking could get a man into trouble.

"Only thing the army will check up on is the criminal history declaration." The clerk raised his eyebrow in a well-practised warning.

Sam made strong eye-contact without a flicker of concern. He'd need to lie. It had been some time since the Victorian authorities had been after him. He'd use a different name.

"Name?" the clerk asked.

"John. John Douglas."

Sam looked around while the clerk filled in the 'office use only' section. They'd painted everything in the room army-green. It was a wonder the clerk could find the large metal cupboard and the filing cabinet. Even the manila folders were camouflaged. Only the clock, with its large, honest face smiled out from the khaki gloom.

The clerk pushed the form across the table, but Sam wasn't ready to sign.

What about Bessie and Louis John? Would they get his army pay when he'd used a false name? If he used Samuel Solonsch, he'd risk the army cross-checking prison records.

The clerk was as good at reading people as Sam. "If you're having second thoughts because you need to change any details. For example—listing a wife and family—you can do it once you're out at sea. Sign an affidavit, and you can change the whole bloody form if you like. There's no rejecting you then."

The clerk stood and busied himself with some filing, leaving Sam alone with his thoughts. He planned to provide the correct details once at sea. Douglas was Sam's name from the Great War. The name he'd used to marry Cecelia. The name he'd given the son he hadn't cared for. Cyril deserved a hero fighting under his last name. John was for little Louis John.

When the clerk resumed his seat, he nodded. "You ready?"

Sam reached for the pen.

"I'm pleased you walked across that busy road. The war needs men like you. Calm men, who consider their decisions, who consider others. We're sending a whole lot of young uns out to fight. A role model like you won't go astray."

Sam signed on the dotted line.

John Douglas: VX15035.

Chapter Forty-Eight
POW Camp, Batavia, 1943

Each time the Japs hauled me back to the interrogation room, the commandant became increasingly impatient. I expected this round of questioning to be my last.

I didn't know where to go next with the retellings. John had coached me on keeping the bait on the hook, revealing details slowly, and not appearing too eager. I'd talked until my throat rasped and I imagined the Dutch translator, who'd told me her name was Lotte, developing blisters on the tips of her typing fingers.

Her expressions proved harder to read than the upside-down, inside-out Japanese alphabet. Sam would have interpreted her face in a split second, but all I got was an impression my respite from the POW camp was coming to an abrupt end.

Pity. They'd served me generous meals compared to camp fare. A Jap doctor cleaned and treated my ulcerated leg. For a short time, retelling John's stories, I felt hopeful.

Until lately.

The Japanese interrogator's mood fluctuated from hour to hour, and I couldn't link what I was saying to his behaviour. His demeanour became disconcerting when he began checking his watch and running the riding crop along the joins of the parquet tiles. His boredom became the new enemy.

An assault of angry voices broke the typewriter's monotonous clack-clack-clack and a rock sailed through the open window, narrowly missing the commandant, jolting us back to life. He raced outside; the guards following.

Lotte stood near the window, her eyes moving back and forth between me and the events outside. "It's a Malayan boy on a bicycle. He's teasing them, but they won't catch him." She spoke Dutch. "Even though I'm fairly sure none of 'them' understand our home language, I'll make this quick. You need to make your accounts war-related. And soon. You were stringing them along nicely, but now with nothing to entice them, you will be cut off."

"Thank you for your kindness."

"I'm not doing this for you. At the end of each day, I'm thrown back in the women and children's POW camp, so it's in my interest to keep them interested. Translating and typing allows me to supplement food rations for my daughter back in the camp."

Lotte breathed deeply through her nose, tilting her head back before resetting her business-like face. "Perhaps you see me as a traitor for helping the enemy, but many women were 'enlisted' into involuntary service. You should see what they're doing to some of the women… they're using their bodies whichever way they please." Her face contorted in disgust. "They are humiliated, treated as no more than animals."

I hadn't thought of Lotte as a POW. I'd imagined her as a paid translator. Her calmness and competence in this situation inspired me.

She reached into her pocket and leaned over the table, sliding something towards my hand. "Take this. I've concocted points of interest and added them to my translations. I'm trying to keep them hooked. It's written in Dutch, so if discovered you must swear for my daughter's sake that it's your own handwriting. Tell them you write the things you think are key to whatever Captain John Douglas is hiding."

Her eyes moved in an arc from me to the goings-on. She made a deep-throated sound, almost a laugh. "The vandal has escaped, they're coming back."

I admired how casually she sat, easing a blank sheet of paper into the typewriter's roller, then clipping the completed pages together without a hint of anything other than pure efficiency.

The commandant glanced at his watch and struck the desk with his crop. Our session was over.

As the guards encouraged me to my feet, the commandant stood in the doorway ready to leave. I deviated from John's script to offer nothing until asked. "I should have known it was all rubbish. You should hear the Captain rattle on. He wanted to tell me what happened when he landed here in Java, but I told him to shut up. I'd been in Batavia for longer than him. Why would I waste my time listening to him describe a place I know well?"

The commandant stiffened and barked orders at Lotte.

"What did he tell you?" she asked.

"Not me. I didn't want to know, but a couple of POWs no longer at my camp discussed those events. There was much secrecy. Maybe you should find them?" To hide my nerves, I channelled a famous John move and raked my hair using my fingernails before slicking it down with my palm. I also copied his easy smile. I didn't have his daring, but I did my best to fake his charisma.

"Stop!" The commandant examined me with renewed interest. He spoke with Lotte in Japanese, then studied my face as she translated.

"You will come back next week, but in the meantime the guards will take you from camp to camp to find these other men." She gave me a barely-there smile. "You must befriend this Captain Douglas. Beg him if you must. I need names."

I wasn't in a position to bargain, but it was now or never. "I agree to find out more, but leave a noticeable bruise, preferably on my face. The men in camp will do worse if they suspect I'm double-crossing."

• • •

Back at the POW camp I sat on the hut steps until dark. The low-slung moon mesmerised me—a glowing, white hammock that offered a comfortable viewing point up near the stars. If only I could get there. Instead, I needed to stay on Earth and own up to my departure from our plan.

When John sat beside me, I jumped.

He patted the wooden tread we used as a seat. "You've spent too long out here. Never make friends with a staircase, Kid. You can't trust 'em."

I raised my eyebrow waiting for the inevitable joke.

"They're always *up* to something and they keep *leading* you on."

I searched for it, but couldn't find my smile. "Talking about leading people on..." I paused to breathe in the fragrant night air and figure out how to word this. "I didn't follow your plan. Now I have to come up with men, with names."

When I'd finished telling him about the plight of Lotte and her daughter, the abuse of women, her additions to the tale and the note, I slumped against the stair rail.

"Don't give up hope. It's not exactly what I envisaged," he said. "I wanted the Japs to find you valuable. To heal your leg, then discount my stories as the ravings of a fool. Then they would send you to a working camp, away from me. But your concern for others is commendable. I'm proud of you. Your father will be proud when you return home."

My voice came out strangled, "If I fabricate the kind of story he's hoping to hear; about your involvement in underground and plans to weaken the Japanese army, then they'll punish you. If I don't... It doesn't bear thinking about."

"There'll be no need to make anything up, but the Japs and I need the same commodity. Names. Real names and serial numbers. Preferably of men who've died in the camps." John rolled a cigarette single handed, seemingly without a care in the world. "I will give you information, and you will pass it on word for word. But the names must be changed. I'm not risking anyone else's lives."

Chapter Forty-Nine
Batavia, Java, 1942

Plans for the battle of Java relied on the Dutch heading into the mountainous jungles, destroying bridges behind them, and making the swollen rivers uncrossable for the Japanese Army. The Dutch would turn back and join the allied troops—surrounding and conquering the stranded Japs.

But the clearest of plans had failed.

A radio message warned the Aussie soldiers of the problem. The Nippon army approached at tenfold the expected speed, providing little opportunity to destroy the second bridge near where Sam's group was stationed. The Dutch weren't doubling back.

The armoured vehicles lugging long-range weapons departed first, to prevent ammunition falling into enemy hands. This left the impossible task of defending the crossing to inadequately armed foot soldiers.

An unusual command was given. "Every man for himself until further orders."

The soldiers scattered.

Most took to the dense jungle, which skirted rivers and rice paddies, intending to camouflage themselves amongst thick foliage while picking off the enemy. No one had reckoned for such a tenacious enemy as the Japanese, who forged ahead, fully prepared to die.

Sam and his two companions lay sideways in calf-deep rice paddy water ready to ambush, but they remained hidden. Survival and common sense beat heroism.

There'd been no time to consider anywhere safer. Sam's Captain had taken this route and they'd waded too far in before realising they stood out like beacons on the unblemished carpet of emerald. Sam, Captain Edmondson and Private Nichols frantically waded between each bed of rice to avoid flattening the plants and creating an obvious trail. They'd dropped at a spot where intersecting rice terraces met with a sparse clump of tall palms. Not enough cover, but better than none. Sam pulled handfuls of thigh-high rice plants from the edges of each paddy then after sinking into the water, layered the long reedy leaves over his flank.

Stay down. Stay down. Sam ordered himself. He heard men giving themselves up, which was probably the wisest move, but Sam stayed put. He wasn't ready to relinquish his chance to become a hero for his sons.

When the water level in the irrigated fields rose, Sam moved his head to one side, raising his nostrils just high enough to breathe. Each movement cautious; he dared not dislodge his blanket of leaves.

"Surrender. Surrender!" A megaphoned Japanese voice rang out over the fields. Sam listened for his mates, a few yards away, but resisted the urge to look.

Eventually, the Aussie rifle shots ceased, sending a strong yet silent message of defeat, competing with muted groans of human submission.

Sam wiggled his arm slowly from his side to touch his chest. His Aussie mates were not four-hundred-yards east. This was his last chance to surrender, but he would not allow it to end like this. He intended to fight in the way he lived—ignoring rules which put him at a disadvantage.

By nightfall, Sam believed the intermittent screams came from men challenging orders and being punished as an example.

The resigned beat of trudging boots signalled a defeated march back to Batavia.

The Nippon soldiers stopped before the bridge for one last hurrah. Aiming into the rice paddies, they shot indiscriminately across the terraces while yelling what Sam believed was a victory cry.

He remained still and silent, half submerged, while a voice inside his head repeated orders. *Do not move. Do not whisper. Do not reach for Captain Edmondson and Private Nichols. Hold the flamin' line.*

The sun had barely risen when Indonesian exclamations shattered the quiet. Rice water rippled over Sam. People were wading nearby.

He lifted his head tentatively. Local men and women carried large wooden baskets, dangling from a pole balanced over their shoulders. In between picking the rice they looked over towards the jungle, no doubt dismayed at evidence of a bloody battle near their fields.

Sam left his rifle in the water and stood, hands above his head to show he was unarmed.

There were shrieks from the villagers, but his companions stayed concealed. Perhaps he should have done the same?

Word on the street had been many Malays hoped the Japanese would win, putting an end to the long Dutch oppression. Fortunately, this group appeared more amused than annoyed, one man gesturing to Sam with one of the broken plants and shaking his head as if to a naughty child who'd ruined a prized garden.

Once Sam determined they weren't carrying weapons, he called in vain to his mates.

No one answered.

Both had taken bullets to the skull. At first, Sam shook his head at their incredible bad luck, then decided death by a single bullet, was a better way to go than most. To Sam's surprise it was the scowling villager who offered to help bury them. The man pointed to a resting place high above the terraces.

Nichols was smaller than the captain, but it was difficult carrying the weight of a man while scaling rice paddy steps. The villager grasped Nichols's ankles and Sam threaded his arms under his shoulders, his head resting against Nichols's deathly cold cheek as they climbed.

When they returned for Captain Edmondson, the scowling man squawked instructions at his workers bent over picking rice. Two young men came to help.

Sam removed his muddied, blood-splattered shirt, slinging it under Edmondson's body. The helpers twisted shirt sleeves and shirt-tails into handles, then the four men scaled the landscape like an eight-legged beast.

As they lowered Edmondson, the shirt gave way, ripping up to the collar.

Sam caught his breath, and the young helpers returned to work, but scowling man paused and touched Sam's bare back, nudging him to turn towards the downhill slope. The villager held his hands thumbs together, then parted them slowly as if opening a curtain.

The big reveal took Sam's breath away. He'd been too caught up in the senselessness of war to look at the view. He sighed at the wondrous scenery— indigo sky, jungle clad mountains, mystical valleys and an ocean promising currents that led back to home.

The villager smiled. A missing tooth adding to his weather-beaten beauty. He pointed to the bodies, then back to the view. Nichols and Edmondson would rest in this heavenly place for eternity.

The villager handed Sam an inadequate digging tool, but slowly, very slowly it did the job. He dug alone, the wooden blade striking the damp earth with a booming thud, thud, thud. The drumming quality conjured Bessie. She was tapping over his bare skin with her fingers, encouraging him. And he knew she *would* encourage him. He'd filled in the affidavit and sent a letter and a photo of himself in front of a carved stone wall in Palestine, before the troops had been summoned to Java.

She'd written back.

S
Do what you must, to survive. I'll always love you.
B

When the holes were dug, Sam whispered to Captain Edmondson, who was roughly his size. "Mate, do you mind if we swap shirts? Mine's done for."

Accepting the trill whistle of a rice sparrow as a *yes*, he removed the dead man's shirt and replaced it with his, dressing Edmondson with the care of a mother for her newborn baby. He fastened every button with a silent prayer for both men. A sprinkling of Jewish and Catholic and even some Mormon; Sam covered as many bases as he could.

After finishing the burial, he took a handful of soil, sprinkled it over the ground then faced the extraordinary landscape that stretched out forever. "Mother Nature, do your best for these brave men."

Sam crossed the fields, the shirt flung over his shoulder, then he knelt beside a man-made water channel. There he cleansed his body, washed the shirt and dressed to move on.

He'd seen a young woman watching from the distance and waited as she approached. "*Rumah aman*," she said several times. He knew *rumah* meant house, it was one of the common words they'd used during their short time in Java. From the pleading and caring in her eyes, Sam assumed the other word meant somewhere safe for him to go.

She picked up a twig and drew a map in the drying mud, then pointed to mountains, the river and back to her map. Marking a cross between the two mountains and a bridge crossing a stream, she repeated, "*Rumah aman*."

The young woman patted her upper chest. "*Angkasa. Angkasa*"

He imitated her gesture. "Sam."

She drew the outline of a house with three triangular roofs, and said "*Maharani*."

Sam nodded his understanding of both the map and the person he was seeking. "Okay. I find Maharani."

She steered him in the right direction, calling out to him when he was a few feet away. "*Maharani. Angkasa*."

Sam wouldn't forget. He trusted this stranger and finding Maharani was his best chance of survival.

The mud map indicated a trek considerably shorter than the actual distance, but despite miles of hiking across open fields, Sam met no one. He was relieved when he recognised the bridge she'd drawn and staying in the undergrowth, he turned to follow the stream which ran crystal clear from high in the mountains, avoiding the cleared track on the opposite bank. Although it meant clambering over rocks and weaving through fern-like plants that looked soft, but had spines, it was worth the effort to remain unseen. Sam could disappear into the thicker jungle if need be, but luck was with him and he travelled upstream.

By the time he saw the three-peaked roof appear above the trees, he was soaked with sweat from the liquified tropical air. He scrambled down the bank behind a huge boulder where the stream swirled in a foam lipped eddy. Sam went in, boots and all, closing his eyes as he took in the water's cooling energy and allowed the horrendous scenes in his mind to wash downstream. He pictured the map again and heard the young woman's voice repeating the names. *Maharani. Angkasa.*

With renewed vigour, he waded through the faster-moving water. It was time to face whatever waited on the other side. His gut churned while he watched, hidden by an enormous tree with roots lifting sections of the carved stone wall surrounding the house. The sun did its job and soon he was ready to enter the compound without dripping. He stopped at the carved columns and open gates, stepping over a stone trough channelling water from the stream into a pond at a courtyard's centre. The place felt safe and for the first time in days, Sam's stomach grumbled with hunger rather than fear

The building to his right had an intricate wooden panel surrounding a door-sized opening. He rapped his knuckles on the timber then waited, coiled ready to jump and run.

A woman appeared.

"*Maharani?*" he asked, pointing back over the mountains to where he'd started. "*Angkasa.*"

She nodded without smiling. Sam couldn't pinpoint her age. Her hair was pulled severely back from her regal Malayan face, in a style an older woman might choose. In contrast, her soft brown skin was unlined and perfect.

"Comethrough. Comethrough" she said, checking behind him. She ran her words together without a gap, so when combined with her unusual pronunciation, Sam, at first, believed she was speaking another language. She repeated herself slowly. "Come through."

He followed her into a large sitting area behind an ornate screen, furnished with round-cushioned cane chairs and low tables. The place reminded him of a restaurant he'd once visited with Bessie.

Maharani crossed her ankles when she sat, the rest of her body covered by a multi-patterned, multi-layered mix of batik clothing. Although cotton, it looked too hot for the day. yet Maharani appeared cool.

"You are a Captain?" she asked.

Sam looked down at his shirt and considered his response. When in doubt, do not tell, but do not lie.

"I'm not anything. Just a man on the run from the Japanese."

Chapter Fifty
POW Camp, Java 1943

It was barely light when Captain John and I ventured into the vegetable garden, to find anything ripe enough for the cook to chuck in with the meagre number of eggs the hens had laid the night before.

John leaned on his shovel and whispered, "Last night, I started the section of my story the Japs are actually interested in. When you retell it, leave out the part where Edmondson and Nichols were shot. You need to deposit these in the name bank. You can withdraw them whenever the Japs are itching for details. Nothing worse can happen to those blokes now. After the war, you can reveal the real names of those who deserve recognition for their bravery."

At breakfast call, the men spread out on the veranda and the stairs, and ate capsicum flavoured eggs, while I waited inside. Unfair of me taking food from men who'd barely been fed.

"Can I have a word?" Double-Double, the dentist, asked in Dutch. "I don't know why the Japs have been taking you out on day trips, but the men are uneasy."

"I can't tell you anything except I'm trying to do the right thing."

"First Captain John seemed too friendly with the Japs. Now, after your big 'bust up', you've taken the turncoat's baton." His bony shoulders tensed. "None of us feel comfortable around you. From the outside, it looks like you're running a traitor's race."

I grabbed my old stabilising chair for the first time since the interrogations. My leg had started to heal, but this traitor label jellied my limbs.

Once Double-Double left, John twitched his head for me to come here. "I've spoken to Silent-G. Silence is part of his nature as well as his name. He'll clear your reputation when it's over.

When I headed outside to wait for Lotte and the guards collecting me for camp visits, the men on the verandah steps leaned aside, a wide path for the stinking rat. I didn't blame them. It looked like I was up to no good, but I trusted John. He wanted to feed the Japs false information. To save those still be on the loose, trying to end the war. That's as much as I'd pieced together.

Having valid reasons for my actions didn't stop me feeling sick to my guts.

On the road to Bandoeng camp, Lotte and I sat in the back of a jeep confiscated from the allies. We were passing a coconut plantation when the car ground to a stuttering stop, throwing us forward.

The taller of the guards squawked like a bird of prey, pointing his bayonet to fallen coconuts on the shoulder of the road.

"He wants us to collect some," Lotte translated.

When the Dutch troops were first stationed in Batavia, I'd marvelled at coconuts in the wild. I'd seen coconuts in fruit shops, piled like small brown bowling balls, but on the tree, they grew green, much larger and elongated. I shook each near my ear as I picked them up, listening for the swoosh and slosh of coconut milk, indicating they were fresh enough to eat.

When we'd almost filled the tray at the back of the car, the tall, coconut-loving guard took one off me and threw it on the ground.

He stabbed it with his bayonet, missing and kicking it when it rolled. Clumsily, he hacked enough to break the fibrous green husk and dislodge the woody nut inside. His companion yelled at him in short, curt words, but the coconut massacre continued.

Lotte whispered, "He's warning his friend he'll ruin the bayonet, and there'll be consequences."

With the coconut in pieces, the guard tentatively bit a piece, then spat it out, waving his hands for us to get back in the car.

Lotte knelt, picked up the broken sections, and put them in her shoulder bag before climbing aboard. When the car took off, she produced two small portions of white coconut flesh.

I scraped shavings with my teeth, savouring the taste. It was delicious. But she didn't hand me another.

At the camp, the guards discussed our purpose with the Japanese soldiers on patrol. The soldiers flicked their hands dismissively.

"They don't want to catch anything from the prisoners," Lotte said. "They are trusting me to translate whatever you say."

"What disease do they have?" I considered pulling my shirt over my mouth and nose.

"Boils. Touch nothing. On their own, boils aren't bad, but you know from your leg how the mildest injury can worsen without proper attention. We have one hour to find what we need, then we're back to the interrogation office."

This camp, although raised from the ground like ours, was made of red brick instead of timber. Possibly once a school, it had a long outdoor corridor with evenly spaced doors, metal numbers affixed above.

I held my palms upwards, spoilt for choice.

"Number six looks lucky." Lotte promptly reached into her bag, producing a square notebook and pencil. "You do most of the talking and I'll take notes."

Everyone in dorm room six looked at us as if we were exotic animals. Correction, they looked at Lotte that way. Before the war, I'd seen men stare at women with longing, but these men looked ashamed, a few rearranging themselves to cover the festering abscesses multiplying on their skin.

When they exchanged suspicious glances, I took a leaf out of Captain John's book and spoke as if I knew what was going to come out of my mouth next.

"We're here to collect information about the POW camps," I improvised, hoping rumours hadn't travelled ahead and blocked my path. "Camp conditions, things like that. If anyone is inclined to tell us about your treatment here, or what you're being fed, or what you do to stay sane, it would be much appreciated."

I almost convinced myself this was true, but the men stayed put. Some laying on their beds, several smoking near the window, and a group of four sitting cross-legged on the floor playing cards.

Lotte held up several pieces of coconut. "There's a small reward."

A bloke who'd been lazing on his bed leapt to his feet and took a piece. "I'm known as Scrounger, for obvious reasons. What d'ya wanna know?"

I swallowed back the bile. Lotte's bribery was ingenious, but it sickened me, too. Like rewarding circus animals for doing tricks.

"I'll start then." Scrounger pointed to the card players. "They're all Yanks. You'd think you wouldn't be able to tell 'til they opened their gobs, but check out what they're using as stakes."

Lotte and I stepped closer. Piles of varying sizes rested near their knees. Rice.

Scrounger explained. "Not enough to eat in here as it is, so these blokes are betting with their lives. That curly-haired one is the capitalist. He's got a stash of more than he needs. Won't share, though. One of them got killed in a fight over rice. Who'd have thought it. Friendly bloody fire."

We watched for a while and Lotte wrote it down, even though it wasn't what we'd come for. Scrounger had an intelligent edge to him. Best not to rush things.

He pointed to a Japanese officer sitting on the steps. "Aikawa looks mean, but he's the least of our worries when it comes to the Nips. Reminds me of a school teacher I had. Funny that. Maybe the buildings bring it out in people. He carries a wooden ruler and lines us up on parade, berates us then slaps our faces. Annoying as all shit, but he's killed no one."

What a lucky change of conversation, taking us where we needed to be. I counted to ten, so as not to seem too eager. "Have any of the men died?"

"What d'ya reckon? Follow me."

There was a back corridor, mirroring the front, and Scrounger pointed to a bank of school lockers. "Our hidden bloody memorial wall, right here."

On the inside of every locker door, nicknames, real names, ranks, and serial numbers were scratched into the wood. This was the impossible treasure we sought.

Lotte scribbled lightning fast while I spoke to Scrounger. "How many from illness?"

"Most."

"Jap beatings gone too far?"

"Course. It's still a bloody war." Scrounger pointed out many names, ignoring me as if I'd lost my mind.

Perhaps I had.

"Did the Japs kill any men because of war related crimes?" I asked.

"Nah. Hang on. Some might be a yes." He tapped two locker doors, four names inside each. "These fellas deaths weren't no accident. Seems the buggers were involved in some daring underground stuff before capture. After the 'trials' there were executions—Nippon style. We watched." Scrounger's breath became an embittered sigh.

I could taste the rancour. A Mother-Lode of Evil.

Even though we had what we needed, the Japs drove us to another POW camp.

"They will search us after we leave the last camp, so you will have to wait for the names," Lotte whispered, her voice barely audible over the rush of wind in the back of the vehicle. She opened her notebook to show me. "These are women who died in my camp, in case you need a female name. And these are business owners who escaped before the Japanese arrived. Drag the Captain's stories out as long as you can."

Most of the men in the next camp were out working; rebuilding damaged bridges, repairing roads and extending the runway for Japanese bombers. Our tour finished early, but our armed escorts weren't in a hurry to leave and after they searched us, they locked Lotte and me in the jeep, while they caught up with a guard they knew.

She opened her notebook at the original page where she'd

written the dead men's names. She copied them quickly. Before tearing it out, she scribbled lightly over the writing, making it look like a useless scrap.

I was mesmerised as she creased the square paper with the back of her fingernail. First diagonally, then square; cross-folds, inside-out turns, all manner of shapes, until she eventually held up the finished product. "Tulips. Origami," she said.

She indicated the coconut murdering guard. "He taught me Origami. He's an expert. Tuck the 'special' tulip into your pocket and I'll show you how to make one of your own. If he finds them, he won't notice the men's names, he'll be too busy criticising the careless workmanship."

Chapter Fifty-One
Batavia, Java, 1943

Sam and Maharani's relationship unfolded like a slow, slow tango. Every conversation or action a step towards discovering the other's particular dance. Each, reserving details of their moves. This was, after all, a war. Once he knew he could trust her, he'd ask where to find the allied troops and rejoin.

He deduced from her interactions she wasn't one of the servants; but the owner of this impressive property, and he took to watching her with curiosity. Sam wasn't in a hurry to leave.

Maharani's mouth curled in a sneer, but her hand trembled when a servant, Kajen, mentioned the Japanese. Sharing the same enemy made Sam feel safe, yet gave rise to questions. Not voicing them maintained the calm. Questions can be the greatest unsettlers in the universe.

Each morning she sat by the courtyard pond weaving a palm-frond basket to fill with flowers. This, she placed in front of a framed photograph of a couple Sam assumed were her parents. With the greatest of care, she lit a stick of incense in offering or prayer.

One morning after completing her ritual, she brought a tray with a sweet gingery drink out into the courtyard and perched near Sam on the long stone bench.

She studied his face as he sipped. "What happened to the rest of your platoon?" She locked eyes, awaiting an answer.

He took a sharp breath. She was changing the rules of engagement. The calm would be broken, and Sam readied himself for his marching orders.

"Dead or forcibly taken by the Nippon army." He spat on the ground.

She smoothed the batik over her knees. "I have news."

"Yes?" Sam watched her eyes.

She blinked slowly. "The allies—all of them have capitulated. The Japanese are in control of The Dutch East-Indies."

Blood pulsed in Sam's temple. It wasn't time to give up, he'd plenty of fight left. "The allies will send planes. There'll be air battles."

"It's done, and it's official." Maharani set her chin firmly. "The allied soldiers are now forced labour and fortifying buildings across Java, turning them into prisoner of war camps. Men who refuse are killed; the others will remain incarcerated until…" She shrugged.

Sam's mouth was sandpaper dry. He gripped the cup with both hands, his arms suddenly heavy. Defeat was crushing.

"The Japanese are making rounds of the villages, searching for soldiers such as yourself. My staff will take turns on lookout, but we won't be able to keep it up forever. It might be safer in the long run if you turn yourself in."

"I am most thankful for your help, but I beg a few days to consider my options. I can work to pay my keep."

She tilted her head attentively, then pointed to the cracked terracotta tiles on the far building's roof. "Are you afraid of heights?"

"Not at all."

"Then I'll find you a set of civilian clothing, and get Kajen, to teach you the repair skills, but first, follow me."

She walked inside and stopped in the library space near the great room, before looking up to the ceiling. "The attic."

The lack of a ladder surprised Sam, but he was more surprised by Maharani's demonstration. Although close to forty, she leapt like a gymnast onto the upturned hands of a black granite statue, then clambered onto a cabinet filled with books and spider-conch shells. She moved a ceiling panel aside, lifting her body on her arms, all while wearing a close-fitting skirt.

He copied best he could. He was agile, but nowhere near as graceful. When he looked for her inside the attic space, high in the thatch's peak, there was nothing to see. She called to him from behind a false wall. "If you hear anyone yell '*Burung*', the word for bird, you must fly up here as fast as you can."

After a roofing lesson from Kajen, Sam set to work. He was eager to restore the Aussie reputation by proving himself capable.

"Good job," Maharani called. "But only work until eleven. After that the sun is too hot."

He continued resealing and layering the tiles as Kajen had shown him until Maharani returned late morning. "I have refreshments."

He climbed down and washed his hands in the water channel, as he'd seen Kajen do earlier.

Sam's woven hat protected his face from the sun overhead, but he removed it and squinted to check his handiwork, hoping the tiles looked neat from ground level. "I'm getting the hang of it, I reckon."

"Kajen says you are a quick learner." Maharani smiled and Sam realised it was the first smile she'd given him. A ray of kindness, erasing thoughts of dark atrocities outside the sanctuary.

Sam scrutinised the tray in her hands—white morsels arranged artfully on a banana leaf. "What is it?" A teasing-smile played across his lips.

"*Gong-Gong*. Flesh from the spider conch. We collect the shells on low tide."

He tried one piece, then followed with another. "Delicious."

She regarded him for a moment. "How do you think you'd go learning Japanese?"

"Without bragging, I'd expect to be good at it." This time, his smile was dazzlingly concentrated. "Do you speak the language?"

"I do. During these uncertain times, some Japanese will be useful. Finish up and we'll go inside for your first lesson."

Sam didn't ask why. The unknown gave him a delectable judder of adrenaline.

The language lessons always took place in the far pavilion—Maharani's private quarters. The first time she'd invited Sam in, he'd been distracted by the curtained four-poster bed dominating the enormous room. He had blinked and cleared his throat, but she'd moved quickly to the end of the room where majestic potted palms broke up a wall of wooden shuttered doors.

From where Sam sat, he could see down the volcanic mountains to the valley and beyond. The rice fields, now clear of plants, were being ploughed by cattle ready for the next crop. It gave them an unobstructed view of the only road so they could keep watch for uninvited guests.

"When you said you pick up languages quickly, it wasn't an idle boast." Maharani leaned against the small day bed cushions, blues and the golds echoing the ocean on the horizon.

Sam grinned. "Like Kajen said, I'm a quick learner."

She checked her notes, flipping pages. "Only six lessons. And you've rarely forgotten a phrase."

"I practise with the statues." He pointed to a stone sculpture of a woman holding a bowl filled with petals. "Pity she doesn't correct me when I make mistakes."

Nothing about Maharani's composure changed; either she didn't understand him or didn't find him funny.

"How did you come to learn Japanese?" he asked.

"My parents owned this land along with several rubber plantations. My father encouraged me into the family business from an early age. He traded with Japanese officials who exported our rubber for years. He paid for private tutoring, training me to become his chief negotiator." She sighed. "He said he didn't trust anyone. Pity was—he did."

"Did the Japanese rip him off?"

She gave Sam a quizzical look.

"Did they cheat him?"

"They cheated all of us. Told us a wonderful fairytale of how Japan, the only non-European industrialised nation, was *The Light of Asia*. We believed them because we wanted it to be true."

Sam raked his thinning hair nervously. He sensed Maharani's parents were dead, but he didn't want to broach the subject. Dealing well with family death was not a skill to which Sam had bragging rights.

"My mother was Chindo—half Chinese, half Indonesian, so my father encouraged her to establish commerce with the Chinese. She was on a trip to Nanking with my younger sister, when the Japanese attacked. So much for the Japanese helping Asians. The *Rape of Nanking* took them both. My father couldn't accept his guilt over their deaths and he took his own life."

Her shoes tapped a sad beat on the stone floors as she left the room. Sam could taste her pain. It brought back memories of his own. In those times he'd preferred to be left alone, so he didn't follow.

She returned with a bottle of rum and asked in Japanese, "Would you like a drink?"

"Yes, please."

His response was met with a teary-eyed laugh. "Now, you're just showing off."

As the level in the rum bottle dropped, their focus shifted. She lifted her knees beside her on the day bed, and he moved his chair closer. They paused their lesson to share silly stories, lulled in into a sweeter, tipsy world.

By the time they heard the Japanese soldiers, it was too late to shout *Burung*. It wasn't safe to venture into the hallway and climb into the attic. They were trapped.

"I'll hide under the bed," Sam whispered.

"They will have heard both voices through the open doors. Hiding will make it worse." She unbuttoned her shirt. "Remove your clothes."

Sam didn't like the plan, but had none of his own.

He and Maharani were in a naked embrace when the soldiers burst through the door, bayonets at the ready.

The Japs sniggered, but did not take their eyes off Maharani.

Sam pulled the sheet protectively around her bare shoulders, eyes scanning the room for a makeshift weapon.

"Names?" One barked in Japanese.

"Maharani," she said, adding other words, not stock phrases from their lessons.

Sam assumed she was passing him off as her lover. This was fraught with danger, and bile rose in his throat at the glint of lust in the Japanese soldiers' eyes. He steeled his nerves and reached for his trousers to buy time. As a deserted allied soldier, he was done for. Even worse was the looming threat of what they might do to a half-naked woman, especially a traitor.

He snapped his belt buckle and introduced himself with the most German sounding name he'd ever heard. "Hermann Schmidt."

The Japanese and Germans were on the same side.

Under different circumstances he'd have smiled in memory of Jacob Feldt, but he had two lives to save. Sam broke into German patter about the black market and how he was the man to ask if they needed anything.

Maharani raised her eyebrows at Sam, while the soldiers jabbered amongst themselves. They asked to see his papers. Sam held his empty hands upward and spoke slowly in Japanese, "Hidden. I will fetch. Next time."

They answered using words Sam didn't know. Maharani replied, then gripping her sheet with white-knuckles, she escorted the soldiers outside.

Sam removed a houseplant stake and held it weapon-ready, listening at the door.

When Maharani returned, she opened it so fiercely that he was knocked to the floor and she fell onto him in a crying tangled mess. "They're coming back in three days. They want to check Hermann Schmidt's passport."

She wrapped her arms around his neck. Goosebumps prickled—

not unpleasantly. The flower perfume was concentrated, and the remains of rum in his mouth tasted smooth. It had been a close call, but they'd survived.

"Thank you." He tentatively touched the fabric draped over her arm. "I can't believe we got away with it."

Instead of answering, Maharani dropped the sheet and drew Sam towards her.

He pulled away, needing to see her face. "Are you sure?"

"Are you?" she replied.

Sam closed his eyes, remembered his vows to Bessie, but couldn't concentrate on anything but the sensations of 'now'. They'd had a close brush with death, and the Japs would return, but in that moment, there was beauty in the face of ugliness and warmth to melt a glacial dread.

He pictured Bessie's note: *Do what you must to survive.* This wasn't her intention, and he knew it.

He blocked the voice questioning whether he was a good role model for his sons. This was more than a matter of survival—feelings had sprung up unprompted. This wasn't succumbing to a beautiful, exotic woman. This was primal.

He kissed Maharani with a passion fuelled by urgency, danger, and bad-seed desire.

The following morning, Sam awoke to an empty bed. He listened as Maharani clattered around in the next room, hoping their night together had not complicated their easy dance. He parked himself in a window-facing chair, monitoring the mountain track in case the Japs returned.

Sam was considering whether to mention what happened, or put their intimacy down to alcohol and adrenaline, when Maharani's small car rumbled away from the house.

He borrowed a book and perched on a rock near the stream. His instincts trusted Maharani, but his head cautioned. *Stay alert.* Hidden behind thick foliage, he unsuccessfully tried to make sense of Dutch words. Sam observed the road, instead.

Sam left his hiding place when she returned alone in the late afternoon, carrying a bag of supplies under one arm. She waved stiffly with the other. Her body language, while not entirely relaxed, did not set off warning bells. *Do not let sex cloud your judgement.* When she offered a drink and a quick smile—her eyes were self-conscious, but her soul pure. Sam felt guilty about second-guessing her motives.

He waited until dark, when it was less likely anyone would risk the narrow mountain road, and snuck up on Maharani who was putting paper bookmarks inside an atlas.

She made serious eye contact. "I had to be sure. I spoke to Angkasa, who confirmed you are an Australian soldier. Sorry about your friends."

Maharani handed him the atlas. "I'm assigning more study. Familiarise yourself with this area of Java, and the countries I've bookmarked. As Hermann Schmidt, you were a German soldier years ago. You'd begun your dream of sailing around the equator, until you became stuck in Java with the outbreak of war. Those are the basics. Create a narrative with rich details because in all likelihood, you'll be questioned again. Your story must be believable."

Maharani gazed at him inquiringly. Trust goes both ways and he owed her some explanation. "I grew up speaking German with my grandmother, and in the Great War I was a sailor with the British Merchant Navy," he said. "I'm sorry for bringing you unnecessary trouble."

"Work on your backstory. We'll discuss this tomorrow evening, when the others arrive."

Sam leaned against the roughly rendered wall of the house, escaping the breeze to light a cigarette when he saw yellow-orange flickering headlights heading up the mountainous road like sparks of fire.

He ran into the house. "Maharani. We have visitors."

Together, they stared into the far distance until the lights came into focus.

"Two sets," she said. "Unlikely to be Japanese. The patrols travel in one vehicle. My associates usually drive two cars, but... best you wait in the attic."

"No. I'll wait with you."

When Sam heard friendly laughter outside, his racing heart slowed and he smiled at Maharani, bending to press his mouth on the sensuous curve where her neck met her shoulders. She lifted her mouth for a kiss.

In the past, Sam had witnessed the Dutch visitors follow the same routine of fetching the rum and the cards. But this time the three men, one a priest, and a blonde woman gathered around him, looking on with the expectation of a crowd waiting for a magician to produce a rabbit from his hat.

Maharani's description must have painted him in a favourable light.

Before introductions, the youngest man produced a camera. "Move next to the wall."

Sam stepped back in surprise.

"Sorry. Not there," the photographer said. "I need a plain background."

Sam moved, but covered his face as the flash went off. "What's going on, mate? Even a bloke with half a brain wouldn't allow a stranger to snap a picture."

Maharani took Sam's arm. "My fault." She held her hand out to the Dutch priest, and he fished an envelope from inside his robe. "Your new passport," she said.

Sam fumbled as he tore the packet. He was both shocked and impressed.

A German passport, khaki green cover, spread-winged eagle carrying a swastika. DEUTCHES REICH REISEPASS. It looked authentic—complete with creased pages and a dog-eared corner. Inside, the official stamping looked genuine and although the photo was missing, the name was complete. *Hermann John Schmidt.*

Sam marvelled at such efficiency. This rum drinking group were well prepared for resistance fighting. He was ready to do whatever they ordered.

He returned the passport with trembling hands. "Where do you want me to stand?"

The photographer, Tom Powell, an Anglo-Dutch interpreter had been working with the Australian Blackforce before the capitulation. Tom snapped several photos, then Maharani showed him into a small storeroom off the kitchen where he could set up a temporary darkroom.

The rest drew wicker chairs around two small tables in the great room. Everyone looked at Sam with wide, expectant eyes.

He offered his hand. "John."

"My apologies, I got caught up in the excitement." Maharani gestured as she made introductions. "Meet Captain Douglas, the man I told you about. This is Mrs Van Leeuwen, Lieutenant Kriek Walters, and here we have Father Aart, our Lutheran priest."

Sam checked out the priest. He was a giant of a man, and his unruly red hair gave him no chance of staying incognito. "Who's in charge?" Sam asked.

They glanced uncomfortably at each other and then at Sam.

Father Aart eventually spoke. "We are all equal under God and hoped you were an answer to our prayers. We have vague notions of helping the war effort, but don't know where to start. We're thankful you're here."

Sam assumed these people were part of an efficient underground organisation. It was no one else's fault he was way off mark. They were brave all right, but they were lost amateurs, battling their way through a haze of fear like everyone else—Sam included. And they were making dangerous mistakes. He narrowed his eyes at Maharani. "You visited all these people yesterday and told them about me?"

"Yes." She crossed her arms indignantly. "You have a problem accepting my help, *now*?"

Her emphasis on the word 'now' constricted Sam's throat. She'd put her life at risk and invited him into her bed. Shame washed over him and he straightened. "How many of you are there?"

"Five," Maharani said. "Before sensing your unwillingness, we had hoped to become a group of six. But you don't have to join us.

You'll have your passport within the hour, and tomorrow you can head out alone."

Sam was about to answer, when Tom, the photographer sauntered out, checking his watch. "Nine more minutes for the film to develop. I needed fresh air. Did I miss anything?"

"Nothing," Lieut. Walters said. "We were discussing who should be in charge. The Captain has the highest rank and I'm ready to take orders."

Everyone, including Maharani, nodded and Sam felt the power of their shared plea.

"Okay," he said, leaning in. "The first thing we need to understand, is that we cannot all know everything. Successful underground organisations need structure and secrecy." He looked at Maharani, his eyes soft with apology. "Could I please have a pen and paper?"

Sam drew a hexagon in the middle of the page, a mixture of letters and numerals.

$$X1$$
$$X2 \quad X3$$
$$X4 \quad X5$$
$$X6$$

"This diagram represents our central group. We can use names when we're together but not beyond this cell. Keep those details to yourself."

He drew new satellite cells linked to the centre. "For example." He pointed to X2 on the chart. "This could be you, Mrs Van Leeuwen. You'll share information with your helpers on a needs-only basis. Reporting back here on generalities. Telling no-one else anything." He made eye contact with everyone. "Am I clear?"

Once they agreed, he continued. "If one person is interrogated, the entire organisation can't be eliminated, because no one knows every name. Safer, too, for us not to grow beyond six clusters of six. Thirty-six people working for the cause is manageable."

The group collectively relaxed and Sam realised they'd moved the weight from their shoulders to his.

"What can we call ourselves?" Lieut. Walters asked.

"The Thirty-Six?" Father Aart suggested.

"I'll get back to the photographs," Tom said. "Get the cards ready."

"Good job, Tom," Mrs Brouwer said. "I'll pour you a glass of rum."

Sam had been itching to do something significant since the day he enlisted in Melbourne. Being part of a resistance group didn't frighten him. That's basically what the army was, one big resistance group. His only concern was their laid-back attitude. Naming the group, planning card games. He wanted to make plans.

"I can't play cards. I don't have any money."

"We don't bet with modern currency." Maharani laughed and lifted a bottling jar from the floor. "My father's collection of old coins," she winked at Sam. "I count them at the end of each session."

Sam helped Maharani sort coins into even piles while waiting for Tom. He turned one over in his hand. NEDERL. INDIE. The same type Bubbe had given him. He was feverishly sifting for one dated 1836 when Tom returned.

"Looking for gold?" Tom laughed and swigged his rum.

"Pardon?" Sam had been thinking of the coin and Bubbe. If he could find the right year, success would be guaranteed.

"Hoping there's a gold coin in there?" Tom asked again.

"No. A particular year," Sam said. "My grandmother gave me a Dutch-Indies coin and I lost it."

They didn't need a group name, but the legend of *The Nistarim* had one for them. *The Concealed Ones*. The thirty-six who hide in their normal lives until it's time to step up and act.

Chapter Fifty-Two
POW Camp, Batavia 1943

I flattened the coded origami paper against my thigh and handed it to Captain John. After he added Edmondson and Nichols to the list, I hid it under the inner sole of my boot, barely daring to remove my footwear to wash, and then only if John guarded them.

I'd become used to regular meals during interrogations. Not only was I starving again, but skittish; jumping at every strange sound, waiting, waiting, waiting for someone to collect me.

The solace I'd taken from John's stories was suffocated by their new purpose. Remember the details, but change the names.

He told about meeting Maharani and the resistance, making it clear he was using their real names, but didn't want their identities known.

"I don't understand," I said, entirely confused. Lack of food—fat melting, muscle wasting, skin hanging, changes that turned men into scarecrows—were obvious on my body. Changes inside the head were unseen, but the mental toll of starvation was real. I struggled to connect ideas that once would have connected themselves. Sam Solonsch becoming John Douglas was one thing, passing himself off as a captain was another. Then changing his identity to the German, Hermann Schmidt, stretched my starving brain cells.

John whispered, "I need your list." He held the crisscross lined paper up to the moonlight, then circled three names.

"Only three?" I asked. "There were six of you."

"We must draw out the reveal. Disclose one at a time, two if you absolutely must. Get them to help you. They will offer fake names to trick you, which you will consider carefully before saying no. Gathering the identities cannot be easy or it won't ring true."

This was important. I rubbed my forehead to dull the pounding, and concentrated on the convoluted task of remembering and forgetting at the same time.

"Repeat the events I've told you, substituting names from the list. You must recite these over and over again so the names you say under duress are of names of people the Japs can no longer hurt."

"Why don't I make up an entirely different story with fake names?"

"Because the Japs will pick a fabrication miles away. The truth has a resonating ring."

"If they've already arrested people, won't they know who they are?"

"It's possible they possess the organisational chart I drew up on the first night. I'll describe it again tomorrow and draw it in the soil so you can recreate it on paper. This information will be most convincing if offered at the point where your gut tells you they're losing faith."

He began folding the paper, then stopped. "We can't keep the original list. It implicates Lotte. Tomorrow you'll copy this on scraps. More convincing, and in your own handwriting."

John stopped to straighten his back several times as he scratched interconnected hexagonal shapes in the earth. It reminded me of molecular structure charts in chemistry lessons. And it was no less confusing.

"Don't look now, but the guards are here." John murmured through gritted teeth. "They're having a cigarette with Widey. Act normal."

"I can't do this." Every cell in my body rebelled. "How does it all end? They'll know this information has come from you."

"I'm not leaving this place alive, Kid." John squinted into the sun, half-heartedly squaring his shoulders. "I'm dying. My kidneys are kaput, and getting worse. My means to immortality is keeping you alive. One day, when this fuckin' war is over, you'll be around to tell people what happened, and if you remember, throw in a kind word about me."

Measured intakes of breath didn't calm me, so I screamed raw emotion into the sky. At least it stopped me from crying.

As Japanese guards marched towards us, John pushed me in a well-rehearsed show of annoyance. I scrambled to my feet and joined the performance, gripping him in a head lock. Bile burned my throat when I rasped in his ear. "I'm not losing you. I need you. You're my father in war."

His back heaved against my chest, and I pulled him closer, scared. If John was sobbing, I'd come undone.

"Halt. *Teishi*."

I dropped my arms at the command. The guard beckoned me to climb into the military vehicle by waving a cigarette instead of a rifle.

We drove the usual route into Batavia, but continued past the interrogation building, pulling into the compound with many Japanese flags. *Kempeitai* headquarters—the dreaded and brutal secret police.

This was where serious 'questioning' took place and they had serious means to extract the answers. Lotte and my usual interrogation officer were waiting outside the principal building and, after a quick exchange between him and the guards, we marched through the corridor. Lotte moved her head in a barely perceptible nod. Now, if I had Sam's or John's or bloody Hermann's powers of observation, I'd have read the significance. I came up with plausible interpretations. The preferred was, 'It's all going to be okay,' while the dreaded option was, 'Nice knowing you.'

I settled on a benign, "Stay calm."

A set of stairs led down the back of the building, a high concrete block wall stood fifty yards beyond. Half-way there, the interrogator stopped to speak. Even if I spoke Japanese, I couldn't have understood because blood-curdling, inhuman screams smothered his words.

Lotte translated, her eyes reflecting my fear. Or maybe her own. "You are about to get a taste of what the next session will be like if you do not cooperate."

Behind the wall, a man hung by his wrists. Two Jap officers flanking him, swung thick bamboo poles taller than a man. As if playing a child's game with a toy on a string, they took enthusiastic turns bashing the man across his torso and legs like a human piñata. Laughter danced around their eyes with every vicious strike. The only participant not having fun was the unconscious, blood-splattered prisoner.

My head moved of its own accord, side to side, surveying the scene with horrified denial. When I shielded my eyes with the back of my hand, one of our guards snatched it away.

"You must watch," Lotte said. Her voice was emotionless, but I sensed steel-will was holding her feelings in check.

A Japanese onlooker, a side referee of sorts, called time, and the guards unhitched the rope, lowering the man to the ground.

Three buckets of water and several boot prods later, the man coughed and spluttered and tried to raise his head from the ground. If the referee had a whistle, he would have blown it to resume the game. They hoisted the man again, and I cringed at the accompanying laughter. How could these Japanese soldiers sleep at night? Was there a point where human decency would kick in?

My interrogating officer flicked his whip dismissively and passed a message to Lotte.

Once he'd stormed off, she pressed her hand to her heart and stared at the bloodied sand. "Today is for you to think carefully.

Unless you provide complete answers to tomorrow's questions, you will become the next battered rat."

Chapter Fifty-Three
Batavia, Java, 1942

Maharani nudged Sam with her dainty foot. "You are a madman."

Stretched out on the hot slate courtyard floor with one arm folded under his head, the other shading his eyes from the midday sun. Sam squinted to look. "I'm preparing myself."

"Can't you prepare inside, or at least find shade?"

"No. I need to bake my creations. I'll come inside once my confession is cooked to perfection."

"I was right the first time. You are a madman."

Sam closed his eyes again, but he could hear the smile in her voice. He lay still, rehearsing the answer to any number of questions the Japs could throw at him. He memorised the town of birth written on the fake passport and wove complicated tales of visits to countries visa-stamped within the pages.

When the sun dipped behind the mountains, he stripped off and jumped into the deepest part of the stream, submerging himself and thinking of his old friend Bert, who'd remained terrified of water the entire time at sea. Thanks to him, Sam had a backstory about being in the German navy during the First World War. Who'd have thought Bert's annoying repetition of German battleship names patrolling the Jutland Sea would prove useful?

By evening, Sam and Maharani were ready. Their eyes wandered over the glorious vista, then back on each other, then on the one track to the house. He kept his arm firmly about her waist and drew her close. She leaned in, touching her face to his, stealing his warmth while he borrowed her coolness. He found strength in the closest human exchange, and she seemed to have been doing the same.

Then they saw it. The potholed mountain road flickered the car's headlights like a Morse code warning: *The Japs are on their way.*

"Come," Sam said, "we'll walk out to greet them. Then the balance of power is ours."

He bowed Japanese style as they got out of the car, and grinned as he spoke in German. "I know how busy you are. Here is my passport."

They bowed in return and Maharani took on the role of interpreter during the short yet respectful exchange.

The soldier in charge added something else, sighing then looking away. The Japanese weren't so different. Sam detected regret.

"They have orders to take you in to headquarters," Maharani said.

He kissed her goodbye and hoisted himself into the back of the vehicle, open to the elements. The tyres stirred up a fog of dust on the dirt track and brought on a sneezing fit. "Dear God," Sam yelled, "I'll choke before they kill me."

Within minutes Mother Nature answered, squeezing the heavy sponge of cloud that had formed in the late afternoon. Rain doused the road and washed dust from his face.

Baptism complete, the rain stopped, and by the time they reached the Japanese headquarters, the invigorating breeze had dried Sam's clothes.

The guards ushered him inside, where he bowed to a Japanese officer squatting on a stool—an intricately engraved samurai sword across his knees. The officer stood to return the bow. He had prominent cheekbones and a stronger jawline than most. His teeth, although too large for his face, didn't mar his unusually compassionate expression. He was a non-threatening fella who didn't seem to fit in. Perhaps shocked at discovering what he'd signed up for.

"I am Satoru." He lowered himself to his seat and indicated for Sam to sit. "Your full name?" he asked in German. "Date of birth?"

Sam answered calmly, leaning back in the chair like little Louis John imitating Bessie in a good mood. Sam's smile was automatic, and the officer smiled back, his teeth taking up more of his face than before.

"Tell me about your family? Where did your grandparents live?"

Sam sighed with relief. He could be entirely honest without affecting his cover identity. "My father lost touch with his family before I was born, so I never met his parents. My grandmother on my mother's side once lived on a farm in Ortelsburg, but then moved into town, near the town hall, a block from the railway station."

Satoru wrote nothing down, but Sam was confident of this officer echoing this information back, word for word.

"Why didn't you enlist for the war?" Satoru asked.

"I served in the first war."

Sam told of the Imperial German Navy fighting in the Battle of Jutland, implying he served on the German side. He provided the name of a ship, the *Lützow*, telling the interrogator about the damage from heavy calibre shells and it taking in so much water they evacuated the crew before German torpedoes sank the boat for security reasons.

Satoru raised himself and signalled to a guard who came into the room to watch over Sam.

With Satoru in the adjacent room, Sam listened to static and indistinct German voices on a radio. He was right. The man had remembered it all.

"Toilet?" he mimed a peeing action.

Sam looked inside every room along the corridor, hoping his memory for details was as keen as the Japanese officer's. There were communication rooms, interview rooms, and offices with doors tightly shut.

He was back in his seat when Satoru returned.

"Your story checks out." He handed back the passport. "Keep it on your person."

"Thank you. Can I ask you a question?"

Satoru leaned forward with an intelligent, curious expression. "What do you wish to know?"

Sam pointed at the sword. "Are you a genuine Samurai?"

Satoru ran his hand over the tiger embossed scabbard. "Not me, but my katana came from ancestors of samurai lineage." He held up the sword. "It is a beautiful piece, unlike those mass-produced swords issued to soldiers who want others to believe they are Samurai but do not follow Bushido, the way of the warrior."

A guard behind Sam cleared his throat, and Satoru frowned at the guard's disrespect.

Studying Japanese expressions wasn't as different as expected. The myth of them being unfeeling monsters didn't match the emotions he saw unfurl across Satoru's face. This man gave back a sliver of faith in humanity, and Sam was in no hurry to leave. "How does one follow Bushido?"

"The principles are courage, integrity, benevolence, respect, honesty, honour, and loyalty. A difficult road to travel, but I try."

Sam held a fist to his chest. "I believe you. I feel it inside."

"I studied business and international languages before the Emperor called." For a moment he spoke to Sam as a man sharing the same language and not just the words.

"Thank you again," Sam said. "In another time and place we could talk for hours."

Satoru bowed in agreement, then made unblinking eye contact. "That may well be true, but even brothers can play on different teams. My instinct tells me there are things I'm yet to learn. Do not underestimate your opponent."

He turned to the guards, issuing an order. Return him to his dwelling.

Chapter Fifty-Four
Batavia, Java, 1942

Sam wasn't officially the leader, but with him in place, the resistance group was no longer a jigsaw with a missing piece. Emboldened by a set of simple rules, the members sought fresh opportunities to help the war effort.

At their previous meeting, Lieutenant Kriek pointed out the danger of regular gatherings. They adopted a haphazard rotating roster, because the consequences of being caught were unthinkable.

Sam suggested randomised routes, meeting halfway near a tea plantation belonging to Maharani's trusted friend, and leaving all but one car inside a disused shed. They parked the last vehicle in a patch of jungle a hundred yards from Maharani's.

Maharani still thought Sam mad, but she laughed when he stood by his theory of heat, helping him think. Out in the sun, he mentally prepared for that evening's meeting and celebrated the growth of the group during the past month. The central six now had purpose. Except for drinking rum, which Maharani provided from her late father's never-ending stash, they'd abandoned their old routines.

With sun-drenched eyelids imprinted in pink and yellow like splattered candle wax, Sam stole a moment to think of his family in

Australia, imagining them warmed by the same sun. He thought of the mountains and how much he'd love to share the jungle with his sons.

The jungle! He scrambled to his feet, realising something that should have hit him on the head like a hammer long ago. Satoru was astute. Wily enough to have him watched.

He raced down the hill to where Kajen was clearing the curved path through the heavy undergrowth to hide the car.

"Stop," Sam said. "Too obvious." He dragged piles of cut branches and dozens of palm fronds, arranging them to disguise the cleared entry. Kajen followed his lead.

Hot from exertion, Sam leaned against a shady tree. He needed to calm before he shared his concern. He was angry with himself. The group relied on him, and his lack of thought was putting them at risk.

Two cigarettes later, his heart slowed and ready to face Maharani, he stooped to stub out the butt. Wedged between a crack in the rock, a glimpse of red and white paper. Fresh. He glanced at Kajen, then retrieved the discarded cigarette packet. Sam flattened it between his hands—rain hadn't washed away the image. Japanese flags with rising suns.

Sam ran inside. Maharani wasn't in the great room, he called out while moving the low tables she'd arranged for the meeting. He dragged the chairs back to their usual position.

"Are you okay? What's going on?"

"We gotta cancel the meeting?" He clutched his hair.

"Too late, they're on the way." Her eyes darted around the room, then searched his face for answers.

"I found this in the clearing." His hand shook as he showed her the packet. "It should have been clear. You have rubber plantations, of course the Japs are watching. They can't afford to lose resources they started a flamin' war for."

"Oh, no." Maharani covered her mouth.

"It's unlikely we'd be ambushed this evening, but we can't risk it."

Maharani spun into frenzied action. Shoving the paper and pens she'd set out under a chair cushion, she reached for the bottle of rum, but it slipped and hit the stone floor, exploding into a broken glass moat around her feet.

She stared at Sam and froze.

For a tangled moment, he caught her confusion. But he forced himself to be the solid base she needed. Once he lifted her out of the mess and set her down, he was back in control.

"There are serious consequences in what we do," he said, pulling her close and stroking her hair. "we've been lucky so far, but I've known a few gamblers in my time and luck always runs out."

"I'll meet the others halfway." Her lip quivered, but her voice was strong.

"It's dangerous."

"We don't have a choice." Despite Maharani's tough talk, an eye twitch betrayed her fear. She straightened her shoulders and smiled, giving Sam a look he read as a fusion of bravery, empowerment and fear. An unfamiliar emotion no less powerful for being nameless.

"You're not going alone," he said.

Sam and Maharani intercepted the cars, turning them around with minimal discussion. Sam needed time to decide their next move.

They drove home by a lengthier path, and when they returned hours later Kajen was waiting a few hundred yards from the house. He signalled the all clear.

"Come on. Let's call it a night." Sam wrapped his arm around Maharani's waist, keeping her close as they walked inside.

"We caught them just in time…" her voice trailed off into a sigh and she sank onto the bed, burying her head into Sam's chest. "If it's safer for us to travel separately, I'll meet Tom alone in the village tomorrow."

He wanted to object, to protect her, to stay by her side, but perhaps she was right. She could be safer if not associated with him.

They curled up together, arms and legs entwined. Maharani broke the silence. "We should meet at Mrs Brouwer's next. What do you think?"

Sam wasn't so sure. "She's already paying her neighbours hush money."

Maharani shrugged. "Where then? Tom and the Lieutenant live in boarding houses, and Father Aart's church is in the busiest part of town. Since the war, people are praying night and day for peace."

"That's where we'll meet, then. The Church. The best place to hide is in plain sight."

"In that case, we will put on a show. The Japanese know us as lovers. So, lovers we'll be."

A week later, they walked boldly, hand-in-hand, along the main street, stopping outside the church for a long kiss. Sam spun her around and checked the surroundings before going in.

Father Aart looked up from the pulpit and beckoned them towards him, without showing recognition. "Welcome. If you're here for prayer, take a pew. If offering help in the working bee for the poor, follow me."

They trailed him down into the crypt. Father Aart had excelled. He'd set up an actual work station to divide rice, flour, sugar, and potatoes into family sized portions. Tom and the Lieutenant were already bagging rice.

Sam picked up a paper bag and watched how many scoops went in. "Mrs Brouwer not here yet?"

"We're staggering arrival times." Lieut Kriek winked smugly.

They were all learning on the run and doing the best they could. They'd all be rejoicing if the fallout of minor mistakes wasn't catastrophic.

Sam shook himself to rid an air of pessimism, then chuckled at a joke he hoped would lighten the mood. "What do you call a person who prefers white rice to brown rice?" He waited for Maharani to translate, then delivered the punchline. "A ricist."

Only Sam laughed.

He worried for a moment he'd offended them, but he realised this joke only worked for those who spoke English well.

Father Aart stapled Sam's bag and moved it to a box. "I've pleaded with my parishioners to volunteer their time or make donations. Most have opted to leave foodstuff near the pulpit. I don't expect them to provide more. Money is tight for everyone."

A bell rang from the church entrance, then it rang again within seconds.

Everyone but Father Aart stopped dead.

"That will be Mrs Brouwer," Aart said. "If I'm not inside the public part of the church, open and close the big door twice. I'll come out at the bell."

Once Mrs Brouwer was safely inside, Maharani pulled a bottle of rum from within her batik sarong. "Some traditions should stay. Do you have drinking glasses?" She raised her eyebrows at Father Aart, who promptly disappeared up the steps.

After pouring everyone a drink, and allowing time to savour the first glass, Sam screwed the lid back on and banged the bottle on the worktable in front of Father Aart. Their usual starting signal for the meeting. "Anything else, Father?"

"I need help delivering food to the women and children in the internment camps. I'm on a warning from the Japanese about dealing with anyone outside my congregation, so I can't approach the camps myself. I'm hardly a man who blends in."

Mrs Van Leeuwen shook in rum-amplified laughter.

Sam slid the bottle to Tom. "Here you go, mate. What ya been up to?"

"Not much to report. Having difficulty sourcing medical supplies. The Japs have cornered the black market. What we need, they need, too. Everything's in short supply and prices are rocketing. I've been storing it down here." He pointed to a corner cupboard, then refilled his glass before passing the rum across the table.

Sam opened his mouth, but Lieutenant Kriek drew his shoulders back and launched in. "I bring good news. A group of Dutch East Indies businessmen, who left the island before the invasion, will pay handsomely for information. They need intelligence of planned military moves and details of the Jap infrastructure. Their intention is to pass it on to someone in the ABDA command."

Maharani held up her hand. "ABDA? I don't know who or what that is."

"The American, British, Dutch and Australian central military coordination. The businessmen believe ABDA is planning to fly the relatively short distance from Australia and bomb vital targets. These men are willing to pay four-hundred guilders a week, for continuing what we're doing."

The collective intake of breath was audible. It was easy to live on a guilder a week, so forty guilders a week would have been generous. Four-hundred opened new doors.

The mood was electric. They had money. One obstacle out of their way. An obstacle the size of a mountain.

Maharani traced her finger around the lip of the rum bottle, she paused and looked at Sam. "I visited Japanese headquarters yesterday."

He dismissed his shock as vanity. They were people thrown together in a war, and they'd made no promises. Yet, it was a gut punch not to be trusted.

"Although the Japanese have a pre-war contract to buy rubber, they stopped paying last month. I feared they might take over the house, too, so I made a friendly visit to keep them onside. I've offered to donate the rubber to the war effort. They were taking it anyway."

She gulped her drink as if clearing a sour taste from her mouth. "Pity, we used the trucks to move supplies from A to B. Too much at stake. Drivers could talk to the Japs."

Her fingers brushed Sam's hand when he reached for the bottle, but she didn't make eye-contact when he spoke. "I've made a point of chatting to a few Japs through fences when the compounds dotted around Batavia are quiet. They're getting to know me because I bring alcohol. It whets their appetite and loosens the tongue. Getting useful info is slower than running through treacle, but there've been enough specks of gold to make it worthwhile. I have stuff that ABDA might find useful. I've sussed out where the bulk of them sleep, where the main control rooms are, the military equipment stored inside."

Mrs Brouwer didn't wait for the bottle. "I'm happier now. I was almost out of bribery funds. I'm turning away injured soldiers because it's too dangerous to take them all in. The more I have, the more the neighbours see. I've upped the hush money and although they're happy for now, Lord knows what would happen without monetary incentive."

Chapter Fifty-Five
Batavia, Java, 1942

In the far corner of the attic, away from curious eyes, Sam sighed at his rough sketches of Japanese barracks and munitions stores. They were less than satisfactory.

Frustrated, he left the cramped area where he compiled his 'intelligence' and edged across the ceiling to secrete the paperwork behind woven wall-lining at a junction of timbers. The action dredged up memories of hiding books from Solomon. Sam gripped the sloping roof beam, his knuckles white. Was that bastard still alive?

Although another time and place, his current problems weren't so different. If, on the day he'd left to enlist in the Great War, he'd lunged at his father with the poker in a blind rage, rather than walking away, there was a chance of missing Solomon and injuring his mother. The same could be said of the information he collated for ABDA. The Jap's positioned their facilities next to schools and hospitals. Providing sketchy details to an allied bomb-laden plane was risky. Killing the enemy required pinpoint accuracy.

At a tune of bamboo tapping on metal, Sam held his breath. With arrests increasing and danger in the air, he and Maharani had moved the wind chimes near the entrance to the attic, agreeing on two signals. Prolonged shaking warned of danger, in which case the plan was for Sam to remove two pre-loosened roof tiles and crawl onto the roof. Fooling the Japs with his German passport wasn't enough. He did not want Maharani implicated. Better if they weren't seen together.

Double shakes with an abrupt break in-between. The signal to come down.

Out in the courtyard, he found Maharani standing with two young, athletic Malay men astride bicycles.

"Captain," she called, waving him over. "Angkasa sent her cousins to help the cause. I've questioned them thoroughly and am convinced of their intentions."

"Pleased to meet you." Sam held out his hand.

The first young man said, "Yudo." But when he turned to introduce the other, Sam held a finger to his lips.

"No. No names. *Tidak ada nama.*" He tried sign language, then pleaded with Maharani, "Please translate. I have too few words."

She laughed lightly. "But you were doing so well."

She passed on Sam's message and the youths nodded.

Sam rang Yudo's bicycle bell. "Did they ride all the way up the steep mountain?"

"Yes," Maharani replied. "Anger is a great source of energy."

"Maybe we can harness it for our cause?" Sam tried to communicate. "*Mengapa. Anda. Marah?* Why. You. Angry?"

The men and Maharani responded, but the braiding of three voices was impossible to untangle. Sam raised his eyebrows imploringly. Then he cast his eyes around the jungle, across the stream and down the track. "Quickly. Come into the house."

Inside, Maharani explained. "The Japanese lured them from the rice paddies with promises of new skills and higher wages. Instead, they were press-ganged into heavy manual labour, chained and fed only enough to maintain their strength. They stole bicycles and escaped. Now they cannot return to their families without endangering them."

"Can you give me a minute? I've rushed too many decisions." Sam walked in circles, clasped hands squeezing the back of his neck.

The resistance group could use help distributing food to internment camps. But that would put these young blokes in danger. What if these boys were his own? He pictured Cyril, not much younger, haggling with prisoners over a camp fence, pretending to trade food for useless memorabilia. Would he send his own sons to do this? Maybe not. But, if he sent these youths away without purpose or money, what would their future be?

Sam joined them at the table. "We will give you enough money to travel east, away from the occupied areas, and provide food until you find safe work."

The boys shook their heads when Maharani told them, looking at their feet and sneaking shy looks at Sam while they whispered.

"They want to know why *you* haven't taken the money and disappeared?" She asked.

Sam was hit by their words. "We need to discuss this alone. We'll decide while they rest."

Sam hid the bicycles while Maharani settled them with sheets and pillows in the attic.

"Poor things look buggered." Sam's shoulders drooped with the weight of a decision they'd yet to make.

"What do you think?" she asked.

"If we send them away, they'll try to help someone else. It could be a trap. End up in greater danger. But if they help, they'll need somewhere to stay. We're already under surveillance."

"There's an abandoned shed at the tea plantation where the group left their cars."

"Let's check it out." Sam said.

Maharani crept into the attic and whispered to the men, returning with her car keys.

When Sam climbed into the passenger seat of Maharani's car, she shrugged. "You look worried."

"I am."

She kept her eyes on the winding track.

"This is an enormous responsibility. Risking my own life, well, that's okay..." Sam's voice drifted off.

"These are not naïve young men. They've seen what the Nippon army is capable of and believe there's no chance of freeing Javanese people by looking the other way."

The turnoff into the plantation was overgrown with thigh-high weeds. No one had driven to the shed for weeks. Sam got out and walked along each side of the track, hunching over to check for signs of unwanted visitors. "Nothing. Not a cigarette butt to be found."

He turned three-hundred and sixty degrees, scanning the surrounding empty fields and encroaching jungle. "Why aren't your friends farming this land?"

"The tea bushes developed a blistering fungus, so they burned the plants to prevent spreading. Replanting now would be safe, but until people know what's happening with the Japanese, nobody will invest."

She unbolted the shed's double gates, and they each dragged one, pegging them open with rocks.

The timber lining planks, though mouldy, appeared waterproof. The concrete floor, with seashell aggregate, had cracked in several places, weeds taking foothold despite the lack of rain. Tjik tjak lizard droppings carpeting the floor appeared untrodden.

Sam took a deep breath. "This place is out of the way. Angkasa's cousins will be safer here than in the attic."

Two days later, Maharani ferried the youths to the safe house. Bicycles, taken apart, were stored on the comfortable back seat while, one by one, the young men curled up in the hard metal boot away from prying eyes.

Sam waited at the plantation; his makeshift toolbox ready to reassemble the bikes. He showed how to bend one spoke on each front wheel inward, almost touching the fork.

"Inwards," Sam yelled, reminding one youth who was bending it the wrong way. Both stopped and looked wide eyed.

Maharani shot Sam a look of disapproval, then fussed about the boys like a hen with chicks.

Sam took a drag on his cigarette. Yelling at people without

names was uncivilised. They at least needed nicknames. Except these boys were cousins, same age, almost the same height, and too alike for him to pick distinguishing features. He could have called a tall one, 'Stretch', but there was only an inch between them. Both barefaced, not a 'Mo' to be seen. He exhaled, his shoulders dropping in a rueful slouch.

As he dug a hole to bury his cigarette butt, a bewdy of an idea struck him. He could name them *Satu and Dua*. One and two. Sam opened his mouth to share his brainwave, but slammed it shut. The allies had joined the war to stop Hitler dehumanising people. The evil man had assigned numbers to the Jews, tattooing their forearms, stealing their names, and Sam had been about to do the same.

Maharani threaded her arm through the crook of his elbow, eyes brimming with concern. "Are you ill?"

"No. Just a grumbling of guilt. I want to call these fellas by their rightful names, but it's too dangerous."

"The Aussies are famous for giving nicknames. If anyone can do it, you can." She looked at Sam with such expectation, he delivered the previously discounted names with finger clicks. "Stretch and Mo."

"Stretch and Mo," she repeated with a laugh.

She ruffled each young man's hair in a casual naming ceremony, explaining in Indonesian these alternative names were to protect them.

Sam studied their faces to remember who was who. When the war was over, he would introduce himself by his real name and he'd call these men by theirs.

"Back to business, gang." He patted an area of low dry grass and the four of them crouched in a circle. He pointed to crosses on a hand-drawn map.

Maharani explained what Sam was saying. "From the air, bombers can discriminate between the church, the blown-up bridge, and the swimming pool, but not between the three similarly sized buildings between the landmarks. This one is our target; the others are a hospital and a school. The Japanese have barricaded the roads to motor vehicles, so we can't measure distances using the car's odometer, so we're making our own."

On each bike's front fork, Sam attached a bent playing card using a peg lashed with string. "Each click you hear as you ride will be the length of your wheel rotation."

Sam got up to demonstrate, and the young men fell about with laughter as he wobbled slowly down the track, counting each click, "*Satu, dua, tiga, empat, lima, enam, tujuh, delapan, sembilan, sepuluh.*" At ten clicks he planted both feet, stopping without sliding, and wrapped a rubber band from his wrist around the handle bar.

After several trials, he handed back the bike. "We will finesse this. Stopping every ten clicks is too often, but we must keep track of the count."

Stretch and Mo took turns riding from the line in the sand, stopping at increments of ten, then fifty clicks.

Maharani and Sam watched from the side as they measured their tracks with a cloth measuring tape. The hefty burden of worry lifted from their shoulders as they worked and laughed amongst themselves. Wearing smiles, they looked less like men and more like boys.

Mo tried to get Maharani's attention without using her name, then huddled with his cousin before whispering in her ear.

The warmth of her smile embraced Sam's soul. "They say it's only fair we have nicknames, too. They've asked permission to call us Ibu and Ayah. Mother and Father."

Maharani slipped her hand into Sam's, and he closed his eyes.

There, in the middle of a tea plantation in Java, with the young men looking to him for guidance and protection; and the tender touch of a woman, Sam felt intimacy deeper than romantic love.

Sam had been called several things in his life—a son, brother, husband, reluctant father, fruit-seller, hustler, even a criminal, but never a role-model. Yet, in this god-forsaken place, up for grabs by the Javanese jungle, he felt what Bob had preached in his sermon. His unique talents were finally coming through. He could make a difference. He was making a difference in these boys' lives. He would care for them like family.

"What is the Malay word for family?" he asked.

"*Keluarga.*"

Sam prayed for both this *keluarga* and his *keluarga* at home. He wished he could pray for the safety of all the sons and daughters in the world, but that wouldn't work. Every soldier fighting in the wars was someone's child.

Chapter Fifty-Six
Batavia, Java, 1942

A stone's throw from the women and children's internment camp, an empty playground beckoned like a toffee-apple dangling from a string. A tease for the poor children who whined and reached small hands through the barbed wire gaps. Even harder for the mothers who carried tenfold the sadness and guilt of their offspring.

Sam and Maharani rehearsed the POW food handover with the Malay boys. Unless it appeared like black market trade, they'd arouse suspicion. Trading was discouraged, but readily ignored when a sweetener was offered to the guards.

Sam arrived first and sat on a park bench pretending to read a Dutch newspaper, which he didn't understand. Several small grey birds with white priest collars and pink beaks sang a whistle-stop sermon that made as much sense as the newspaper. Sam recalled times when his thirst for adventure had not been life or death.

When his old mate Sparra offered him dodgy deals, there was the choice to walk away. 'No questions. No trouble,' Sam whispered under his breath. Good advice then, great advice now.

To the letter of the plan, Maharani and the boys sauntered down the street carrying baskets of food, appearing to scout out places to set up trade. As they passed a Japanese guard, Mo said something Sam couldn't hear, but Maharani swiped the back of his head in a show of a mother keeping unruly sons in line.

Mo and Stretch rattled the fence next to POW women cooking on an open fire, while Maharani, playing her role as distractor, headed for the Japanese guard. She complained loudly of her sons, of her lot in life. She offered the guard a packet of sweets, and it shocked Sam when he tipped them into his mouth without question.

He shook his head in disbelief. ABDA was planning bombs when they could airdrop bags of poisoned fruit gums. They wouldn't even need to be poisonous. A sedative would do the job.

A hand signal from Stretch got Sam's attention, and he watched Maharani join the boys, then whisper discreetly to a woman who'd approached the fence. Although Sam couldn't hear, he knew what she was saying. They'd practised it many times. The women would be told to bring useless trinkets to the fence for trade. These would be pushed back under the fence so they could trade repeatedly. A never-ending currency for supplementing food.

The guard, who'd been busy eating, finally paid attention to the job. He grabbed his bayonet and hurried over.

This could go two ways. The guard could demand payment to look away, or use his weapon. Sam yelled at the birds, sweeping them into the air with his newspaper and singing in German like a crazy man. His distraction was enough for his *keluarga* to step back from the fence.

Sam reached inside his inner pocket for the concealed knife. He stood and steeled himself to use it, even though the thought made him ill. Like most soldiers, he'd killed in war, but there's a big difference between shooting long-range at human sized shapes, and grabbing a man by the hair, forcing a blade into his throat, and seeing the whites of his dying eyes.

Maharani twirled and laughed, reaching into her basket for one of her father's finest bottles of rum. Her composure, startling. The guard smiled and rested his bayonet against his leg, eager for the gift.

Sam sat and sighed so loudly, he startled the birds who'd been watching the goings on. He couldn't bloody blame them. It was quite a show.

They weren't the only audience. A man, possibly Chinese-Indonesian, watched from further down the street. Something about his manner, the way his feet were ready to pedal and his hands gripped his bicycle, set Sam's gut to high alert.

He watched Bicycle Man watching Maharani, and as if he knew he was under surveillance, the man turned to look at Sam.

Sam never forgot a face. This face belonged to a soldier from the Orcades; the ship which had transported him and the Aussie soldiers to Java. He'd passed him a few times walking on deck.

"Guten tag," Sam called, waving hello.

Bicycle Man rode slowly towards Sam, but his muscles were coiled—wild animal like—ready to escape or attack.

"Orcades," Sam said when he was close enough to speak English.

Bicycle Man stared open-mouthed. "I not know you." He stuttered in a fake Malay accent.

"We were on the ship together," Sam whispered, keeping one eye on the guard chatting to Maharani. "I recognise you."

Sam watched Maharani and the boys pack up and waited until they'd walked away before gesturing for Bicycle Man to meet at the far end of the park.

He followed Sam, laying his bike on the grass. They both leaned over a concrete bore.

"I no know what you talk about." He continued the broken English act.

Sam laughed. "Fake accents are difficult to sustain under stress."

He laughed and extended his hand. "Sapper Lum. Ronald. What do you want from me?"

"Nothing." Sam offered a handful of guilders. "Take these. They'll help you get by."

Lum needed no further prompting. "Thanks. I've been in the plantations passing as Chindo. Running out of money."

"Cigarette?" Sam tapped two out of the packet and gave one to Lum.

Lum told Sam of the battle he'd seen and how the other soldiers had turned themselves in. He could talk the leg off a bloomin' chair. There were men he thought Sam might know, but used names like Goathead. He talked about places back in Australia and told of his gorgeous fiancée who he bloody well hoped didn't think he was dead.

Sam could listen to the reassuring twang of the Australian accent forever.

But when Lum said he'd worked as a draftsman before the war, Sam's ear pricked with interest.

"I've drawn a few maps," Sam said. "They aren't as accurate as I need. I've got fairly good measurements, but I need a professional drafting job. You up for it?"

"Maps of what?" Lum asked.

Sam rubbed his throat and did a Sparra, "No questions. No troubles."

Chapter Fifty-Seven
Batavia, Java, 1942

Sam was more than impressed with the precision of Lum's drawings. Lieut Kriek, who barely smiled, had beamed at the meticulously labelled plans—all drafted in perfect scale.

Their last exchange included detailed diagrams of The Hotel de Indes, which the Japs commandeered for officer accommodation. Sam's *keluarga* boys had taken turns loitering on street corners, recording numbers of officer comings and goings, while Sam got ready to cause a distraction should things take a bad turn.

Kriek's business associates paid handsomely and passed the plan showing exits and frequently used routes to a well-compensated go-between with connections to ABDA command.

Today's meeting with Lum included drawings of the armoury. Sam checked his watch. Delivery hand-over was planned for half an hour ago, yet Sam was three smokes down and no sign of Lum.

One more ciggy and Sam would have to leave. His hand trembled at the thought of any accomplices being caught.

He'd barely lit up when Lum appeared, shaking his head. "Had to circle the bloody block waiting for a pair of mangy watchdogs to disappear."

At the mention of watchdogs, Sam's eyebrow shot up like a red flag.

Lum was quick to quell Sam's concern. "Just checking documents. Not much of a worry for me." He angled his head like a pinup girl. "Face like mine blends in. You, on the other hand, stand out like a sore bloody thumb."

Sam shrugged. "I'll be right, mate."

Lum checked they were alone and parked behind the closest tree, before deftly kicking the crossbar of his bike and dislodging the end which slotted into the seat post. He extracted a roll of papers—his latest assignment.

Without inspecting them, Sam wrapped them with his newspaper and handed over payment. "Meet you in two days with the next instructions. Same time, behind the hospital. Remember, more than an hour late—take off."

If he and Lum hadn't been spying in the middle of a Jap occupied zone, Sam would have bought him a beer and bragged about his fake passport. He'd have spun a fantastical yarn interspersed with German phrases. After a bit of fooling around he'd have spat out a corny punch line. But with increased surveillance, fun was a dangerous luxury.

Wary of the watchdogs, Sam took a circuitous path to his appointment with Kriek. The meeting place, a bare plinth, had once displayed larger-than-life iron statues. Along with decorative metal on landmark buildings, the statues had been removed, The Japs needed iron more than art.

Despite cutting the Lum meeting short, Sam hadn't made up the time, and Kriek was waiting. From a hundred yards away, Sam saw Kriek flicking his fingers, burning off nervous energy.

When Kriek heard the whistled signal, he stood straighter, yet relaxed.

Without so much as a nod, the men checked they weren't being followed and took separate routes to the safe café. At the very back table, partially hidden behind a carved wooden screen, Kriek inspected the documents.

Between sips of tea, he said, "More impressive than the last lot."

He could not contain his smile. "This information is enough to set the wheels rolling." He lowered his voice. "Soon there'll be planes with bombs. On the ground we'll set the POWs free."

Sam's insides vibrated with excitement and he stifled a throaty laugh as Kriek scrambled to his feet, nodded a serious goodbye, and patted his jacket over the inner pocket concealing the papers.

"When will you know more?" Sam whispered.

"This afternoon. I'll leave a message in the hymnbook on the pulpit."

Sam continued to drink his tea. "Don't let down your guard. This is the time for our group to lie low.'

With hours to kill until Maharani collected him, Sam walked the city's back streets, feet barely touching the ground. He imagined the Japanese flags gone, and the buildings restored to their former glory. It was a bloody good feeling to have played a part.

Such favourable news would be difficult to keep from Maharani, but group rules were set for safety. Better to wait until Kriek got confirmation.

He raced eagerly into her car. His first kiss delivered with a grin. The second fiercely passionate. She threw him a quizzical smile at an attempted third kiss. "We'd better get home."

He shrugged playfully and whistled a tune.

Maharani glanced at Sam several times as she drove. "Something big has happened. I can feel it."

Compared to the trip down the mountain, the world seemed to have exploded with unfurling flowers, newly born leaves, and uplifting scents carried on whispers of breeze.

Maharani looked between Sam and the road, touching his forehead when they were almost home. "No fever. Not delirium, just bottled-up happiness. I hope you don't explode."

"That's why I'm whistling. A release valve on a kettle."

"Perhaps, to release the tension you could nod and let me know if I'm on the right track."

Sam affectionately squeezed her arm. "You're not usually impatient."

"I've been waiting a long time for good news. I'm guessing from your manner that we're closer to winning the war?"

He nodded like a carnival toy.

"Really?" She sighed. "After I heard about the dissolution of ABDA command, I thought we were stuck with Japanese rule."

Sam's smile evaporated. "Where'd you hear that? Kriek's contacts deal directly with the command."

"Perhaps he's using an old acronym for a new organisation." Maharani didn't sound convinced.

"He definitely said ABDA. He said it again today. Turn around. We'll wait for Kriek at the church."

In tandem with the depressed mood, grey clouds blemished the sky. Sam fixed his eyes on the road and concentrated on slowing his breath. There had to be a mix-up. That was the only feasible explanation. Kriek's contacts had praised their resistance effort. Yet, in the time Sam had known her, Maharani had never been wrong.

He crossed his fingers, hoping this was a first.

Inside the Lutheran church, Father Aart was consoling a young parishioner.

To give them privacy, Sam and Maharani sat in a pew near the back, while the woman's toddler ran up and down the length of every pew.

The child broke the tension, and Maharani smiled at Sam, then rested her head against his shoulder to watch the boy skidding along the pew in front of them, singing a nonsensical song. Sam decided it was more bawdy rugby ballad than hymn. He would normally have laughed out loud, but the melody barely dented the hollow in his chest.

When the lad clambered up the seat rails and spread his arms to fly, Sam leapt sideways to catch him.

Rescuing the child reminded Sam why he was fighting. So children could have trust. To make a better life for his sons. Rather than inheriting the world, fathers are tasked with handing it to their children in a better state.

The woman thanked Father Aart and said goodbye, apologetically retrieving her son.

"Goodbye, little one." Maharani waved. "Thank you for entertaining us." She whispered to Sam, "I needed it."

Father Aart beckoned. "Come downstairs. Quickly." His voice carried an ill-omen.

Sam clasped Maharani's hand firmly and the tiny spark of optimism he'd borrowed from the child, dwindled with every step.

The crypt stairs were inadequately lit, a bare light bulb losing its fight against the dark. The worktable still showed signs of food repackaging.

When Father Aart switched on a standard lamp, Tom Powell materialised from a shadowy corner.

"Mrs Brouwer's been taken in for questioning."

Sam portrayed bravado he did not feel. With his shoulders back and a measured voice, he took charge. "Tom, tell us the facts. When did this happen? How do you know? Talk us through it slowly."

Tom took a deep breath. "She was treating a wounded soldier and contacted me for medical supplies." He slumped and covered his face with his hands. An extended silence passed before he lifted his head. "I knocked on her door this morning, and when she didn't answer I waited in her garden. A neighbour whistled over the wall and beckoned me. Told me I was wasting my time. Mrs Brouwer was gone. The Japs had come for her and other occupants during the night. The neighbours were woken by shouting."

"Did the neighbour say why?" Sam asked.

"No. He passed on the message, then hurried back into his house. I came straight here."

Sam hoped one of the other three would speak. No ABDA. Mrs Van Leeuwen taken in. He was defeated, a frightened boy, staring at a cane on the back of a door, preparing for the horrific beating which was coming.

The church doorbell rang. Once. Twice.

Father Aart tramped upstairs and Tom switched off the light.

Sam thought the light should stay on, but didn't have the strength to argue. If the Japanese came now, there'd be no pretending to package food for the poor while huddled in the dark. He wrapped his arm around Maharani's waist, pressed his cheek against hers, and buried his face in her silky hair.

"It's okay," Father Aart called down. "Lieutenant Kriek has news."

The bare bulb highlighted Kriek's ghostly expression, dark circles that weren't there earlier in the day, a distraught cast to his eyes.

"I'm sorry to report that our intelligence collecting is for naught. My contacts have severed all ties. Seems the chap at the end of the communication chain was desperate to keep the money, even though he'd run out of options to pass it on. Apparently, after finding ABDA defunct, he'd offered our intel to each allied country in turn. They provided the same response. Only fools accept information from unapproved sources without multiple checks and cross-references. Since they have none of their own operatives in the zone, they can't act. At least not in the foreseeable future."

Sam's skin crawled, and he scraped his back against the chair, despite knowing the sensation was fear. "We have bad news, too. Father, do you mind explaining?"

As Father Aart described Mrs Brouwer's disappearance to Kriek, a moan escaped. "After the first meeting we had, where Captain John drew up the hexagonal cell formation and joked about us being the concealed ones. Well, Mrs Brouwer took the chart home. She wrote her name in one of the cells while we were in the car. I warned her to destroy it, but she insisted she wasn't doing anything wrong. If anyone searched her house, she said, they already knew her name."

Tom patted the Lieutenant's arm reassuringly. "She probably burned it. If not, she's right, it was only one name on a silly piece of paper."

Father Aart nodded in agreement. "It was scribble."

Sam and Maharani exchanged looks. Then she spoke. "If the Japanese have found it, they know she wasn't working alone. They'll look for a central group of six and all the offshoot cells."

Sam rose slowly from the chair. "Gentleman, Lady. Many thanks for your help. Unfortunately, this must be the last time we meet." The others whispered amongst themselves, but Sam couldn't hear them. The alarm bells in his head drowned out their voices.

Chapter Fifty-Eight
Batavia, Java, 1942

The following morning, Sam and Maharani clung in a melancholy dance, fear heightening every touch. Neither said a word. Not wanting to break the spell, the pretence of paradise.

But reality closed in. They listened to tuneless songs, shared tasteless food, then gave up to clear the house of everything connected to Sam. By that afternoon, they'd wiped every trace of their sweet liaison.

"It's as if we never were," Maharani whispered through tears.

"It exists in here." He brought her hand to his heart.

Sam fanned a stash of guilders across the table. "I was saving these for after the war." His voice quavered. "Take the money to the keluarga boys. Tell them it is from Ibu and Ayah to help with the next leg of their journey. They would do best to leave today, to ride far from here and find rural work away from Japanese-occupied towns."

She touched his lips, then rose from her chair. "Your other contacts?"

Sam massaged his forehead. Lum and the others knew to

skedaddle if anything happened. "We made a contingency plan. They'll take off."

With Maharani gone to the boys, it was easier for Sam to pull his emotions into line. Wanting none of the sun's misleading warmth, he stripped off and waded into the deepest part of the stream, whirlpools swirling about his legs; chilling him inside and out.

With his head underwater, he imagined himself hiding beneath his bed, away from his father, reading The Merry Adventures of Robin Hood.

He remembered most of the words on that magical first page. *IN MERRY ENGLAND in the time of old, when good King Henry the Second ruled the land, there lived within the green glades of Sherwood Forest, near Nottingham Town, a famous outlaw whose name was Robin Hood.*

Sam surfaced and hauled himself over a boulder, pressing his cheek against the smooth, hot surface. The rock reminded him of the smallness of his life, it—like all the other rocks around him—had formed over five hundred million years before. Sam's time on earth was but a speck.

He wanted to be like Robin Hood, and in some ways he'd succeeded. He'd moved money from the rich to the poor and he'd been an outlaw much of his life. He thought of Cecelia and Bessie, but Maharani was his Maid Marion.

With an unexpected smile, he rewrote the words.

IN BUSTLING West Java in the time of war, when Japanese tyrants tried to steal the land, there lived within the mountainous green jungles near Batavia Town, a little-known outlaw whose names were Sam Solonsch, John Douglas and Hermann Schmidt.

When Maharani returned, Sam was waiting in the living room, a sarong wrapped around his waist, rum bottle in hand. "One last drink?"

"One last everything." She threw her arms around his shoulders, her lips onto his.

The saltiness of tears mingled with her sweet mouth and Sam carried her to bed.

They made love with careful brushstrokes and splendid colours. Two artists painting a shared masterpiece on skin.

Maharani lifted herself on her elbows and whispered. "Only now, am I brave enough to ask a question." She pressed her finger to his lips. "I'm not sure I want this answered, but a man like you must have a wife and family waiting in Australia?"

Sam wiped the tears streaming over her cheeks. "I'm sorry for not telling you."

She wept as she continued. "Ask your wife to forgive me. I've been selfish. I needed you and I needed your support, but I didn't need to take you to my bed. That's something I wanted." She slipped from the bed to the floor, her body shaking in a sob.

"Come back." Sam took her hand. "I want to hold you. You needn't feel bad. The guilt is all mine. I knew I was married, you only suspected. I didn't tell you because I needed and wanted you, too."

"Then you must never tell your wife." She closed her eyes and lay vulnerable, naked on the floor.

Sam's heart ached—not with an understanding of her pain—he'd learned humans could only guess such things. He couldn't take back the hurt he'd caused, but he owed Maharani an explanation. "My wife is called Bessie, and I will tell her and my sons about the beautiful, brave woman who saved me. I don't think Bessie will ask about us being lovers, but if she does, I won't deny it. I will tell her I loved you."

He reached down and pulled her back to bed. She curled up in front of Sam and they nested like spoons until first light.

Sam gulped at the sight of her sleeping face and took a sharp breath at the thought of what he must ask her to do.

"Wake up, my love."

She opened, then closed her eyes quickly.

"Maharani. You are brave, but this might test you. Go to the Japanese building where I was asked to show my passport. Request a meeting with Satoru. Tell him I mentioned Satoru by name. Break down as if battling with what you are about to do.".

"Tears will come easily enough," she said. "Words might not."

"Tell him I'm your lover, but you recently discovered my deceit. I'm an Australian soldier and it pains you, but you feel you have no choice other than turning me in. Tell Satoru you plied me with alcohol and left me to sleep it off."

She blinked back tears. "Why can't you just run away?"

He brushed her cheek with his fingers, then wiped the tears from his own eyes. "The Japanese have seen us together. This is the safest option. You must distance yourself. Set yourself up in case names are revealed."

"What will the Japanese do to you?"

"They'll put me in a POW camp." He kissed the top of her head. "But you, my Maid Marion, will be safe."

Chapter Fifty-Nine
Batavia, Java, 1942

Kajen sprinted into the bedroom, short of breath but forcing words. "Nipponese. *Jalan*. Road."

"Go. Go. *Pergi*." Sam pushed Kajen, hurrying him through the back of the house. "Jungle. *Hutan. Pergi*."

When Kajen opened his mouth to speak, Sam pushed him harder, looking over his shoulder for the enemy. "Go."

As Kajen fled, Sam clutched his sides, trying to catch his breath. He and Maharani had forgotten about her worker. Sam had waited, feigning sleep and ready to feign surprise, expecting to be dragged out of bed without warning.

Now, the script needed a quick rewrite.

Lifting his arms high above his head, he walked through the courtyard, his bare feet matching the splat-splat of soldiers' boots on slate as they approached.

Sam registered their shock to find him waiting, arms in surrender, dressed in nothing but a knotted loin cloth.

"Hermann Schmidt?" One asked.

Sam nodded.

A guard brought down the butt of his rifle on Sam's bare foot, crushing the flesh of his big toe, splitting his nail like a crab's claw smashed by a hammer. He screamed, eyes watering, but held out his wrists for the shackles.

The car bounced over pot-holes, and without steadying hands, his shoulder bashed against the back of the vehicle. His toe screamed, and his shoulder groaned, but the voice in his head stilled. The thing Sam feared most had begun, and his mind stopped the useless self-bargaining and doubt. He was in a place of painful peace.

When the guards hauled Sam along the Japanese flag lined path of the *Kempeitai*, then into the interrogation chair, Satoru clucked his tongue and closed his eyes. This Japanese man, whom Sam respected and with whom he'd imagined a shared understanding, sat still for some time. Satoru moved his hands slowly in front of his chest, in and out as he inhaled and exhaled with purpose.

Sam matched the rhythm of his breath, and the synchronicity gave him a clearer sense of what he should say.

His confession must have truth at its core.

Satoru opened his eyes but stared, glassy-eyed. "A woman came to see me. Her account does not match the one you provided."

Sam nodded. "I had selfish reasons for not telling the whole truth. One of them was losing the love of a woman."

"Go on." Satoru's inscrutable expression gave nothing away.

Sam was so used to reading other people's reactions and using them as a map, he found this nothingness a challenge. He was a lost man calling for help into a void that didn't return an echo.

"I'm disorientated. I've reinvented myself and now I'm not sure who I am or where I fit." Sam stuck to facts, not only because it was the best option, but he didn't wish to insult Satoru. "I took on the name John Douglas to join the Australian army because my German-sounding name would have stood out. I'm a German speaking Jew, so I would never ever fight under Hitler or any leader who believed whole groups of people were inferior."

There it was, a rapid blink, but in that flicker, Sam saw a crack in Satoru's veneer. Satoru understood. More than a technical knowing, a visceral response.

Sam kept talking, desperate to break through.

"What I shared about my grandmother in Ortelsburg, was true.

What I didn't say was I grew up Jewish and have spent much of my life hiding my parentage and religion. Even from my wife." A sob escaped, and Sam gulped. It wasn't a prop: it was an overwhelming wave of grief in memory of poor Cecelia.

"I admit to being inferior, but not because of my ancestry or beliefs. My flaws are of my own making."

Satoru leaned forward, arms on the desk. He understood.

The commonality between these men became clear. Satoru didn't fit in with the rest. From the first meeting when the guard had sneered at Satoru owning an ancestral sword. His face shape: the stronger jawline, the higher cheekbones. This man wasn't purely Japanese. Probably part Korean. Satoru knew what it felt like to be on the inside, yet feel on the outside.

Sam wanted to keep talking, not to deceive, but to forge a bond with this man who represented the enemy. What else in this world is more valuable than a human connection, a shared experience?

"How did you end up with the woman?"

"When the Nippon army caught our men by surprise, a few of us fled into the jungle. Not to run away, but because fighting face-to-face in that place was futile. We planned to circle back and take your men by surprise, but none of us reckoned on the jungle being another foe. It swallowed me whole and when it spat me out, I was alone and completely lost."

Satoru inhaled deeply through his nose, but didn't say a word. Sam continued. "I walked for days, trying to find my way back while staying unseen. I stole clothes off a washing line and got rid of my uniform. Then I saw Maharani. A beautiful woman, struggling to fix broken tiles on her roof. She looked so helpless in the rain. I offered my help."

"I've heard enough." Satoru stood and bowed.

Sam did the same.

"I would prefer to send you straight into a POW camp with your contemporaries, but that isn't procedure and unlike you, I follow rules. The Imperial Japanese Army requires information checks. What is said during passive questioning rarely matches what is said under duress."

Sam harrumphed. "Is it like the ancient Romans, where slaves' testimonies were only considered truthful when given during torture?"

Satoru smiled. Not the smile of someone who found torture amusing, but a fondness for his prisoner.

He escorted Sam through the building and asked, "Do you know where we are headed?"

"The torture yards?"

"Yes."

They sat together on the waiting bench. Sam imagined the audience of the Colosseum bloodthirsty for the release of lions. "Can I jump the queue? I hate waiting." Sam laughed, not because it was a joke, but because it was true.

"I'm afraid not. Watching others is the psychological part of your torture."

"Like an appetiser at a restaurant?"

"If you will."

Two guards ordered a British soldier to strip out of his uniform. He protected his genitals with his hands. One guard struck his head and shoulders with a baton, then seized his arms, tying his hands behind his back. The other Jap bashed him with a bamboo stick until he fell to the floor. Then he stomped on the prisoner's testicles until they swelled like bizarre fruit.

Sam instinctively brought his knees together and Satoru, who until this point had been a statue with a chiselled chin, did the same. Without moving his head, he said, "I won't demand this treatment for you."

"Good." He thought of Bessie and how they both preferred other people's meals. "This isn't the beating I would have chosen from the menu."

Satoru turned to Sam, a half-smile playing on his lips. "What sort of beating would you prefer?"

"A brow beating."

"I don't understand?"

"In English it means to intimidate with a mean look, maybe some abusive words."

"English is a complex language." Satoru braced his shoulders and watched the guards remove the maimed prisoner.

"Trust me on this," Sam whispered. "If you and I were in an Aussie pub drinking beers, that joke would have got a right laugh."

The guards called John Douglas, and Sam stood immediately, bowing to Satoru.

He was escorted to the arena and raised by the wrists on the gallows.

Nothing happened until Satoru gave the orders.

A tall Japanese guard wearing a white shirt, which seemed a poor choice for persecution, beat him across the buttocks, lower back and legs until Satoru ordered an interrogation break.

After two sets of beatings and repeats of the same questions Sam had already answered, the white-shirted guard tripped over his beating stick, and Sam started to laugh. He couldn't stop. The third beating was frenzied, and he slipped into the disassociation he'd learned to shelter his mind from his father's beatings. Between strikes, he saw the faces of everyone he loved. He began a stream of regret but when he questioned his past actions, he heard Sparra say, 'No questions, no trouble' and for once he did as he was told.

He watched the guard's white shirt layering with splatters of blood until there only red.

He was inside the building when he regained consciousness, Satoru standing over him. "Laughing almost cost you your life. Instead of going to one of the work camps, you'll now be sent to the Hospital Camp in Bandoeng. Hospital is an unfortunate word choice. There is little in the way of medical care, but they will not expect you to clear the jungle or build roads until you recover."

Chapter Sixty
POW Hospital Camp and Tjipinang Prison, Batavia, 1943

The interrogation ended and my gut knew they'd decided John's punishment. I closed my eyes and pictured the road from Batavia back to the Hospital Camp. My memory showed lumpy mountains and sloping plains smeared with the same homogeneous green. But when the guards took me back to camp to collect my things, I was determined to take on John's trait of viewing the world more eagle-eyed, and the green showed its true colours—mixed shades of yellow-green, black-green, brown and even blue. I hoped, one day, to develop his gift for seeing people in all their different, wonderful hues.

I dragged myself inside the POW hut, swallowing the razorblade sharpness of guilt and helplessness. Although I'd done exactly as John instructed, I wanted this to end differently.

He was at the window, his usual spot, but during my ten-day absence, where I'd repeated his stories and signed his death warrant, he'd withered like a plant deprived of water. He looked up and smiled, reaching for my hands. Tears pricked my eyes as I embraced him like a child clinging to his father.

"Thank you, Kid," he said.

Remorse wrapped cruel fingers around my throat until I gasped to breathe. I reached into my shoe to retrieve the origami-folded note on which John and I recorded the dead men and women to replace the real identities. "Do you still remember the names we chose?"

"You think I've bloomin lost it?" He tapped his forehead then winked.

The old John was there all right and I smiled through the heartache.

I'd long known his real name wasn't Captain John Douglas, but my brain refused to boot out the old and make room for the new. Sam Solonsch? I kept thinking of the man in my barracks as John. He thought he'd cornered the market on telling lies, but my brain told me many lies, too. That they were sending John to serve a harsher sentence. That we'd meet up after the war. That planes would soon arrive and save us all. My lies were kinder than the truth.

He hung an unlit cigarette from the corner of his mouth and got himself performance ready. As sick as he was, he summoned the strength for a joke.

"The POW doctor visited while you were gone and I told him about my memory loss. He asked how long I'd had the problem. What problem? I asked."

When he laughed at the punchline he gasped for breath. "Key information is locked in here." He tapped his head again, then gripped my hands tighter. I realised with shock I was still holding him. "I'm honoured to have shared my time in here with you," he said.

"I'm sorry I won't be coming with you to the prison at Tjipinang. The Japs are sending me to a work camp. My leg's much better, and I'll be digging ditches alongside the other able-bodied." The tendons in my neck tightened. "Thank you for keeping me sane."

"Sama-Sama," he said in Indonesian.

I repeated it in English, "Same-same."

"Right-eo Kid, I've got a lot of gear to pack for my holiday." He flicked his hand dismissively, and forced a smile but I didn't miss his tears.

"Don't die in prison," I said. "I plan to meet up with you in Australia. We'll catch those crayfish you bragged about, and eat them until we're ready to burst. Wash it down with Aussie beer, too. I'll meet your sons, tell them about their father the hero, then I'll dance while your wife plays the piano." I laced my fingers on top of my head to stop my hands trembling. "I don't want you to die."

"I won't now. I can't," he said matter-of-factly, "I've spent years searching for the meaning of life and the secret to immortality, and I've found it just in time. You're taking my life story with you," he whispered. "You can pass it on. No one ever dies if there's someone left to tell the tale."

The guards came for John with a Japanese officer in tow, one with high cheekbones and wide jaw. Satoru.

"We meet again," he said in English.

The guards waited outside, and I took backward steps to slink away.

"Don't leave," Satoru said firmly.

Lightheadedness travelled to my legs and I stumbled onto an empty bed, shaking my head with dread as John struggled to his feet and bowed. There was no fear on John's face, instead he wore a look of pure respect.

After all this time in his company, I was learning the subtle art of reading faces—perhaps even the hue. John's expression was gold.

"Do either of you have anything to tell me?" Satoru asked. "If so, now is the time. While our conversations are not being recorded."

"You've read everything I told Young Dutchy?"

Satoru nodded.

"Then, yes, I have more to say." John offered Satoru a chair and perched on the edge of his bed. "What do you want with the kid?"

"He must accompany you to prison, those higher up will be watching you both. Checking for reactions to match that of a traitor and the man who turned him in."

"I have a favour," John said.

"If you are asking me to free you, I cannot."

"No, I'm not as silly as I look." John crossed arms against his chest. "There comes a day for everyone to either step up or walk away. Please don't walk away from me. I realise my actions are at odds with your side of the fight, but I'm asking to die at your hands. You are worthy and I trust you to help me die with dignity. I want Young Dutchy to appreciate the beauty in death."

The guards took me from the holding cell to the 'last stop' room. There Satoru asked again for the name of the man who led the resistance group.

"I don't know that name," I said. "John didn't tell me."

As weak as John was, he managed to muster energy from somewhere, yelling for me to shut up, calling out traitor and trying to strike me.

I glanced at Satoru who nodded. He agreed with me. John's final performance was painfully convincing.

Satoru flinched when the guards restrained John and I closed my eyes.

Satoru made an announcement in Japanese and the guards pulled John into a kneeling position.

"I have pronounced him guilty of treason." Satoru surprised me by speaking in Dutch. "These guards don't understand what we are saying. I will tell them I've found you innocent and commended for your assistance. Is there anything you want to tell John before he dies?'

My voice quaked and Satoru held up a warning hand. "Hold yourself together, Kid. Do not let the guards sense regret."

I stared at a stain on the floor, arranging my mouth into a cold sneer, the opposite of my feelings. "Please tell him that I have been proud to be an adopted son. Tell him his mother was wrong about the bad seed. We have all met dishonourable men, but he is not one, never has been. I wish for him to go peacefully with whichever version of God takes his hand first. If he's met by more than one, they'll start a fight to claim him."

After translating, Satoru produced a sharpened bamboo spike

which he placed in John's hands. "You lived as a warrior and you deserve to die as one. Hold the sharpened end to your gut and prepare to take your own life. I give my word to follow quickly and cleanly with a blade at your neck. I await your signal."

Satoru stood ready with his samurai sword and John mouthed words to me, "See you in heaven, Kid. Now look away."

My heart pounded in my ears, but I shut my eyes to start a silent count.

Een. Twee. Drie.

The swish of a blade.

A deep falling thud.

The spurting hiss and sugary scent of blood.

A numbness I'd never forget.

Samuel Solonsch.

His real name ran through my head.

Tot ziens. Goodbye.

Goodbye Sam. Goodbye John.

THE END

Dear Readers

Dear readers,

I hope this story has been as rewarding for you to read as it was for me to write. Your support means the world to me, and I'd like to ask a small favour. If you found this story engaging and meaningful, I invite you to share your thoughts by telling friends and leaving a review on Amazon or Goodreads.com. Your feedback not only brightens my day, but also helps other readers discover the tale of Sam's remarkable journey.

Additionally, if you're interested in receiving copies of some of the source articles that inspired this book, I encourage you to sign up for my newsletter at www.miladouglas.com.au

The newsletter is a way for us to stay connected, and I'd love to share more about the incredible research journey that brought Sam's story to life. Thank you for being a part of this literary adventure, and I hope our paths cross again in the pages of another story soon.

Warm regards,
Mila Douglas

Acknowledgments

I owe a debt of gratitude to my dedicated critique partners, Sue and Linda, who not only embraced the story but also clamoured for more, pushing me tirelessly to finish it and share it with the world.

A special thanks to my editor, Lidija Hilje, whose unwavering belief in me and my writing, coupled with her impeccable editing skills and intuitive grasp of storytelling, breathed life into Sam's character and helped shape this narrative.

To my incredible circle of friends and family, who never once yawned while I obsessively enthused about Sam's extraordinary tales, your unwavering support means the world to me. You sat wide-eyed through recitals of newspaper articles, excerpts from war diaries, and a multitude of other documents that sometimes portrayed Sam with awe and at other times with disdain. Your enthusiasm and encouragement sustained me throughout this journey.

A heartfelt thanks also goes out to the dedicated group of individuals who took the time to read the final manuscript, providing invaluable feedback and picking out the annoying typos.

www.ingramcontent.com/pod-product-compliance
Lightning Source LLC
Chambersburg PA
CBHW011149290426
44109CB00025B/2539